Harish Dhillon describes himself as a 'compulsive story writer' and his short stories have been published on a regular basis in journals and magazines all over the country for almost 40 years. He is also the author of two novels.

THE LIVES AND TEACHINGS OF THE
SIKH GURUS

HARISH DHILLON

UBSPD

UBS Publishers' Distributors Pvt. Ltd.

New Delhi • Bangalore • Kolkata • Chennai • Patna • Bhopal
Ernakulam • Mumbai • Lucknow • Pune • Hyderabad

UBS Publishers' Distributors Pvt. Ltd.

5 Ansari Road, New Delhi-110 002
Phones: 011-23273601, 23266646 • Fax: 23276593, 23274261
E-mail: ubspd@ubspd.com

10 First Main Road, Gandhi Nagar, Bangalore-560 009
Phones: 080-22253903, 22263901, 22263902 • Fax: 22263904
E-mail: ubspdbng@eth.net

8/1-B Chowringhee Lane, Kolkata-700 016
Phones: 033-22521821, 22522910, 22529473 • Fax: 22523027
E-mail: ubspdcal@cal.vsnl.net.in

60 Nelson Manickam Road, Aminjikarai, Chennai-600 029
Phones: 044-23746222, 23746351-2 • Fax: 23746287
E-mail: ubspd@che.ubspd.com

Ground Floor, Western Side, Annaporna Complex, 202 Naya Tola,
Patna-800 004 • Phones: 0612-2672856, 2673973, 2686170
Fax: 2686169 • E-mail: ubspdpat1@sancharnet.in

143, M.P. Nagar, Zone-I, Bhopal-462 011
Phones: 0755-5203183, 5203193, 2555228 • Fax: 2555285
E-mail: ubspdbhp@sancharnet.in

No. 40/7940, Convent Road, Ernakulam-682 035
Phones: 0484-2353901, 2363905 • Fax: 2365511
E-mail: ubspdekm@asianetindia.com

2nd Floor, Apeejay Chambers, 5 Wallace Street, Fort,
Mumbai-400 001 • Phones: 022-56376922, 56376923
Fax: 56376921• E-mail: ubspdmum@mum.ubspd.com

1st Floor, Halwasiya Court Annexe, 11-MG Marg, Hazaratganj,
Lucknow-226 001• Phones: 0522-2294134, 2611128
Fax: 2294133 • E-mail: ubspdlko@lko.ubspd.com

680 Budhwar Peth, 2nd floor, Appa Balwant Chowk, Pune-411 002
Phone: 020-4028920 • Fax: 020-4028921
E-mail: ubspdpune@rediffmail.com

NVK Towers, 2nd floor, 3-6-272, Himayat Nagar,
Hyderabad-500029 • Phones: 040-23262572, 23262573, 23262574
Fax: 040-23262572 • E-mail: ubspdhyd@vsnl.net

Visit us at www.ubspd.com & www.gobookshopping.com

© Text: Harish Dhillon
Illustrations: Rathin Mitra

Reprint 2005

All rights reserved. No part of this publication may be reproduced or transmitted in
any form or by any means, electronic or mechanical including photocopying, recording,
or any information storage and retrieval system, without permission in writing from
the publisher.

Cover Design: Ilaksha

Designed & Typeset at: UBSPD in 11 pt. Souvenir
Printed at: Nutech Photolithographers, Delhi

*To my Children
Jason, Priya, Naina, Jai and,
of course, Tegh*

Preface

At the time of our story, the Panjab was a much bigger geographical region than it is today. The north of this area was marked by the high Himalayas, the Hindu-Kush and the mountains of Afghanistan. In the west it was bounded by the river Indus. The south was marked by the desert of Rajasthan. The eastern boundary was not very clearly defined. But, broadly speaking, Panjab was a region of large plains watered by the rivers Jhelum, Chenab, Ravi, Sutlej and Beas.

This is the area where Indian civilization, one of the oldest civilizations in the world, was born. Stone implements dating back to almost 500,000 years have been found here. Copper and bronze implements dating back to 25,000 years have also been unearthed along the banks of the Indus. The ruins of the Harappan culture found at Ropar prove the existence of a flourishing urban culture dating as far back as 2500 B.C. It was also in Panjab that the Aryans evolved Vedic religion and composed the great works of Vedic and Sanskrit literatures.

The Aryans were followed by wave after wave of conquerors: the Greeks, the Bactrians, the Scythian tribes, the Huns and then after the beginning of the eleventh century tribes who differed greatly from one another but had one common factor: their religion, Islam. The Ghaznavis, the

Ghoris, the Tughlaqs, the Suris, the Lodhis, the Moghuls —
all invaded North India and ruled for a time.

The Muslim tribes, when they had settled down in Panjab,
directed much of their energies towards destroying non-
believers. For over three hundred years, Islam and Hinduism
existed side by side in Panjab in a state of constant conflict.
Hinduism had a pantheon of gods and goddesses who could
be worshipped as idols, and a society that was based on the
caste system. Islam believed firmly in monotheism, abhorred
idolatory and believed in the equality of all men.

Some attempts were made to bridge this divide. The
bhaktas preached that there was only one God and He was
without any form or feature. They advocated that all men
were equal and preached against the caste system. The Sufis
too tried to bridge the divide. For the first time, music was
introduced into Muslim religious practice. The Sufis welcomed
non-believers both in their homes and in their mosques and
believed that all men had a right to observe their own form
of worship.

But both these attempts were tentative in nature and any
popular acceptance they had found was destroyed by Taimur's
invasion in A.D. 1398. The Muslim ruling class turned once
again to killing and robbing the Hindu masses and to
destroying their temples. The average Muslim believed that
he could gain merit in the eyes of God by converting non-
believers, even if it was at the point of a sword. Religious
practice in both religions degenerated into the performance
of empty rites and rituals. The Muslims believed that
circumcision, abstinence from pork and fasting during
Ramzan were the attributes of good Muslims. The Hindus
once again reverted to idol-worship and an even more
determined belief in the caste system and the rituals of
washing away their sins in holy rivers, eating vegetarian food
and wearing a thread to make themselves sacred.

In 1499 Nanak embarked on an attempt to define what
was common between the two religions and to purify religious

practice from all the rituals and the hypocrisy that had come to surround it. His teachings were soon accepted by thousands of followers and the faith embodying these became the youngest of the great religions of the world.

This book is an attempt to relate the birth and growth of this great religion during the first two hundred years of its life through the life-stories of its ten Gurus, i.e., spiritual preceptors. This work claims no originality; everything it contains has been culled from the sources listed at the end. It has been written solely for the young readers in a simple narrative form; but unlike some other such efforts, the present attempt carefully eschews all those elements that may be considered supernatural and miraculous in nature, as the performance of, and belief in, miracles are against the basic tenets of the teachings of the Sikh Gurus.

The only justification for retelling a story that has already been told so often is the firm belief that a story so beautiful and inspiring needs to be retold as often as possible. If a small fraction of the great charm of this story can communicate itself to the reader, the effort will have been worthwhile.

First of all, I am greatly beholden to Dr. Wazir Singh for editing the text, meticulousy at that, and also for suggesting improvements.

I would like to express my grateful thanks, to Dr. S.S. Dhillon for obtaining all the source-material for me, to Sohan Singh for deciphering the terrible handwriting and typing out the various drafts and to Neeta Sibia for patiently reading through each draft and giving me her quiet but very valuable advice. My grateful thanks, most of all, to K.S. Bhalla for having gone through the text so very carefully, word by word, and suggesting important and meaningful corrections and modifications. To Rathin Mitra I owe a special thanks for the use of his exquisite illustrations.

— **Harish Dhillon**

Contents

PART 1

Guru Nanak
(1469 – 1539)

Birth and Childhood

Guru Nanak was born in Talwandi, now in Pakistan, which later came to be known as Nankana Sahib. The village of Talwandi lay in Central Punjab between the rivers Ravi and Chenab in the direct path of the invaders who came to India. They had destroyed Talwandi thirteen times, and each time, like a phoenix, Talwandi had risen again from its ashes. The last time, it was rebuilt under the supervision of Rai Bhoe, a Bhatti Rajput who had converted to Islam.

Rai Bhoe and his son Rai Bular, who became the village chief when his father died, did a great deal for the development of the village and seeing this development more and more people migrated to the village. They were attracted not only by the prospect of earning a better living but also by the greater security that Talwandi now provided. One family which came to Talwandi was the Bedi family which migrated from a village close to Amritsar. During Rai Bhoe's time the family was headed by Shiv Ram. He was an honest, hardworking man and good at handling money matters and keeping accounts. He was given employment by Rai Bhoe and was put incharge of the revenue accounts of the Bhattis. Shiv Ram's son, Kalyan Chand, was also an intelligent, hardworking boy and his father trained him to follow in his footsteps. So when Shiv Ram died, Kalyan Chand quite naturally became the Bhattis' accountant. The Bhattis paid their accountant well and the Bedis had one of the biggest houses in the village, their own fields and a herd of cows and buffaloes. Kalyan Chand had married Tripta, daughter of Rama of Chahalwala, a village south of Lahore.

Most biographers and historians are agreed that Guru Nanak was born on Vaisakh sudi three (corresponding to April 15) A.D. 1469, though the Guru's birthday is celebrated on the full moon (Purnima) of Kartik occurring in November each year. The Guru's father, Kalyan Chand, is popularly known as Mehta Kalu. On the night of Nanak's birth, Mehta Kalu was worried about his wife. All kinds of thoughts ran through his mind. What if something went wrong? Perhaps he should have let Tripta go to her parents the way she had gone when their daughter Nanki was born. At last he heard the baby's cry. The midwife, Daultan, came out and said, "Congratulations Kalyan Chand, it is a boy."

Kalyan Chand took out a silver coin from his pocket and gave it to the midwife and only then did she let him take his son into his arms.

Soon after, he hurried towards Pandit Hardyal's house. The pandit was a great scholar who had made a deep study of many religious books. He was also a wise man who helped the villagers solve their problems by giving them simple, practical advice. He led a simple life and as a result was greatly respected by the villagers, both Hindus and Muslims alike. "I have been blessed with a son, panditji," Kalu said with some pride as he bent himself to touch the pandit's feet. "And I have come to ask you to make his horoscope."

"Good," the pandit said, after he has studied the horoscope, prepared by him, adding, "Kalu, your son, will sit under a canopy. Both Hindus and Turks will respect him and his name will be famous on earth and in heaven. I will return on the thirteenth day and name the child. May God bless him."

As the village of Talwandi awoke to another day, the news of the birth of Kalu's son and of the pandit's predictions spread like wild fire. The next few days were exciting for the Bedi household. Several people from the village and friends and relatives from neighbouring places came to congratulate them. On the thirteenth day, Pandit Hardyal returned and named the baby 'Nanak'. It was after Nanak's name that the village of Talwandi came to be known as Nankana Sahib.

In the early years of his life there seemed little to mark Nanak out as being special or different from the children of his age. But soon enough he displayed traits of character and temperament that were to remain with him throughout his life. He was polite to everyone. He liked people for what they were and always wanted to do things for others. He shared everything he had, his food, his toys, with other children and found great happiness in giving what was his to others. Though he played games with the other boys he was a quiet child who preferred to be by himself and seemed always to be lost in deep thoughts.

The village of Talwandi was small, much of which was covered with the forest and thick low bushes. Nanak loved to wander in the forest and he often met "faqirs" and "sadhus" and "sants" who stopped there for a few days. He was profoundly influenced by what they did and said. There was a big mound outside Talwandi; he loved to sit on the top of it, looking at the countryside around him. He noticed the changes that the different seasons brought about and enjoyed the gifts of nature, which are reflected in the sacred compositions (Bani) in good measure.

Early Years

When Nanak was seven, Mehta Kalu, on Rai Bular's advice, decided that it was time for Nanak to learn how to read and write. Kalu went to Pandit Hardyal and the pandit after consulting Nanak's horoscope gave Kalyan an auspicious date on which to start the boy's education.

In Nanak's village there was a small school run by Pandha Gopal. There were a dozen children of different ages who sat outside the Pandha's house and learnt to read and write and do simple sums of arithmetic.

Pandha Gopal was happy to accept Nanak as a pupil. Not only did he have a lot of respect for his father, Kalyan Chand, he had also heard about the boy's character and behaviour. Nanak was a very intelligent, hardworking boy. He learnt the alphabet quickly and was soon ahead of the other boys in Gopal Pandha's school. The other boys were at first jealous of Nanak and made fun of him. But he always smiled and was never angry and soon they learnt to respect and like him.

Seeing Nanak doing so well in his studies, Gopal was sure that he would be a great man one day. Like Kalyan he thought that greatness lay in becoming an officer in the Lodhi's court. So he now began to teach Nanak arithmetic and accounts.

Talwandi came under the rule of the Governor of Sultanpur who at that time was Nawab Daulat Khan. Periodically the Governor sent one of his officers to collect revenue from the Bhatti landlord, Rai Bular. While Nanak was studying with Gopal Pandha the officer who used to come to collect the revenue was a Khatri by the name of Jairam. Jairam was treated with great respect and affection by Rai Bular, not only because he was the representative of the Governor but also because he was a very polite and friendly young man. Rai Bular and Jairam soon became good friends.

One day after the evening meal, when they were sitting together, Rai Bular said to Jairam, "It is time, my friend, that you got married and started a family."

"I too have thought of this," Jairam said, "and my parents want me to get married very soon. But I have not found a suitable Khatri girl."

"What kind of girl are you looking for?" Rai Bular asked.

"I am looking for a girl from a good family, a girl who is good at household work, a girl who will respect and love my aged parents. She must also be a girl of intelligence and strength." He paused and his face lit up with a wistful smile. "Am I asking too much?" "No, my friend, you are not asking for too much."

"Then will you find me such a girl?"

"I will try," Rai Bular said. "There are many Khatri families in Talwandi. I am sure we will be able to find the girl you are looking for." But in his heart Rai Bular already knew the girl for Jairam; this girl was Nanki, the daughter of his accountant and old friend Kalyan Chand.

Nanak's family respected Rai Bular so much that the moment he made the suggestion of marriage between Nanki and Jairam, it was readily taken up by both Kalyan and Tripta.

Nanak continued to go to Gopal Pandha's school, but he was not interested in learning how to keep accounts. He composed a poem for his teacher and when the teacher read this he was very impressed and knew that there was nothing more that he could teach the boy.

Kalu was disappointed. Beautiful poems were all very well but how could Nanak begin climbing the ladder of success if he did not learn practical things like keeping accounts? After a few days he came to the conclusion that his son's path to greatness might lie in studying ancient religious texts. So Nanak was sent to Pandit Brijnath Shastri, a famous Sanskrit scholar. He had heard of the beautiful poem that Nanak had composed and was happy to have such a gifted boy as his pupil.

In the meantime the day for Nanki's wedding drew near. As in all weddings, there was a great deal of singing and dancing for days before the actual ceremony. When the marriage party arrived, the whole village came out to see the wonderful bridegroom and his relatives. There were feasting and a lot of singing. The ceremony was performed according to the Vedic rites. Rai Bular took part in the wedding as an important member of the family and gave many presents to the bride and to Jairam.

Then it was time for the "doli" to leave. For Nanak it was a poignant moment. From his sister he had always received special love and affection. She, before anyone else, had come to respect and admire her brother and this had given him great emotional strength, and now she was going away.

Nanki went away with her husband and the village returned to its humdrum routine of everyday activities. Nanak returned to Pandit Brijnath Shastri and resumed his studies. As with Gopal Pandha, he learnt everything quickly. He became fluent in Sanskrit and knew many of the texts by heart. But he realised that he did not want to build his life on this. He said goodbye to his teacher and came away, much to his father's disappointment. It was true that his son had learnt a lot with Gopal Pandha and Pandit Brijnath Shastri and it was also true that both of them admired and respected him. But this was not enough to help Nanak achieve the greatness that the father wanted for him.

He made one last effort to provide some direction to his son's life. He took him to Maulvi Qutab-Ud-Din who taught Persian and Arabic. Both these languages were court languages. Perhaps if Nanak showed interest in these two languages and became a master of them, Rai Bular would help him find a job either with the Governor in Sultanpur or with the Emperor in Delhi. There was still hope that Pandit Hardyal's predictions would come true. Once again Nanak proved to be a good pupil and learnt both the languages easily.

Nanak was now thirteen years old. It was time to perform the ceremony of sacred thread. Once again Pandit Hardyal was asked to set a date on which the ceremony would be performed.

Pandit Hardyal sat on a special platform made of bricks and mud and in front of him sat the young Nanak, his legs crossed, his back straight, his body bare from the waist upwards. Lamps had been lit on the edge of the platform and there was the strong smell of incense as the smoke from the sticks curled to the sky. The pandit sat chanting *mantras* and all the guests and family members sat in hushed silence. At last the pandit finished his *mantras*. He blessed the cord and then, unwinding it, reached out to put it across Nanak's shoulder. Nanak put out his hand to stop him. "What are you doing with this thread?" he asked.

"This is the sacred thread which marks out the upper-caste Hindus." The priest explained patiently: "You are a high-caste Hindu." By wearing this thread you become a pure Hindu."

"Can a person become pure only by wearing a thread?" Nanak asked. "Is it not our actions that make us pure? The wearing of a thread will not make a difference. I will not wear it."

The people in the courtyard were too shocked to say or do anything. Pandit Hardyal was confused and angry with Nanak for creating this embarrassing situation.

He got up from the platform, shuffled into his wooden sandals and went away from Kalyan's house. Nanak sat on, quiet now, with a soft smile on his face. All around there were murmurs of resentment. No one had ever done this before, the pandit was angry, and Nanak had disgraced his family, his parents and his caste. One by one the guests left the house, not wanting to be part of this break with tradition, custom and religion. The feast that was to follow the ceremony did not take place. Kalyan was hurt and angry but he knew his son well by now, knew that there was no point in scolding or punishing him. Tripta was frightened: frightened at what her son had done. She was apprehensive that the gods would be angry with him and the priest would curse him.

If Nanak felt in his mind the effect of his action, he did not show it. He continued to go to the Maulvi for his Persian and Arabic lessons. When he had become almost as proficient as his teacher, he decided that there was nothing more that he could learn from the Maulvi and gave up his studies.

Kalyan turned to his friend Rai Bular for help and advice and the Bhatti sent for Pandit Hardyal.

"Panditji, our friend Kalu is very unhappy on account of his son Nanak. Do you remember what you predicted when the child was born?" The priest smiled his quiet, peaceful smile.

"Yes," he said, nodding his head.

"I remember. And I say again: he will be a great man. But let him find his own path. Do not push him."

"Yes, I think panditji is right," Rai Bular said. He had always liked the quiet boy and had often told the father to be more polite and gentle with him.

"If he does not want to study any more do not push him. Let him start working at something."

It was decided that the boy would be encouraged to take on a job. Kalyan returned to his home with a sinking heart. In spite of what Pandit Hardyal had said, he could not help thinking that no greatness could come from doing any of the work that was available in the village.

Search for an Occupation

Nanak had reached his fourteenth year and Kalyan Chand was still not able to decide what job his son should take up. He knew that there was no point in asking Nanak to take up work he did not like; he would only give it up, as he had given up his studies.

He watched Nanak closely. Nanak was spending more and more time all by himself in the forest and shrubs around Talwandi. This activity seemed to give him the most pleasure. The Bedis had a large herd of cattle and taking them out to graze was an important task. It would give Nanak the chance to be by himself in the forest and shrubs which he liked so much. When this idea was broached to him Nanak was happy to take on this task.

Nanak drove the cattle out to the forest. All day he would let them feed on the grass and the fresh leaves of the bushes, and in the evening he drove them back home. Day after day he followed this routine. He was able to spend a long time alone with his thoughts and he loved the animals and made sure that each of them fed well. He was no longer restless and his mother was happy to see this.

From Kalyan's point of view there seemed to be a general improvement in Nanak's attitude. He performed his duties well, he spent more time at home with his mother and his father and was more friendly with the villagers. He carried out errands for his father and performed them well. This brought the father and son closer together.

Kalu felt that his son was now ready for greater responsibility. He called the boy to him and gave him twenty silver coins.

"My son," he said gently, "you must go to the town of Chuharkana, it is market-day there today. Take your friend Bala with you. Buy something cheaply and then bring it back and sell it at a higher price so that you can make a profit."

Nanak, in his new mood, was eager to please his father. "I will do so, father," he said and, accompanied by his friend Bala, he set out for the nearby market town.

When they had reached the outskirts of the village they came to a little path that led through the forest and was a shortcut to the market town. In the middle of the forest there was a clearing where saints and faqirs rested when they passed Talwandi. Nanak would often visit this place and listen to the holy men as they held their discussions and exchanged ideas. As a result, at a very young age he had learnt a great deal about different religions and different religious movements. It was here that he met the Muslim scholar Sajjid Hussain and first learnt about Sufism. Now too he stopped at the path which led to the clearing and after thinking for a moment or two he said, "Let us take the path through the forest."

"No," Bala replied sharply knowing that Nanak wanted to take the path not because it was the shorter way but because he hoped to meet some holy men in the forest. They would spend many hours here and would be late for their shopping.

"No," he said again, "Let us take the main road." Nanak smiled at him and walked quickly down the path and Bala had no choice but to run after him. Nanak had heard that there was a group of holy men in the forest who belonged to the Nirbani sect. He had never met any holy men from this sect before and was anxious to meet them.

They came to the clearing in the forest and stopped when they saw a large group of sadhus. All of them were naked and stood in different postures absorbed in meditation and prayer.

Nanak and Bala stood at the entrance of the clearing, looking at this strange scene. Bala was impatient to get to the market.

"Come," he said, pulling at Nanak's sleeves. "Come, or we will be late."

"I will only take a few moments," Nanak said and strode through the clearing and stopped before the sadhu who was the obvious leader. The leader's eyes were closed and his lips moved in silent prayer. At last, his prayers over, he opened his eyes. Nanak bowed to him and the holy man held the palm of his right hand in blessing. Then he signalled to Nanak to sit down.

"Maharaj, why do you not wear any clothes?" Nanak asked.

"We are Nirbanis," the holy man said, a gentle smile playing at his lips. "We do not want anything that will bind us to this world. So we do not wear any clothes. We do not look for food and eat only when God sends us food."

"And when did God last send you food?"

"For me it was three days ago. For some," he pointed to a group of four men standing on one side, "it has been eight days."

Nanak was sad that these holy men should have gone hungry for so many days. Perhaps God wanted to use him as an instrument to feed them. He bowed to the sadhu and took his leave and hurried to the market town.

When they reached Chuharkana, Nanak spent all his money buying food. He bought flour, oil, sugar and many other things. He bargained fiercely and beat the prices down to a considerable extent. Bala was sure that when they sold these things in Talwandi they would make a good profit and Kalyan would be very happy.

The two friends were much slower on the return trip because of the heavy loads they carried. They reached the clearing in the evening, and when Nanak took the load from his head and put it on the ground Bala was happy to do the same. He was tired and was glad that Nanak had stopped to rest. As the wiped the sweat from his forehead he saw Nanak approach the leader of the Nirbanis and bow to him.

"Holy one," he said, "God has sent food for you and for all the other holy men of your group." Bala was shocked beyond words when he heard this.

Nanak bowed to the holy men once again and, with Bala following, made his way out of the forest. When at last they reached the small mango grove just outside Talwandi, Bala stopped.

"Your father is going to be very angry because you have thrown away his money. He wanted you to make a good profit, but see what you have done!" He stopped to catch his breath and then went on. "I will tell him the truth. I will tell him that it is all your doing; that I tried to stop you but you did not listen."

Both friends were quiet. They were both thinking of Kalyan's anger.

"You go ahead, Bala," Nanak said. "I will stay here." So Bala left his friend and made his way to the village. Because he loved Nanak very much and was afraid of what Kalyan would do to him, he went quietly to Nanak's house and first told Nanki what had happened. It was only after this that he went to report to Kalyan. Fortunately Rai Bular was present when Bala told his story.

Kalyan was very angry.

"Take me to him," he said.

"Take me to where he is hiding." They both hurried to the mango grove, followed by Rai Bular and Nanki. Kalyan caught hold of Nanak and shook him hard.

"You waster, what have you done with my money?" He sounded so angry that Rai Bular was afraid he might strike the boy. He held his friend back.

"If the loss of twenty silver coins troubles you so much," Rai Bular said in a soft, gentle voice, "I will give you twenty coins. But don't berate the boy".

Kalyan was quiet for a little while. But the whole thing had been too much for him. He saw that all his dreams for his son now lay shattered.

"Greatness!" he said bitterly. "Pandit Hardyal said my son would be a great man, and look what he has become! He cannot be trusted even with twenty silver coins."

Rai Bular put his arm around the boy's shoulders and spoke kindly to his friend. "Pandit Hardyal was right. Tell me, my friend, what greater merit can a man earn than from feeding the hungry? He has invested your money wisely."

The Bhatti's words softened Kalyan's anger a little.

Nanak was upset by his father's anger. When his mother gave him his evening meal he refused to eat it.

"What?" his mother said, pretending to be angry with him.

"You, who have earned so much merit by feeding twenty hungry men, will you not let me earn some merit by feeding just one hungry boy?" She smiled and caressed his hair. Nanak felt the sadness lift from his heart. In spite of his father's anger he was glad that he had fed the holy men. He smiled at his mother and ate his food.

At Sultanpur

After Nanak had spent the money on feeding the holy men, Kalyan barely spoke to his son. Though he did not scold Nanak, Nanki, who was on a visit to Talwandi, knew it was only a question of time before his anger erupted again. She was frightened of what would happen. One night, while the men slept, she spoke to her mother about it.

"I am frightened too," Tripta said in a whisper. She added, "I am also frightened that Nanak will go away. He spends so much time listening to the holy men who go from place to place. I am frightened that one day, like them, he too will want to wander off on pilgrimages." Her voice broke as she spoke and she began to cry softly in the dark. Nanki reached out and held her mother's hand.

"Don't be frightened, mother," she said, caressing her mother's work-worn hand. "I will think of a way out." She brought her mother's hand to her lips and kissed it.

Nanki's touch brought comfort to Tripta and her fear was stilled.

Nanki thought of a way to resolve the difficult situation. Perhaps Nanak should go away from Talwandi for a while.

He would be away from his father's anger and also from the influence of the holy men. He had never been to visit her in Sultanpur. Perhaps when the time came for her to go back she should take him with her.

The more she thought of this the more she felt it was the right thing to do.

When Jairam came to Talwandi a few days later, Nanki told him everything that was on her mind.

"Yes," he said, "it is a very good idea. Nanak should go away for some time. It will be good to have him with us in Sultanpur."

"Ask my parents if he can come with us. They might say no to me, they will never refuse you."

So the next morning, when Kalyan had gone to work and Nanak had gone for a walk, Jairam seated himself close to his mother-in-law. Tripta was spinning cotton yarn. Nanki left them alone and went into the kitchen.

"Mother, I have been thinking of Nanak." Tripta paused in her spinning.

"He spends too much time with the holy men."

"Yes," Tripta said with a sigh. "Sometimes I feel afraid that he will start going away on pilgrimages with them and be away from home for great lengths of time."

"If you permit, mother, I want to take him with me to Sultanpur." The thread broke and Tripta suspended her spinning. Her son had never been away from her for a single day and she felt sad that he would go away now. But at the same time she knew that this was the only way to keep him from being influenced by sadhus and faqirs and to protect him from his father's anger.

"Yes, yes of course," she said, still not looking up, afraid that Jairam would see the sadness in her eyes.

"You are his brother, you know what will be best for him." She looked up at last and smiled at her son-in-law, but he saw the tears glistening in her eyes.

"Do not worry, mother," he said, "it will only be for a short while. He will come back to you with his mind cured of all these thoughts and after having achieved something in life. Then his father will not be angry with him."

Yes, Tripta thought, God was kind. He would help. She resumed her spinning.

In the afternoon Jairam carried his father-in-law's lunch to him. As Kalyan sat eating, Jairam suggested that Nanak should go with him to Sultanpur.

"It is a good idea," Kalyan said. "I have not been able to do anything for the boy here. He might find some useful employment in Sultanpur and finally settle down. You must first go back to Sultanpur and see what chance there is of his finding a job."

Fifteen days after Nanki and Jairam had left for Sultanpur, a messenger arrived with a letter for Kalyan. Jairam had spoken to Nawab Daulat Khan Lodhi and the Khan had promised to help Nanak. It was imperative that Nanak should come to Sultanpur at the earliest.

A few days later Nanak set out on his journey to Sultanpur accompanied by Mardana. Nanak never really returned to Talwandi again. He came back on short visits but it was never again to be his home.

Sultanpur was at that time a rich and prosperous town. This was mainly because of Nawab Daulat Khan. He beautified the city and built many gardens and grand buildings. He also brought learned people to Sultanpur and the town became the home of teachers and scholars who taught in the many Islamic schools that had been set up.

Nanak and his companion were given a warm welcome on their arrival. Nanki and Jairam extended every hospitality to them and the next morning Nanak went with Jairam to the Khan's palace. As they were getting ready to leave the house Nanki offered her brother a bowl of curd and sugar. Said Nanak, "I know you do this because you love me, you believe that this will bring me luck and the Khan will give me employment. But tell me, sister, if merely by eating curd and sugar we could ensure good luck no one would need to work. No one would believe in God!"

The Khan's palace was very grand. There were signs of great wealth everywhere: in the furniture, in the decorations and in the clothes that the people wore. Nanak came into the Khan's room with a gentle smile on his lips. Like Jairam he bowed before the Khan in greeting, but when he looked up again he looked the Khan straight in the eye.

"Come and sit beside me," the Khan said, pointing to the small stool by his side.

"How many days is it since you left Talwandi?" he asked.

"We left five days ago, sir," Nanak spoke in a strong, gentle voice.

"Did you have any trouble on your way?"

"No, sir. God was with us, we had no trouble on the way." The Khan was pleased by the young man's manner. He was polite and well-behaved, yet there was no fear in his eyes and voice, fear that other people showed when they were in his company.

The Khan was a busy man. Yet he put all his work aside and sat and talked to Nanak for a long time. He remembered what Sayed Hassan, a Muslim scholar from Talwandi, who came to teach at one of the Islamic schools in Sultanpur, had told him about Nanak. Sayed Hassan had praised Nanak's knowledge and interest in religion. By the end of the meeting the Khan had appointed Nanak as the officer incharge of his *modikhana*.

The *modikhana* was the Khan's granary. It was a very important part of the Khan's office because in those days farmers were given the option to pay their taxes in cash or in kind and most of them chose to pay in kind. Part of the salary of the court officials was also paid in grain. So Nanak had to measure and record not only the grain that came into the *modikhana* but also the grain that went out. Nanak had always been quick to learn and soon he was adept at his work. Nanki was happy that her brother seemed at last to have settled down.

The Khan noticed how well Nanak worked and, in appreciation of his good work, gave him a house near the *modikhana*. Nanki felt sad that her brother would now be living away from her, but she was satisfied that Nanak had got a job and would be living in Sultanpur itself.

The new house was a small one but Nanak was quite happy. He had never wanted anything more than a roof over his head. Nanki helped her brother settle into his new home, and Mardana, who moved in with Nanak, took charge of the household.

Soon Nanak's life established a pattern. He would wake up before the break of the day and go to bathe in the waters of the Bein rivulet. After this he would spend some time in meditation. Then he would come home and take his breakfast and go to the *modikhana*. The day would thus pass quickly in work. He was very sincere, honest and hard-working, and recorded all transactions scrupulously. At the end of the month he carried out a physical stock-taking to ensure that the stock of grain in the store tallied with the quantity entered in his account books. All through the day he would work and in the evening he would return home. Sometimes he would go to his sister Nanki's house and spend an hour or two with her. Then he would compose hymns in praise of God.

According to biographers of Guru Nanak, he was about 35 years of age when be moved to Sultanpur. He had got married in the year 1487, and had been blessed with two sons. His father-in-law was Mulchand Khatri of the Chona sub-caste, who lived in the town of Batala. He had a daughter Sulakhni who was said to be polite and soft-spoken. Both Jairam and Nanki had felt that she would make a good match for Nanak. It was during his stay at Sultanpur that his sons Sri Chand and Lakhmi Das were born in the years 1494 and 1496.

Sulakhni was as gentle as Nanak and made friends easily, though her best friend was Nanak's sister, Nanki. She was also very hard-working. From an early age she had helped her mother with the household chores and knew exactly what was needed to ensure that her own household ran smoothly. She had to prepare an evening meal without knowing how many people would be eating, because the number of people who came to listen to Nanak's *kirtan* varied everyday. But she never showed any surprise. She followed her husband's life; she woke before Nanak was awake, and made all her husband's guests welcome to her home.

Nanak had become so absorbed in his pattern of life that he had not been to see his sister for many days. One day she cooked *kheer* for her husband's evening meal. As she served him his meal Jairam noticed that something was troubling his wife.

"What is it," he asked, "what is on your mind?"

Jairam was a sensitive man. He knew that Nanak was very fond of *kheer* and Nanki wished that her brother was there to eat it.

"Put some *kheer* in a bowl, Nanki," he said after finishing his meal. "You know how Nanak loves *kheer*. We will take it to him."

So Nanki took a bowlful of *kheer* and husband and wife walked through the streets of Sultanpur to Nanak's house, where the *kirtan* session was on. After the *kirtan* Nanki helped her sister-in-law with the serving of the food. She was happy to see Sulakhni's cheerful face, she seemed to find pleasure in all the work. After this Nanki and Jairam came often to attend the *kirtan*.

Close to Sultanpur was a village, Malvian, and in Malvian there lived a man named Bhagirath, who spent a great deal of time in the company of saints and holy men. He heard that Nanak, who looked after the Khan's *modikhana* in Sultanpur, was a holy man. So he came to Sultanpur and attended the *kirtan* at Nanak's home. The *kirtan* deeply touched his heart and he was so influenced by Nanak's teachings that he took up his abode in Sultanpur and became Nanak's first disciple.

Eleven years after Nanak's wedding there was another wedding in the house — Mardana's daughter's wedding. Bhagirath was entrusted with the shopping. He went to Lahore for this purpose and came in contact with a trader named Mansukh. Mansukh was so impressed by what Bhagirath told him about Nanak that he too travelled to Sultanpur Lodhi and became Nanak's disciple. He wrote down many of Nanak's hymns and took them back with him to Lahore and every evening people would gather in his house to listen to the hymns.

Professionally too Nanak was doing well. The Khan was very pleased with him and showed him many favours. This aroused jealousy in the minds of some of the courtiers and they began to spread false tales about Nanak. They said that he was stealing from the *modikhana* and this was how he was able to feed so many people every evening. Some people complained to the Khan that Nanak was misusing his position.

Nanak too heard these stories and one morning he went to see the Khan.

"What is it, Nanak? What has happened?" he asked after greetings were exchanged.

"There are people who say that I have stolen grain from the *modikhana*," Nanak said, coming at once to the point. "I would like you to have the stores checked." He held out the keys of the *modikhana*.

"I do not believe these accusations," the Khan said, putting his hand on Nanak's shoulder. "I know that you are honest, that you sometimes give out more grain than is their due to the poor people. But I also know that you keep a careful account of all this and make it up at the end of every month. But yes, it is important that your name should be cleared and all these people who make up these stories should be shown up as liars." The Khan took the keys from Nanak and asked his treasurer to check the stores and the accounts. Everything was found in order.

A few days later Nanak did not return home after his bath in the stream. When people went to look for him they found his clothes on the river-bank but no other sign of him. So they concluded that he had been drowned. The Khan heard the news and came galloping to the spot, his officers riding close besides him.

"Get the fishermen's nets," he ordered. "Drag the waters. Hurry," he shouted. While his orders were being carried out he thought of Nanak. Nanak was a good swimmer, so it was not likely he could have come to any harm. But perhaps Nanak had been perturbed by the recent happenings. Lost in his thoughts, he might perhaps have swum into an unsafe part of the stream. Hours passed and one by one his officers returned.

"Did you find anything?" he asked each of them, and each shook his head to say "no". By now all his followers had gathered in Nanak's house. The men sat in silence, frightened of what was believed to have happened. Sulakhni was dazed with grief and her little sons broke into tears.

Only Nanki did not believe that her brother had died. She comforted Sulakhni and her nephews and brought strength to them.

"You wait and see," she said, "Nanak will soon return." And on the third day Nanak did, indeed, return.

While swimming in the rivulet, Nanak had heard a voice, a voice with a strange dream-like quality to it. The voice told him that he must travel from village to village and bring his teachings to the people. When he woke from the dream he found that he had been meditating in the jungle. This was where he was found by the Khan's servants who brought him back to the town.

His disciples were very happy to see that their teacher was alive. The Khan too was very happy to learn that his official was alive. The first words that Nanak spoke on the occasion were:

"There is but one God. There is no Hindu and no Musalman."

This was the proclamation of Guru Nanak's new faith.

He had also composed a few hymns while meditating in the forest.

Guru Nanak was now ready to go out beyond Sultanpur and spread his message to all the people who cared to listen to him.

Travels

So Nanak set out on his missionary sojourns. His travels started in 1507 and lasted for nearly fifteen years. He travelled to many far-off places in India, Lanka, Baghdad, Nepal and Tibet. He put on a dress which was not the dress of the Hindu "sadhus" or the Muslim "faqirs", but a bit of both. People would stop him and ask:

"Are you a Hindu or a Musalman?" and he would reply with a smile. "There is no Hindu, there is no Musalman."

On most of his journeys he was accompanied by Mardana, the Muslim bard who played the reback (*rabaab*).

During his travels he met many kinds of people, rich and poor, simple village-folk and learned scholars and saints. He passed through small villages and big towns and cities. He visited many famous temples and mosques and places of pilgrimage. He saw farmers working in their fields, potters working at their wheels and merchants working at their trades. Everywhere he went, people found peace in his words of love and in his gentle, smiling face. In the evening he sang hymns in praise of God and people came to listen to his songs and to his teachings and learnt the lesson of love and kindness.

Nanak's travels can be divided into four major journeys. The first journey was towards the east. He is believed to have begun this journey by crossing the Beas and going first to what is now Amritsar. It was the month of "Sawan", the month when the sky is covered with dark clouds and the winds that blow are cool and fresh. Nanak came upon a beautiful spot. There was a large stretch of water, and all around were thick groves of trees. Pleased by the beauty of the place he stopped to rest under a tree. This was the spot at which Guru Arjun Dev, the fifth Guru, later built the Harmandir Sahib, the holiest Sikh temple. In the compound of the Golden Temple, the tree under which Nanak sat still stands, old and shrivelled but very much alive.

Nanak went to Lahore and then on to Talwandi. He spent a few days with his parents, with Rai Bular and with his old friends. Mardana too was happy to be with his family. He was the centre of attraction because he told many wonderful stories about life in the town of Sultanpur.

"How are my grandsons?" Tripta asked her son as she sat beside him while he ate his food.

"They are fine," Nanak said, "Sri Chand is with my sister is Sultanpur and Lakhmidas is with Sulakhni in Batala."

"Do you not miss them?" Tripta asked again.

"I travel on my soul's command," Nanak replied, looking straight into her eyes. "I cannot let earthly bonds tie down my feet." His mother watched him as he ate, her heart full of love, and as she watched, tears came to her eyes. She knew that her son was a saint and already people had begun to call him Guru. But she felt sad that he had to leave his wife and sons and go away. Kalyan Chand too came to be reconciled. He listened with pride when Nanak spoke to the people who came to see him. There was great wisdom in the answers he gave to their questions. And in the evenings when Nanak sang his hymns in praise of God, he too felt close to God as he listened. At last he knew what Pandit Hardyal had meant when he said that Nanak would be a great man.

Nanak spent time with Rai Bular, and the Bhatti, who had sensed his greatness before anyone else, was happy to be with him again.

It was time for Nanak to start on his journey again. His parents knew that it was God's will that he must go and so they made no effort to hold him back.

Nanak and Mardana reached the town of Saidpur and Nanak stopped at the door of Lalo's house. Lalo was a carpenter and was at that time working in his courtyard. He saw a shadow fall across his doorstep and looking up saw Nanak. He came forward to greet him.

He saw the glow on Nanak's face and folding his hands, bowed his head in greeting. Nanak reached out and took Lalo's hands in his own. The carpenter's hands were hard and calloused and Nanak knew that here was a man who earned his living by the sweat of his brow and the labour of his hands.

"I am a tired traveller," he said. "Will you give me a place to rest?"

"All that I have is yours," Lalo said. "You have done me great honour by coming to this abode. But I belong to the lowest of the low castes and you will be defiled by staying in my house?"

"There is no low caste, there is no high caste," Nanak replied and stepped into Lalo's house.

Malik Bhago was an important official who worked for a Muslim landlord. It was his son's birthday and he had arranged a great feast for all the sadhus and faqirs and for all high-caste Hindus. By feeding these people he thought he would earn merit in the eyes of God. There were many who came to the feast and Bhago was sure that God would be happy with him for having fed so many worthy people.

"Did all the holy people of the town come to my feast?" he asked one of his servants after the feast was over.

"All, you honour," the servant replied, "except one."

"Who is that?" Bhago asked, surprised.

"It is the strange faqir from Sultanpur who goes by the name of Nanak."

"And why did he not come?"

"It seems, sir, that he prefers the simple food in Lalo's house."

"Lalo? That low-caste carpenter?" Bhago was truly angry.

"Go and summon him to my presence."

When Nanak arrived, Bhago spoke to him in anger.

"What is so special about the food of the law-caste Lalo that you would rather eat the simple bread than all the rich dishes served at my feast."

"There is no low caste and no high caste. Our caste is formed by our actions." Then Nanak went on to prove to Bhago and all the assembled people that Lalo's bread was special. Lalo worked hard with his own hands and earned very little. Yet he was ready to share his bread with others even though he might himself go hungry. Bhago earned his money by exploiting the poor. When he shared it with others it was with a motive. He thought that he would earn favour with God. Lalo's bread was full of the milk of human kindness whereas Bhago's food was replete with the blood of the poor.

Nanak stayed for many days in Saidpur, and made many disciples, among them Malik Bhago. When Nanak left Saidpur, Lalo took upon himself the task of propagating Nanak's message.

Nanak and Mardana crossed the Punjab through Harappa and came to the town of Tulamba. Near the main gate of the town was a rest house run by a man named Sheikh Sajjan who seemed to be a holy man. He dressed in white and spent a lot of time in prayer. He wore a *tilak* on his forehead which was the mark of Hindus and a rosary around his neck. He had built a mosque and a temple near his rest house. As a result both Hindu and Muslim travellers came to his rest house and he looked after them very well. But whenever a rich traveller came, Sajjan would wait till he was asleep and then he would kill him and steal all his money and his belongings. Nanak and Mardana too came to Sajjan's rest house. Nanak's face had a glow, but Sajjan thought the glow came from eating rich food. So he concluded that Nanak was a very rich man. He fed Nanak and Mardana well and was very kind to them. He expected Nanak to go to sleep after his dinner and then he would be able to kill him and steal his belongings. But instead of going to sleep Nanak decided to conduct *kirtan* and he invited Sajjan to attend. Sajjan had no option but to accept the invitation. The music touched his heart and the words made him see the evil of his ways. He fell at Nanak's feet, told him of his evil deeds and begged to be forgiven. He gave away everything he had and spent the rest of his life in the service of others.

The hymn Guru Nanak sang with the accompaniment of music is in the musical measure *suhi*. It runs thus:

Bronze is bright and shining
But, by rubbing its sable
Blackness appears
Which cannot be removed even by washing a hundred
    times.

Nanak travelled to Kurukshetra and then to Panipat where he spent a few days in discussing religious matters with the Sheikh of Shah Sharof. He then went on to Delhi and from there travelled to Hardwar. Here he saw many people, who first bathed in the river, then stood and prayed and offered water to the rising sun by throwing it towards the east.

"Why are you throwing the water towards the sun, my friends?" he asked a young man who stood in the river close to him. "I am offering this to the spirits of my ancestors. It is to quench their thirst."

Gurdwara Sri Nankana Sahib

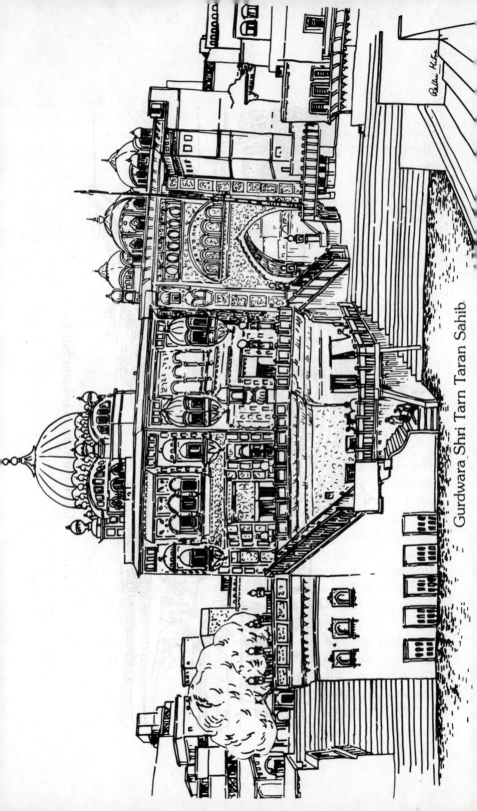

Gurdwara Shri Tarn Taran Sahib.

Nanak stepped into the river, bathed, then turning his back to the sun began to toss water towards the west. All the people who were standing on the river bank were amazed to see this.

"What are you doing, strange man?" they said. "Have you gone mad? Why are you throwing water in that direction?"

"Why," Nanak answered, smiling softly, "my land is near Lahore, and Lahore as you know is towards the west. There has been a drought there, the land is dry and my crops will be ruined. So I am irrigating my land."

They all laughed at Nanak and Nanak pretended to be angry.

"Why are you laughing at me?" he asked.

"You are truly mad," they said between peals of laughter. "How can the water reach as far as Lahore?"

"How far is the land where your ancestors live?" Nanak said.

"It is 49½ crore kos away," a learned pandit replied.

"Well if the water can reach a spot which is 49½ crore kos away, it will surely reach my farm which is only 250 kos away."

From Hardwar Nanak and Mardana travelled eastward through the lower ranges of the Himalayas. They passed through Almora where people offered human sacrifice to their goddess. Nanak knew that if he was to make the people give up this custom, he would have to spend some time with them and teach them the lesson of love for each other. In the beginning the priest was suspicious of him. He thought that Nanak would try to undermine his position among the people. But Nanak did not talk about religion at all. He went quietly among the people bringing help and comfort to all those in need. Gradually the people began to think kindly of the stranger who had come to live amongst them.

The days slipped past and soon it was the day of the next sacrifice. A young seventeen-year-old boy was being offered as a sacrifice. He was bathed and dressed in new clothes and made to kneel before the goddess and the priest said all the special prayers that had to be said. The large crowd of people waiting for the sacrifice to be made were sure that the goddess would be kind to them.

At the last minute Nanak stepped forward from the crowd. "Stop," he said to the priest. The crowd turned to look at Nanak. They respected him and they were sure that he would not have stopped the ceremony without adequate reason.

"Why do you offer this sacrifice?" he asked the priest.

"To please the goddess." "Your goddess is your mother: she is kind and gentle and you are all her sons and daughters. Do you think the pain and suffering that is caused by human sacrifice would please her? Do you think she would be happy to see one of her children being killed? Your religion teaches you to love one another like brothers — to treat your neighbour's pain and suffering as your own. Your religion says that there can be no happiness, no success if it is based on someone else's tears. Why then should you take part in causing such pain and suffering to another? Think of what the boy's mother would go through if he were to die. You are all like her, you would suffer with her." The priest was won over by Nanak's arguments and actively supported Nanak's campaign against human sacrifice and the people soon abandoned this terrible practice.

Nanak stayed for some time in Gorakhmata near Pilibhit, the seat of the Nath Yogis. Many people became his followers and in later years the place was renamed Nanakmata.

From the hills Nanak and Mardana came down to the Gangetic plain and travelled along the river. They passed through Ayodhya, the birthplace of Sri Ram; Allahabad where the Ganga and Jamuna meet, and then they came to Banaras. In Banaras they were the guests of a very learned pandit by the name of Chatur Das. Chatur Das and Nanak had along discussions on religious and spiritual matters. Nanak and Mardana now travelled on to Gaya where Lord Buddha had gained enlightenment. It had by then become less important as Buddhist Centre and more a place of pilgrimage for the Hindus.

From Gaya the travellers went on to Patna and then to Bengal and Assam. There is to this day a temple at Dhubri on the Brahmputra river which marks Nanak's visit to this place. From Dhubri, Nanak and Mardana travelled to Guwahati, Manipur, Imphal and Dhaka and down to the Bay of Bengal and then to Puri. Here the people at first did not like Nanak but as they listened to his hymns and his teachings, they realised that he was a true Guru. He taught the people that God did not live in the stone and wooden statues they worshipped but in their hearts. At Puri, Nanak also met the famous saint Chaitanya.

It was at Puri that Guru Nanak composed and sang his famous hymn *Arti* in the musical measure *dhanasri*, in 1510.

Mardana had now become home-sick and wanted to be back with his family and friends. To spare him any more pain Nanak started on the homeward journey. They passed through Central India where Nanak came across a man-eating tribe. Nanak stayed for some time with this tribe and weaned it away from cannibalism.

They travelled south, through the thick forests and across the desert of Rajasthan and came to the river Satluj. They crossed the river at Pakpattan and spent some time here, meeting with Sheikh Ibrahim, the descendant of the famous Sufi Saint Sheikh Farid.

They came at last to Talwandi. Tripta and Kalyan were overcome with joy to see their son again after so many years.

Then, after some days, Nanak visited Sultanpur. He was greeted warmly by Nawab Daulat Khan, Nanki and Jairam, and his son Sri Chand. Jairam sent a message to Batala and soon Sulakhni and Lakhmidas returned to Sultanpur, and for a little while the husband and wife and the two sons were together again.

For some time Guru Nanak was content to be among his loved ones. Then the restlessness came upon him again, and saying goodbye to his family and friends he set out on his second journey. According to Prof. Sahib Singh, this journey commenced in September 1517.

The Guru crossed the Satluj at what is now Goindwal and came to Bathinda. He stayed there for a short time and then when on to Sirsa where he spent a few months with some Sufi saints before going south to Bikaner. He also spent time with the monks in a Jain monastery there. He next stopped at Ajmer and visited the shrine of Khawaja Muin-ud-Din Chisthi and was in Pushkar at the time of the annual fair. He passed through many towns and reached Rameshwaram where he crossed the sea to Sangaldeep, Sri Lanka. (According to some biographers, the Guru's visit to Lanka formed part of his first *udasi*.)

In Sri Lanka there was at that time a king named Shivnath. One of Guru Nanak's merchant disciples, possibly Mansukh or Bhagirath, had made many trips to Shivnath's city and the king had been impressed by his simple religion and wished to meet his Guru.

At last the king's wish was granted and Guru Nanak and his followers set up camp in a grove outside the king's city. The King came and greeted the Guru and was accepted as a disciple. It is said that the queen who was a very intelligent woman asked Nanak many questions about God, religion and the meaning of life and also became his follower. Guru Nanak crossed the Palk Straits and travelled along the western cost passing through Tanjore, Trichinopoly and Palghat. The Guru passed through many important towns like Nasik, Baroda, Somnath, Madhopur, Junagarh, Porbander, Dwarka and Bhuj. He stayed for some time at Onkaar on the banks of the Narbada.

Guru Nanak came finally to Pakpattan and after spending some time with his old friend Sheikh Ibrahim, he came back to Talwandi. Because of Nanak's teachings which had spread all over Punjab, Talwandi had become famous. Now, when Kalyan saw his son returning with such a large group of followers, he knew he had been wrong to doubt the path Nanak had chosen as a boy. Tripta was very happy to see her son but got little time with him because she was kept busy arranging food for his followers and looking after them. Rai Bular was very ill. Every day the Guru spent many hours with him, comforting him. Rai Bular wished to hear his hymns and Nanak sang for him. A few days later, Rai Bular drifted off to sleep while Nanak sang. It was a sleep from which he did not again wake up.

After a few days Nanak returned to Sultanpur, amidst great rejoicing. This second journey had taken five years.

This time too Nanak's stay in Sultanpur was a brief one. When he expressed his desire to set out on his third journey, Daulat Khan, his old employer, pleaded with him to stay on.

"Stay here with us, Nanak. Be done with your travelling. We need you here. Stay here and bring the true message to my people."

"I cannot stay still till my soul tells me to. I hear an inner voice telling me to go and I must obey." So Nanak set out on his third journey.

His first stop was at Pakhoke where Sulakhni and his sons were staying and he spent some time with them. He was attracted to a spot across the Ravi and wanted to set up a *dera* there. Ajit Randhawa of Pakhoke, who had become a disciple of Nanak, gave the Guru the land and a village was set up here which he named Kartarpur. Word spread that the Guru had set up a permanent home and people flocked to Kartarpur to meet him. The village prospered and as more people came to live there more and more houses were built. The Guru's parents and family also came to live in Kartarpur, as did Mardana's family.

After a few months the Guru set out on his third journey, accompanied by Mardana. Nanak travelled to Sialkot, then on to Jammu and then to Kashmir. He met many pilgrims on their way to the cave temple of Amarnath. One of these pilgrims was a very learned Brahmin by the name of Brahm Das, who was greatly respected for his learning. He was not only a devoted Brahmin but was always trying to learn more about other religions. He noted Guru Nanak's strange dress and began to question him. They spent some days together in discussions on the essence of life and religion which impressed Brahm Das. At Maltan there is now a Gurdwara which stands at the spot where the Guru and Brahm Das met.

From Srinagar Nanak went on to Ladakh, where there is a Gurdwara called Pathar Sahib which has been built to commemorate Nanak's visit. From here he followed the upward course of the river Indus into Tibet, where he stayed in a monastery for a few days. The Head Lama was so pleased with his teachings that he went with him to Mansarovar, the holy lake. Nanak went on to Nepal and Sikkim. From Sikkim he came back, following as closely as possible the route that he had taken on his way out. Nanak reached Sultanpur in 1518.

His brief stay in Sultanpur was a sad one because during this time both his sister Nanki and his brother-in-law Jairam passed away. They had no children, and it was Nanak who performed the funeral ceremonies. It was also the last time that he met Nawab Daulat Khan.

Guru Nanak stayed for a few days in Kartarpur. People who were troubled and unhappy came to meet the Guru. They asked him questions, listened to his teachings and his hymns. Their pain was soothed away and they returned to lead their lives according to the Guru's directions. But soon his soul prompted him to move on again and he set out on his fourth and last journey.

The Guru travelled north to Multan, then to Sukhur. Then he travelled south along the river Indus till he came to Thatta. From here he went west to Hinglaj. Here he met a group of pilgrims on their way to Mecca. He joined them and crossed the Arabian Sea with them. Nanak was dressed in blue robes, a colour that is sacred to the Muslims and carried everything that a Muslim pilgrim on his way to Mecca carries: a staff, a prayer mat, the holy book and a pot for his morning wash. The boat brought them to Jeddah and the pilgrims travelled with a caravan towards Mecca. Soon they were joined by many other caravans and when they camped at night fires were lit to keep the travellers warm against the cold of the desert night and also to cook their food. Nanak sat outside his tent talking to all the men who would listen to him. Some men were suspicious of him and thought he was trying to turn them away from their own religion and convert them to a new religion. Others understood what he was saying and respected him and he came to be looked upon as a great teacher.

When they reached the outskirts of Mecca, Nanak stopped for the night in a mosque. He was very tired from his travels and after saying his prayers he went to sleep. He did not know that his feet were pointing towards the Kaaba, the holiest shrine of the Muslims. Because he was tired he slept till late in the morning. When it was time for the morning prayer one of the attendants in the mosque discovered the traveller fast asleep with his feet pointing towards the Kaaba. The attendant was so upset by what he considered to be an insult to God that he went quickly up the steps and brought Qazi Rukn-ud-din, the mullah of the mosque, to witness this act of sacrilege himself. The Qazi was very angry. He struck Nanak with his staff and shook him awake.

"Wake up, wake up," he said in anger. "Look at the terrible thing you have done. You have pointed your feet at

God's house, God will be very angry with you. You must rub your face in the dirt and beg him to forgive you."

"You are right O, Qazi. I have indeed insulted God. But I am an ignorant man and to avoid making a mistake again, I would be grateful if you could point my feet towards a place where God does not live."

The Qazi was taken aback by Nanak's request. He understood what Nanak was trying to tell him: God was omnipresent and His home was everywhere, so it was wrong to designate any one place as the house of God. The Qazi and Nanak became good friends.

From Mecca Nanak travelled to Medina and then on to Baghdad on to the banks of the Tigris. There is a stone slab outside Baghdad with an inscription on it which tells us that Nanak came to Baghdad. The Guru set up his camp near a tomb outside the city. In the evenings he would conduct a *kirtan* and many people came to hear him and appreciated the beauty of his hymns. But many others became angry because in the orthodox Muslim religion, music was not used in worship. This anger spread and one day a large group of men came to stone Nanak to death. But when they came close they saw him at prayer and the prayer he was reciting was a Muslim prayer. The stones fell from their hands and one by one they knelt and joined in Nanak's prayer. They understood now that here was a saint who respected all religions.

From Baghdad, Nanak travelled to Iran. From there to Kabul and Jalalabad and over the Khyber Pass to Peshawar. He crossed the Indus into the Punjab and went to Saidpur to visit his uncle who lived there.

This was the time when Babar invaded India. He had captured Sialkot and now Saidpur. The people of Saidpur had put up strong resistance and this had angered Babar. As a result he was very cruel to the people of Saidpur. Many

Gurdwara Sri Dera Baba Nanak, Gurdaspur

Gurdwara Kotalgarh Sahib, Chamkaur

were killed and many taken prisoner. Nanak was also amongst the prisoners. While in prison he conducted prayer meetings. The prison warden listened to Nanak and came to the conclusion that he was a great saint.

"Your majesty," the warden said to Babar, "we have committed a sin. Baba Nanak is a saint and we have made him a prisoner."

Babar thought for a while.

"If this is true, we must ask his forgiveness. I will go to see him myself."

Babar came to the prison, and asked Nanak a number of questions and from the answers Babar was convinced that he was a holy man. He bowed to him.

"Forgive me, O saint, for this terrible mistake. I did not know what I was doing. As from this moment you are free, as are all your men."

"These are all my men," Nanak said, pointing to all the prisoners. "I cannot leave the prison without all of them."

Babar smiled, "You are truly a great man." Then, turning to his officer, he said, "Release all the prisoners."

"Ask me for something," Babar said, "so that I may know you have forgiven me."

"I seek nothing," Nanak said. "But if it will make you happy to do something for me then return all the wealth and property and money of the people of Saidpur that have been confiscated by you and also all that has been looted by your soldiers."

This was done and soon afterwards Babar returned to Kabul. Nanak stayed for a few days in Saidpur in the year 1521, and then returned to Kartarpur.

Kartarpur

*I*t was that lovely time of the day which in English they call 'dusk' and in Hindi *goudhuli*. It is the time of the day when the tired farmer, the herdsman, the worker, the labourer, the merchant, all return home from work to the warmth of their homes and a hot meal and the comfort of spending a few hours with their wives, their children and their families, before they go to sleep.

Sulakhni sat near her cooking fire, lost in thought as she waited for her sons to come home for their evening meal. It was winter, the darkness set in early and there was a chill in the air. But she sat close to the fire and did not feel the cold. She thought of her sons and how different they were from each other. Sri Chand, the elder, now twenty-six years old, was saintly like his father. He had no need for things. His clothes were those of a hermit, simple and plain and just enough to cover his body. He ate little and that too only the simplest of food. He was always praying or reciting from the holy books. While he was a boy, he had lived with his aunt, Nanki, and when he had shown some interest in religion it had made Nanki proud and happy. "He is just like Nanak," she would say and because she loved her brother so much she encouraged Sri Chand to spend more time in learning about religion. Sri Chand grew up and became a "sadhu". Like father, like son, Sulakhni said to herself with a smile. Then stopped her thoughts. No, she told herself, be honest; he is not like his father. He did not care about worldly things and spent a lot of time in prayers. In this he was like his father. But in many ways he was very different. She had watched him once while he was in discussion with some other holy men. When one of them disagreed with what he said, his eyes flashed and his face became ugly with anger and he raised his voice at the other sadhus. He was proud of his knowledge and this pride made him arrogant. She had watched her husband too when he had his discussions with other holy men and though they did not always agree with him she had never seen anger or pride in her husband's eyes. No, Sri Chand was not like his father. But then neither was their younger son, Lakhmidas.

She had kept the younger son with her and watched him grow. Every time he had shown interest in matters connected with religion or in holy men her heart had filled with fear. She was afraid that he would take after his father and she would lose him too. So she did everything to keep his mind fixed on worldly things. In this she was helped by her parents. They were always giving him new things — new clothes, new toys, new shoes and all kinds of rich food to eat. He grew up with no interest in God or in prayers. She had succeeded in keeping him with her but she had paid a heavy price for this success. Her son had grown to be a selfish young man who thought only of himself and showed no feeling for others. So in a way she had lost him too. If it had not been for Kalyan and Tripta her life would have been lonely. Like her they too spent their days in waiting for Nanak's return. She smiled to herself as she thought of the soft quiet lives that the old couple led and of the love that had grown between them and her.

As she waited for her sons' return she heard, very faintly, footsteps coming up the long quiet street that led to her home. Her head came up with a start. They seemed so familiar. But it couldn't be: So many times during these long years of waiting she had thought she heard this familiar step. Yet when she had run to the door to look for Nanak there had been no one there. She heard the sound again. The blood rushed to her head. Yes, there could be no mistaking it. Even after all these years she remembered the sound of Nanak's footstep. She got up and ran to the door, and there he was, thin and gaunt, dressed in those strange clothes, his cheeks hollow, his beard now half grey. He smiled at her and she fell at his feet and shed tears of joy.

"Sulakhni," she heard Tripta's voice call out to her. "Sulakhni Putar, who is it? Who has come?" And the weak tired voice which was normally only a whisper now came loud and clear with a strength that only hope can bring.

Nanak drew Sulakhni up, put his arm around her shoulder and together they went into the house to meet his parents.

It was a joyous home coming. As news of Nanak's return spread through Kartarpur, people flocked to the Bedi house to meet their Guru.

Nanak was happy to meet his sons again, but they were so different from him, from everything that he believed in, that they were strangers to him. He was a stranger to them too because he had spent so little time with them while they were growing up.

Nanak never put on the sadhu's clothes again. He wore the ordinary clothes that all the other people wore. He started the day as he had always done by having a bath and then spent a few hours in prayer and *kirtan*. The Guru's compositions, the *Japuji* and *Asa-di-war* were recited in the morning. Mardana, who had played the rebeck for so many years while Nanak sang, continued to play even here in Kartarpur. He was joined by his son Shahzada who had become as good a musician as his father. Large groups of people came to listen to the *kirtan*. Then Nanak ate a simple meal and went to work in the fields around Kartarpur. These fields were all part of the area that had been gifted to him by his disciple Ajit Randhawa. Some of these fields had been cultivated by a few of Nanak's followers who had settled down in Kartarpur. Other fields remained fallow. Now Nanak began to cultivate these fields. He worked in the fields himself and this set a good example for all the other people who lived in Kartarpur and they too worked hard and enjoyed the fruit of their labours.

In the evening there was a discourse or a discussion on religion and then there was *kirtan*. The Guru's compositions

Sodar or *Aarti* would be sung. Then all those who had attended the prayers sat down and ate the evening meal together.

The number of pilgrims who came to Kartarpur grew steadily. People who came from far-away places had no place to stay because the people of Kartarpur had already taken in as many guests as they could.

One day Nanak sent for one of his disciples who was a master builder.

"I want to build a *dharamsala*," Nanak told him. "A place where all the people who come from outside Kartarpur can stay in comfort. The *dharamsala* must have a big hall where our meetings can be held when the sun is too hot or when it rains, and of course you must also build the *langar* and a *langar*-hall."

Word of the project quickly spread and by the time the master builder had finished making his design, cart-loads of bricks and lime and wooden beams had already been brought to Kartarpur by the Guru's followers. By the time the foundations were marked an army of men with all the necessary implements descended upon Kartarpur. By the end of the year the *dharamsala* was ready. All the followers now had a place to stay. There was enough covered space for the religious meetings and the big *langar* served meals twice a day to all who came. His disciples now brought vegetables and grain and food for the *langar* in carts and there was always plenty of everything.

More than a year had passed since Nanak's return to Kartarpur and his life had become so settled that people felt that he would not go away again. Sulakhni too believed that he would stay always with her and stopped looking at him with worry and fear. In the mornings and evenings when he went in and spent some time with his parents they were at last content.

One day while Nanak was tilling the fields Sri Chand came running to him. "Father, come quickly. Mother wants you at home." Nanak felt the fear in his son's voice and knew that something was wrong but he did not ask. He untied his oxen and turned them loose in the nearby meadow. Then he wiped the sweat from his brow and hurried home with his son.

There was a crowd of people near the door and in the courtyard. They all stood there in silence and when they saw Nanak they made way for him. He went into the room and saw that his father had been lowered to the ground. His mother cradled her husband's head in her lap. Kalu's breath came in long gasps and his whole body shook as he breathed. He looked so weak and thin and tired that Nanak knew the end was near. Kalyan raised his head as he saw Nanak come into the room and tried to smile. Then he held out a trembling hand to his son and Nanak, bending down, clasped it in both of his, and thus, his head cradled in his wife's lap, his hand held firmly by his son, Kalyan breathed his last. When the breath stopped, a calm look came upon his face. It was as if he knew that he had not died, that he would live always in the hearts and minds of men as Nanak's father.

There was a deep silence for a moment and then some of the women who stood outside the room began to cry. But Nanak did not cry, nor did Tripta. Nanak gently closed his father's eyes, then taking his father's head from his mother's lap he helped her to her feet and led her from the room.

The next few days were taken up by the funeral ceremonies. Through all these days Tripta sat in silence, not weeping, not speaking, eating only a few mouthfuls of food and that too when she was forced to. There was no outward sign of sorrow on her face as she sat praying, always praying. "What is it, mother?" Nanak asked one day. "Why have you become so quiet?"

"I must pray," she said and again her voice was clear and strong. "I must prepare myself — I have to go to join your father. I cannot leave him alone for long." And the day after all the ceremonies were over, Tripta too passed away peacefully in her sleep.

Gradually, over the months, the people in Kartarpur became one community. Those who were farmers tilled the land but the grain was shared by all. Those who had skills like the potters, the weavers, the carpenters and the masons used them in the service of the *sungat*. The women worked in the *langar*. They cut and cooked the vegetables and made the *chapatis*, and men who could make no other contribution served the meals and washed the utensils. Those who had medical skill treated the sick and the injured and those who were learned and had musical ability joined Nanak in the discourses and the *kirtan*. All the members of the community, those who stayed in Kartarpur and those who came to visit, served the *sangat* in one way or other.

During his travels Guru Nanak had set up centres in many places, some of them very far away, and he had left these centres in the charge of his followers. Now his followers came from these centres to Kartarpur to learn more from their Guru and take back new strength to their own centres. Kartarpur, the city of the Creator, became the centre of the Sikh world.

Many of the Guru's disciples became famous and earned respect not only for their learning but also for their good, kind deeds.

Bura was a young boy of twelve when he first met the Guru. He belonged to a family of Randhawa jats and lived in the Amritsar district. Like Nanak, when he was young, Bura too took the family cattle out to graze. Like Nanak he too liked to spend his time in deep thought, thinking of religious matters. When on his travels Nanak stopped in a jungle just outside Bura's village, Bura greeted the Guru with great respect and brought him refreshments. When it was time for the Guru to move on Bura asked for a boon. Nanak smiled at the young boy.

"What is it that you seek?"

"Oh, holy one, I seek to be freed from the cycle of birth and rebirth."

"You are too young for such thoughts. From where did this idea come to you?"

"When Babar's army came to our village his soldiers camped in his jungle. They took whatever they wanted from the villagers. Then they cut the corn in the fields. They cut the ripe corn with the unripe corn and made no distinction between the two. Watching them I realised that death also makes no distinction between the young and the old."

The Guru hugged the boy.

"You are not a child," he said. "You speak with the wisdom of an old man."

So Bura came to be known as Bhai Budha. When the Guru set up his home in Kartarpur, Bhai Budha too moved permanently to Kartarpur. He was respected for his wisdom and his kindness and people came to him with their problems. He lived to the ripe old age of a hundred and twenty-five and was fortunate to work with five successive Gurus.

Another famous disciple of Guru Nanak was Moola Keer. He lived a simple life according to the Guru's teachings. He worked hard during the day and spent his time in reciting the Guru's prayers and hymns in the mornings and evenings. He was a honest man and he spent most of his savings in looking after the Sikhs as followers of Guru Nanak came to be known, who stopped at his home on their way to Kartarpur. One day a Sikh while resting in his house saw Moola Keer's wife putting some money and jewellery away in her cupboard. The Sikh waited till all in the house had gone to sleep and then he stole the jewellery and the money from the cupboard and put it in his bag. Early next morning he woke up Moola Keer and asked him to open the gate as he was in a hurry to start on his journey again. While they were walking to the gate, the Sikh's bag fell to the ground and the jewellery and money fell out. Moola did not say a word. He put the money and the jewellery back in the bag and gave the bag to the Sikh.

The Sikh was so ashamed of what he had done that on reaching Kartarpur he told the story to Guru Nanak. Guru

Nanak sent for Moola Keer and when he reached Kartarpur and came into the Guru's presence the Guru asked him, "This Sikh told me of your strange behaviour. Why did you give the jewellery and money back to this thief? You should have caught him and taken him to the *kotwali*."

"He is a Sikh," Moola replied in a quiet voice. "If I had handed him to the police, everyone would have come to know and people would say that a Sikh had done an evil deed. This would have brought disrepute to all Sikhs." The Guru was pleased by what Moola said and asked him one last question.

"On his return from Kartarpur this Sikh will stop in your village. Will you take him into your house?"

"Yes, master," Moola said without hesitation. "I will take him into my house and give him food and shelter and serve him as well as I can. You have taught us that serving others is the best way in which we can worship God."

Perhaps the most well-known of the Guru's disciple was Lehna. Lehna came from the village which is now known as Sarai Nanga in Muktsar district. From Sarai Nanga he moved to Khadur. He had been a great worshipper of the Goddess Durga. There he had heard Nanak's hymns and had come to Kartarpur. He was twenty-eight years old at the time and served the Guru and the Guru's *sangat* with great devotion. For Lehna the Guru's word was a command and the service of the *sangat* was a prayer. Though all members of the *sangat* were equal, Lehna was respected by all the others because of his great spirit of service. Ever since he had returned from his journeys, Nanak knew that neither of his sons could be his successor. Sri Chand lived a life of renunciation and Lakhmi Das was too proud. He chose Lehna as his successor. He brought him to the banks of the Ravi and embraced him. "From now on you will be known as Angad which means one who is of my limb." Then Guru Nanak placed five copper coins before him and bowed to him. Thus Angad became the second Guru of the Sikhs.

In 1530 Nanak made one last journey. It was a short journey across the Ravi to Achal, a small village in Batala district. In Achal there was a very old and famous temple in which Shiva's son, Kartik, was worshipped. So during Shivratri there was a very big fair in Achal. Like all village fairs it was very colourful with a great deal of music and dance and games. During this fair many holy men came to Achal and had debates and discussions with each other on subjects connected with religion. When Nanak was sixty-one years old, he too came to Achal to take part in the Shivratri fair. By now his fame as a Guru had spread far and wide and there were many of his disciples amongst the crowds of people thronging the fair. As Nanak approached Achal news of his coming spread and people came out to greet him. Some asked him for his blessings, others asked for his advice. Most stayed to listen to his *kirtan* and his teachings. So many people came to listen to Nanak that a few of the "sadhus" were jealous. They debated with him and tried to make him look small in the eyes of the people.

"You have done an unholy act," one of the sadhus said, "You were a sadhu for twenty-three years and you wore the sadhu's clothes and travelled far and wide. Now you have given up the sadhu's dress and returned to your home and started working in the fields. The sadhu lives on a far higher plane than the farmer and others like him, work with their hands. You have demeaned yourself by giving up the sadhu's life." But Nanak only smiled.

"Tell me, O holy one, what do you do when you are hungry? Where do you get your food from?"

The sadhu was surprised by this simple question.

"Everyone knows that we earn nothing. The only food we eat is what we get when we go begging."

"And who gives you this food?"

"The worker, the householder, of course."

"Then I think the householder is greater. You become a sadhu and then go with your begging bowl to the householder. You would starve to death if he did not give you anything to eat."

Listening to such debates the people were converted to Nanak's teachings. He was a simple farmer himself and what he taught was a lesson that even ordinary people who did small jobs or worked in the fields could understand. On the last day of the fair Nanak said goodbye to the other holy men and to his disciples, and with Mardana by his side returned to Kartarpur.

When Mardana was seventy-six years old he fell ill. Many famous *hakims* and *vaids* came to see him and gave him medicines but to no avail. Nanak was always by his bedside. He caressed Mardana's hair and this brought comfort to Mardana and he drifted off into a tired sleep. And still Nanak sat by his side and caressed his hair. He looked closely at his friend's face and saw him as he had been when they had first returned to Talwandi, surrounded by an admiring group of friends, as he told them funny stories about their life in Sultanpur. He saw him as the rather plump young man who had gone with him on that first journey. He had not been happy to go because he loved good food and on their journey he often had to go without food. Nanak smiled as he remembered that Mardana had always been hungry, had always asked for food. Through all his long journeys, Mardana had travelled with him in sun and rain and snow, over hills and plains and mountains, to regions that were strange and unfamiliar. He had looked after Nanak in every way, attended to all his needs and found joy in that service, and through it all he had been able to laugh at all their troubles and to laugh at himself. Then when they sang their songs, he played his rebeck with such feeling that those who listened were moved by the music. He had been with the Guru for so many years that he had become part of the Guru, of the Guru's way of life and of his teachings.

All these memories came chasing one another through Nanak's mind as he looked at this sleeping companion.

"God," he prayed silently, "be merciful to my friend. He is a good man."

Though the illness continued to eat into him day by day, Mardana seemed to be at peace with himself and with his approaching death.

Early one morning he opened his eyes and saw the Guru still sitting by his side, the way he had sat when he went to sleep.

"Master," he said, without fear, "my time has come."

"So be it," Nanak said, "I will build a tomb over your body so that you will be famous."

"No," he said with a small sad smile. "My spirit is attempting to find release from this cage of bones and skin and flesh. Do not seek to hold it in a prison made of stone." He paused for breath. "And fame: I have all the fame in the world that I need. In years to come, whenever people talk of you, as I know they often will, my name will be mentioned too."

Nanak caught his friend's hand in both of his and squeezed it gently. In Mardana he had found the respect and devotion that a disciple gives to his Guru, the love a friend gives to a friend, the support and affection that a brother gives to a brother and the companionship and care that a wife gives to her husband. They had been together for so long and been through so much that their souls were bound together with a bond that the world has rarely seen, a bond that even death could not break.

Mardana closed his eyes and it seemed that he was sleeping again. Then suddenly he opened his eyes and said, "Go, go Master. It is time. It is time for the morning prayer." His eyes fixed on his Master's face, Mardana left this world. Nanak closed his eyes and drew the sheet over his face. Someone in the room began to sob and Nanak saw that it was Shahzada. He drew him into an embrace and consoled him. Then he went quickly to bathe so that he could be in time for the morning prayers.

Nanak began his discourse. When it was time for *kirtan* he remembered that Mardana was no more. Who would give the music for his song? He looked, as he had always looked when he began his song, towards the spot where Mardana had sat. He saw Shahzada, sitting in his father's place ready to start playing on his *rebeck*. Nanak smiled and began his song.

The years rolled by. Older disciples passed into the shades and younger faces took their place, and yet the number of those who believed in Nanak and his teachings grew every day. People all over Punjab began to live the way Nanak had taught his Sikhs to live. They were free from the empty customs and rituals that they were being forced to observe in the name of religion.

Nanak heard the voice of God calling out to him: his time upon earth was now nearly over.

He went to the banks of the river and lay down under a tree. Word spread quickly that the Guru's end was near. His disciples hurried from far and wide for one last *darshan* of their guru and he was constantly surrounded by his disciples. The end came peacefully on 27 September 1539 and Guru Angad Dev took over the leadership of the Sikhs.

Teachings

Guru Nanak did not claim to be an incarnation of God or even a special messenger of God. He claimed only that he was a teacher, trying to teach people how they could live good, simple lives which would bring them closer to God.

The appeal of Nanak's teaching was instantaneous, and almost from the first time he began to preach, he was able to win converts. By the time he died, he had built up a strong community of Sikhs not only in Kartarpur but also at other centres all over India.

The reasons for the great and instant appeal of Nanak's teachings are not far to seek. The two major religions being preached and followed in the Punjab at that time were Hinduism and Islam. Hinduism was taught in Sanskrit, a language which had been popular in ancient India but which was now archaic. In fact all the sacred books of the Hindus are in Sanskrit and most people could not understand them unless they were interpreted by a scholar or a priest. Islam was taught through old Arabic, the language in which the Koran is written. No one in the Punjab used this language and as a result it was beyond the comprehension of the average man. When Nanak composed his famous hymns, which contained all his teachings, he did so in the language spoken by the people of Punjab at that time. They could be understood even by an illiterate person. As a result people naturally veered away from the older religions, which they found difficult to understand, and towards the Guru's teachings, which they could understand on their own.

Another factor that brought an immediate appeal of Nanak's teachings was his use of music. Music formed the medium of his teachings. All his hymns are set to various *rāgas* of Indian classical music and to this day they are sung in the *raag* in which he composed them. Music has always been an integral part of Indian culture, and of the Indian way of life. It is also a well established fact that people will respond more readily to a song than to a speech. So when Nanak began his discourses with the singing of beautiful hymns he found many willing listeners, who, overwhelmed by the beauty of the song, stayed on as a captive audience to listen to his speech.

The starting point of all Nanak's teaching is his concept of God. He says that there is one God who is without form, who is not born and so cannot die. As such when we worship

God it is not necessary to deify pictures or statues. By doing this we are not worshipping God because God is formless.

Nanak went on to say that God was Truth. By saying this he made God a standard by which men could judge their actions and their behaviour. If God was truth then to behave in an untruthful manner would be to go against God. Behaving in an untruthful manner included telling lies, stealing, being dishonest in our conduct and doing things that hurt other people.

Since it is difficult for an average man or woman to understand the concept of God as formless or a force that lives everywhere and in everything, it becomes essential for all of us to have a "Guru". It is the Guru who will help the disciple to understand God and to love Him. It is the Guru who will give his followers strength so that they are able to bear all the sorrow and pain that life brings to them. It is the Guru who shows us the path of Truth. He is like the captain of a ship who will guide us carefully through the troubled waters of life and bring us safely to God.

Because the Guru plays such an important part in our pursuit of God we must obey him in everything and follow his teachings and his instruction with complete and unquestioning faith.

Again and again Nanak stressed the importance of the role of the Guru in the disciple's life and the need for the disciple to have total trust and faith in the Guru. At the same time Nanak also stressed that we must never forget that the Guru is only a teacher who shows us the path to God. He is not God. As a result we must follow his teachings, listen to his advice, but must never make the mistake of worshipping him.

Nanak says that all men must choose a Guru. This would imply that after one Guru's death his disciples would have to choose another Guru. Nanak appointed Angad as his successor during his lifetime.

Nanak preached a complete adherence to the Guru's instructions. So on his death his followers became Angad's followers because Guru Nanak had said that Angad was to be their Guru. Angad could now carry on Nanak's work. So by appointing a successor Nanak introduced a very special feature to the new religion. Each Guru in imitation of Nanak's example would choose his successor during his lifetime. This ensured that the leadership of the Sikhs remained uninterrupted. Because of this Sikhism became a strong, unified religion. This saved Sikhism from breaking up the way other sects like the Kabirpanthis and Vaishnavas broke up into splinter groups after their Guru's death.

Guru Nanak taught that it is essential for every man to perform the duties of a householder. Earning a living, getting married, bringing up one's children, looking after one's parents, all these were duties that we must all perform. No real good could be achieved by giving up the world and going to the mountains to live alone and to pray. Man must live amongst the impurities of the world and yet try to remain pure, just as the lotus remains dry even though it grows in water. True prayers, Nanak said, were good actions and good actions can only be performed towards other men. If we take *sanyas* we will not get a chance to do good deeds to others and no matter how much we close our eyes, and no matter how many *mantras* we recite, our prayers will not be true prayers. We must live amongst men, perform our duties to the best of our ability, always do good towards our fellowmen. Only by doing this could we come close to God.

Nanak lived the life of a householder himself. He lived with his wife and sons and worked in the field to earn a living. When the time came to choose his successor, he chose Angad who was also a householder with a wife and children. From this simple act it followed that all the Gurus would be householders and that an ascetic would not become a Guru. This meant that all the Gurus lived the same life that their followers lived and shared in their joys and sorrows. The human side of their personalities and their lives made them greatly loved by their followers.

Nanak believed in the equality of all men. In Hindu society caste and religion have always worked side by side. But two *bhakta* saints from the South, Ramanuja and Ramananda, said that it was possible to have a society without the caste system. The Muslims too had no caste system and Panjab had been familiar with the idea of casteless society since the eleventh century. Nanak's mind was influenced by both the *bhaktas* and the Muslim saints. He taught that by treating the lower castes as untouchables we were hurting them. When we do things which hurt other men we are moving away from the truth and from God. So all men, no matter what their caste, must be treated equally. We must give a man of the lowest caste the same respect that we would give to a man of the highest caste. Nanak preached that all his followers must sit side by side with no consideration of their wealth, their social position or their caste and become one united *sangat* by praying together and taking part in *kirtan*. And with the passage of years the *langar* became a visible representation of Nanak's most important teaching. By sitting side by side on a mat and eating together his followers put aside all distinctions of caste and creed and wealth and reiterated their faith in their Gurus' teaching that all men are equal and belong to one caste and one race.

Nanak was against empty rites and rituals. A Muslim could not be a true Muslim by just praying in the mosque, fasting or going on a Haj at the Kaaba. A Hindu could not be a good Hindu by only giving feasts, performing *yagnas* and other forms of worship, or going on a pilgrimage. A true Muslim and a true Hindu must be kind, honest, truthful, polite and good. True religion is a way of life. He summed up this way of life by saying that people should work honestly, pray sincerely and be charitable.

Nanak built a bridge between the Hindus and Muslims, but in so doing he created a new community of people who had their own way of life. Nanak's followers lived the way their teacher had taught them to and their way of life was different from that of the Hindus and Muslims of the time. They had a separate place of worship and did not go to the temple or the mosque. Their way of worship was also different. They did not bow before stone idols or repeat Sanskrit prayers. Nor did they turn towards Mecca and pray in Arabic. They sang Nanak's songs and prayed in their own mother-tongue, Panjabi. Even their greetings to each other were no longer Hindu or Muslim greetings but the Guru's greeting of "Sat Kartar" or "True Creator" which later became "Sat Sri Akal".

It is often said that most of Guru Nanak's teachings, his ideas, have been taken from other religions and other religious leaders. This may be true but he gave to all these ideas a new form which was his own. He made his ideas a way by which human personality could be developed. So powerful are his teachings that they have remained strong and clear five hundred years after his lifetime. They have helped the Sikhs to overcome every difficulty that they have been faced with. The cruelty of the Mughal government and the great military strength of Ahmad Shah Abdali could not eliminate the Sikhs because they had Nanak's teachings to give them strength. Nanak's teachings brought out the best in his followers and gave them the strength to face and survive all hardships.

The Guru who was capable of giving such great strength to his followers has left behind a memory of gentleness and love. He has often been described as meek and gentle. He did not try to impress people with his spiritual strength by performing miracles and used only personal example and gentle persuasion to win followers. He was also a great poet and used his poetry and music to reach the hearts of his people. The poetry he left behind ranks among the great literatures of the world. He was truly one of the greatest teachers the world has ever known.

The *Janamsakhis*

Most of what is written about Guru Nanak has been learnt from *Janamsakhis*. The *Janamsakhis* are stories from the Guru's life. These stories have been put together in a chronological form and when we read them it is like reading a biography of the Guru. There are many such sets of stories but the more important ones are the *Bala Janamsakhis*, the *Puratan Janamsakhis,* the *Meherban Janamsakhis* and the *Janamsakhis* that are supposed to have been written by Sewa Dass and some others. Many stories are common to all the sets though they differ from each other in details.

It modern times *Janamsakhis* do not enjoy the importance they had till about a hundred years ago. Till then people believed everything that was in these stories. Now the readers realise that all these stories and all the details are not altogether authentic. The first of these sets of stories was written more than a hundred years after the Guru's death. Till then they were handed down from father to son by the word of mouth. As a result each time these stories were told the story-teller modified or changed the story a little. By the time they were written the stories had become very different from what they were originally. Also these stories were told by people who were not highly educated and they were told to simple village-folk who were at best semi-literate. To impress the villagers who believed in magic and miracles, the writers brought in these two elements in their stories. It is well known that the Gurus were against performing miracles or showing off their spiritual power.

So when the *Sakhis* tell us about the Guru performing miracles to impress his followers, we naturally doubt their authenticity.

Yet we cannot reject the *Janamsakhis* altogether. They are very important, because each of these stories is an illustration of some aspect of Guru Nanak's teachings.

There are many interesting stories about the Guru in the *Janamsakhis*. It is possible to relate only a very few of these.

When the Guru disappeared while he was bathing in the river, many believed that he had been drowned. When he reappeared and said he had heard a voice many believed that a miracle had taken place. But when Nanak said again and again, "There is no Hindu, there is no Musalman," many believed that he had lost his reason. News of what Nanak was saying was brought to the Qazi, the head of all the Muslims in Sultanpur.

"Your holiness," people said, "this 'Kafir' is saying, over and over again, there is no Hindu, there is no Musalman. What does he mean?"

The Qazi was very angry. He knew that Nanak had already won respect among many of the people in Sultanpur, both Hindus and Muslims, because of his kind, gentle ways and his concern for the poor, and if he kept saying there is no Muslim many Muslims would believe him and stop doing all the things they should do as devout Muslims. He went to see Daulat Khan, the Lodi ruler of Sultanpur. "Lord, this mad man must be stopped immediately. He is saying dangerous things." Daulat Khan could see that the Qazi was angry, so he did not interrupt him. "He can say what he likes about the Hindus but he has no right to make comments about Islam. How can he say that there is no Musalman?"

Daulat Khan loved Nanak dearly and he had been very happy when Nanak had reappeared. But he had heard about the strange things Nanak was saying and now that the Qazi had come to him he knew that he had to do something to stop Nanak.

So the Nawab sent for Nanak.

"Tell us, Nanak, what do you mean when you say there is no Hindu, there is no Musalman. Are not the Qazi and I followers of Muhammad?"

"There is no Hindu, there is no Musalman." Nanak repeated himself. "There are only true followers of God. We must be firm in our faith, our hearts must be clean, we must not have any greed or pride. We must not be troubled by life or death. We must accept the will of God. We must be unselfish and kind to all. Only then can we call ourselves true Musalmans."

This made the Qazi even more angry.

"And what are you?" he shouted at Nanak.

Nanak only smiled and in his soft, gentle voice said, "I am neither a Muslim nor a Hindu."

"Why?" asked the Qazi.

"Because I try to live according to the teachings of all religions. To me all religions belong to God."

The Qazi felt this was a good opportunity to trap Nanak. "The time has come for offering the Friday prayer. If to you all religions are one, join us in prayer in the mosque."

"That I will do with pleasure. I will follow when you lead the prayer."

So the Nawab, the Qazi and the Guru set off for the mosque. The Qazi took his place in front of the congregation. During the *namaz* when all the other worshippers knelt, Nanak remained standing. The Qazi saw this from the corner of his eye and the moment the *namaz* was over he turned to the Nawab.

"See, my lord. This man is a liar and a cheat. He said all religions are equal and he would join us in *namaz*. But he did not do so. He must be punished." He spoke very loudly and in anger and a crowd of people collected around him.

"Tell me, my friend," the Nawab said to Nanak in a quiet voice, "what do you have to say to this?"

Nanak did not reply to the Nawab's question. He turned instead to the Qazi. With a smile on his lips and a twinkle in his eyes he said, "You are a man of God, in the house of God, and you have just led a congregation of a thousand men in prayer. I know you will tell the truth. Tell me what was on your mind while you prayed?"

The Qazi thought for a while, then he saw Nanak looking at him and the smile from Nanak's lips had spread to his eyes. The Qazi knew he must tell the truth. "I was thinking of my mare." He spoke softly but the silence around was so complete that everyone could hear him. "My mare had a foal last night. It was a difficult birth but all went well and I now have a beautiful foal. The stable is next to an open well and I was worried that the foal may fall into the well. This would be a great loss to me and so my mind was on my mare and her foal."

"So tell me, O learned one," Nanak asked, "does prayer consist only in kneeling and bowing and saying a few words?"

"No," said the Qazi, now understanding why Nanak had not joined him in prayer. "Prayer is to control the mind so that when you praise God you think only of Him and of nothing else. You are right, Nanak, while my body was bowing to God, my mind and spirit were full of other things."

Nanak and Mardana were on their first journey. It was the beginning of the monsoon and they travelled in the heavy rain. From the forests of the foot-hills of the Himalayas, the two travellers moved slowly down to the Gangetic plain. They stopped to rest in a little village and in the evenings, if it was not raining, Nanak conducted *kirtan* in the courtyard of his host's house. His fame spread quickly and people came from far and near to listen to his songs and to hear his teachings. Amongst the people who came was a shopkeeper from a nearby town. At first he came because he had heard so much about the Guru and wanted only to see who this strange holy man was. But once he heard Nanak's teachings he became a disciple and came every evening without fail. The moment he closed his shop he would rush home, spend a few moments with his family and then hurry to the village where Nanak dwelt. He knew the Guru would soon move on and he did not want to miss a single day. He spent hours not only in the service of the Guru but also in the service of other members of the *sangat*. In this service he found more happiness than he had ever known before.

One morning he was a little late in opening his shop. As he walked up the step, he was humming one of Nanak's hymns. His neighbour, the shopkeeper in the next shop, had already opened his shop and called out to him.

"You seem very happy these days, my friend. Your business must be very good indeed."

"Yes," the shopkeeper replied. "My business is very good these days but it is the business of the mind and spirit."

"What do you mean?" asked the other shopkeeper.

"I go everyday to listen to the teachings of my Guru and he has brought me great wealth of the mind and the spirit. He has brought me close to God."

"Take me also to meet your Guru — perhaps he will make me rich as well."

"You can come whenever you choose. You can come this evening when we close our shops," the Guru's disciple offered.

But in the evening the second shopkeeper turned to pleasures of the flesh and did not go with the Guru's disciple.

Every day he would call out to his friend to take him to his Guru and every day he would stay back. So the Guru's disciple led the life of a saint, serving his Guru and the other members of the *sangat*, showing kindness to everyone, spending his spare time in prayer. The second shopkeeper led a selfish life in which he thought only of his pleasure and his thoughts, words and actions were full of sin.

One day the second shopkeeper was waiting for some friends under a tree just outside the town. As he waited with nothing better to occupy him, he picked up a stick and began to dig up the earth. He saw something shining in the soil he had dug up and on picking it up found it was a gold coin. He ran home and brought a pickaxe and began to dig, sure that he would find more gold. At last his pickaxe struck something hard. He dug up the loose soil with his hands and found a big earthen jar buried in the ground and was sure that he had found a buried treasure. He held the jar in his lap and loosened the lid, but when he opened the lid he was disappointed to find that the jar was full of ash. He turned the jar over and emptied all the ash on the ground besides him. Then very carefully he felt through all the ash, a little at a time so that he would not miss anything. But there were no more gold coins to be found and he was very disappointed. But then he consoled himself with the thought that one gold coin was better than none at all.

He returned to his shop. After some time, he saw his friend and neighbour coming to open his shop. The Guru's disciple walked with a limp. He carried his left shoe in his hand and his left foot was bandaged.

"Why, my friend," the second shopkeeper called, "what has happened to you?"

"Today, while returning from my Guru's village, a thorn went into my foot. It went in deep and when I pulled it out my foot began to bleed. I had to have it bandaged." The second shopkeeper began to laugh.

"You are the one who talked about wealth and look at the wealth each of us has got. You, who are good and kind, have been given a thorn in your foot while I who lead a life of sin and debauchery have been given a gold coin. I wonder how your Guru will explain this."

The Guru's disciple smiled.

"Come with me this evening and you can hear what he says."

So, that evening the second shopkeeper at last came into the Guru's presence. He listened to the *kirtan* and to Nanak's teachings and when the *sangat* moved away for the evening meal his friend led him up to the Guru and introduced him.

"Master, this is my friend and neighbour. He has the shop next to mine and he has a question to ask you."

The Guru listened to the question, looking carefully at his disciple as the other shopkeeper spoke. Then he smiled and turned to the speaker.

"You are right — you can think of the gold coin as a reward and the thorn as a punishment. But let me put it another way. I say that you were destined to find a big jar full of gold coins but because you lead a life of sin, the coins in the jar were turned into ash and you found only one coin. Your friend was destined to be impaled by a sharp spear but because of his good deeds the spear was reduced to a small thorn. Man's life is made up of the actions he performs. If his actions are bad even the good that comes his way is reduced. If his actions are good the harm that comes his way is reduced."

The Guru came to the *sangat* at Prayag which is now called Allahabad. Here the three rivers, the Ganga, the Yamuna and the Saraswati meet. This point is considered very holy and special merit is attached to bathing in the river at Allahabad. It is felt that by doing this all one's sins can be washed away, especially so on days that have been designated for this purpose. On these days the banks of the river are crowded with thousands of people all waiting to bathe in the river, at the time which the priests have said is most auspicious, and this is usually at about four in the morning. On these special days holy fairs are held in Prayag and people come from all over the country to bathe in the holy waters.

At the time when the Guru reached Allahabad the biggest of these holy fairs was in progress. This was the "Kumbh Mela". It is held once in twelve years and marks the special configuration of the stars during the month of "Baisakh", and commemorates the dropping of the holy nectar at this spot when the Gods carried it away from the *rakshas*.

For fifteen days every bit of open land is covered by the camps of holy men and pilgrims. Each group says its special prayers and practises its own customs. But at the appointed time they all come to the river to bathe.

The Guru arrived on the banks of the holy river and set up his camp on the empty space he could find. Mardana played on the rebeck and the Guru sang a song in praise of

God. The music was so sweet, Nanak's voice was so strong and pure, and the words of the song so beautiful that crowds of people gathered around to listen.

"Who is this holy man?" A whisper went around the crowd. "We have not seen him here before."

Then someone answered: "He is Nanak, the great Guru from the Punjab. He travels far and wide to bring his teachings to people even of distant lands." So in a few days Nanak had drawn many followers to his teachings. There was a *mahant* who had his camp close to Nanak's camp. His jealousy was aroused when he saw that his followers were abandoning him to listen to Nanak's teachings and he began to say nasty things about Nanak, but no one would listen to him.

Guru Nanak sat in meditation. Suddenly he heard a great commotion around him. It was *Brahmmurath*, early morning, the time which was considered most holy by the pandits for a bath in the holy waters. So it was thought that anyone who bathed in the Ganga at Prayag at this time would become so pure that he would surely go to heaven when he died.

Everyone ran to the river to bathe but Nanak sat on, lost in his thoughts. One by one the pilgrims and the holy men returned, sure that their dip in the holy waters had made them so pure that they would go to heaven. When the *mahant* returned he saw that Nanak had not taken a bath and the auspicious time has passed. He felt this was his chance to belittle Nanak and win his followers back. He stood outside Nanak's camp and called out loudly.

"Look, look! Look at this foolish man. He has come all the way to Prayag but at the auspicious time he has not bathed in the river." He repeated these words many times and soon a large crowd collected. Nanak's new disciples were surprised that their Guru had been so careless. They had thought that like all of them he had also come to Prayag to bathe in the holy waters to wash away his sins.

"Why should I have bathed in the water at this time?" Nanak asked the *mahant* in a clear strong voice.

"You know why," the *mahant* shouted in anger. "To wash away your sins. You know that anyone who bathes in the river at this time becomes pure, as all his sins are washed away by the holy waters."

"We cannot become pure by washing our bodies. We can become pure by making a place for God in our hearts. If our minds hold evil thoughts towards other men, if we are ready to cheat and to steal, how can the washing of our bodies in the holy waters make us pure? We will be like a brass untensil which has been polished from the outside till it shines but which is filled inside with poison. Saints are pure and holy even when they do not bathe and thieves remain thieves even if they bathe four times a day."

When Guru Nanak set out on his journey to Lanka he passed once again through Lahore. This time word had already reached Lahore that the Guru was coming. In Lahore there lived a very rich merchant by the name of Duni Chand. Once a year Duni Chand performed memorial ceremonies for his dead father. It so happened that during that particular year these ceremonies were being performed at the time when Nanak came to Lahore. Among these ceremonies was a grand feast for Brahmins and holy men. When Duni Chand heard that Nanak the Guru was coming to Lahore, he personally escorted the Guru to his house and offered him great hospitality. Nanak saw signs of great wealth around him and Duni Chand himself boasted about his great riches.

The Guru stayed with him for a few days. He took part in all the ceremonies and Duni Chand and the Guru got to know each other well. One evening while the Guru took out a needle and gave it to Duni Chand. "Duni Chand," the Guru said, "you have been a very good host and you have looked after me very well. You are now my dear friend and I have great trust in you. This needle is important for me. Please keep it with you, keep it very carefully and after our deaths when we meet in the next world give it back to me."

Duni Chand went back to his room quite confused. He did not understand why the Guru had given him something as ordinary as a needle to look after carefully and carry into the next world.

At night as he was getting ready to go to bed, his wife spoke to him. "What is it that is troubling you? I have never before seen you with such a serious look on your face."

"You know Guru Nanak?" Duni Chand asked.

"Who does not know him?" his wife said with a smile.

Duni Chand took out the needle and held it to his wife. "He gave me this needle," he said.

"He told me it was important to him, and asked me to look after it very carefully and when we meet in the next world to give it back to him. I cannot understand why he has asked me to look after a needle in this way."

Duni Chand's wife was a wise woman. She smiled at her husband's confusion.

"It is so simple, my husband. Will you be able to take this needle with you when you die?"

Duni Chand thought for a moment.

"No, of course not. I will not be able to take it with me when I die."

"And all your wealth? If you are not able to take a small thing like a needle with you, will you be able to take that with you?"

Duni Chand understood at last what the Guru was teaching him. The food he had fed to Brahmins and holy men would not cross the barriers of death and reach his father, just as all the money he had collected would not go with him when he died. What would go with him were his good deeds. Far better to feed the hungry than to feed the Brahmins, far better to use his money to help the poor than to keep it locked up in the hope of carrying it into the next world.

Duni Chand opened up his treasure chests and used all his money for the welfare of the poor.

Perhaps the most beautiful *sakhi* is the one about Nanak's last moments on this earth.

Nanak lay under a tree on the river-bank just outside Kartarpur. Angad sat with Nanak's feet in his lap, his heart heavy not only with the grief of the approaching end but also with the burden of the responsibilities that he would soon have to carry.

All day people from distant places came to see their Guru one last time. Sometimes, Nanak would close his eyes and sleep, sometimes he would be awake, but his eyes did not see any of his followers. His breathing was heavy now and the end was very near. A wind struck up and shook the leaves of the trees. Some of the dry leaves rattled as they struck each other. Nanak opened his eyes and looked up at the leaves. Then he looked at Angad and smiled. And Angad understood the meaning of that smile. The old leaves must fall off and make place for new leaves to grow, just as the old must leave the world to make place for the young. Then the Guru's eyes became clouded again and he seemed to lose awareness of the world around him, and of the people who sat by his side.

A murmur started amongst the Guru's Muslim followers who sat on his left. At first Angad could not make out what they said. Then as their voices became louder he heard the words clearly.

"He is ours, our *peer*, our holy man. So when he dies his body must be handed over to us so that we can give it holy burial."

The Hindu followers who sat on the Guru's right were very upset by this claim.

"No, no," they protested. "Nanak was born a Hindu. His father's name was Kalyan and his mother's name was Tripta. In his teachings is a great deal that he has taken from the Hindu way of life. Besides, he has never said that he is a

Musalman. So how can you say he is yours? He is our Guru and his body will be ours so that we can give him the funeral rites that all true-born Hindus need in order to go to Heaven." The Guru opened his eyes and chuckled softly and Angad held up his hand and the quarrelling disciples fell silent.

"You are both right," he said, looking first towards one group and then towards the other. "I belong to both of you. But there is a way to solve this difficulty. Each of you must bring flowers, lots of flowers, and put them beside me. The Muslims must put their flowers along my left side and the Hindus must put their flowers along my right side. You must leave them there through the night. Then tomorrow morning you must look carefully at your flowers.

If the Hindus' flowers are fresh then I belong to the Hindus and they can cremate my body, and if the Muslims flowers are fresh then I belong to the Muslims and they may do with my body as they wish."

Nanak was tired; he closed his eyes again and drifted off to sleep.

The Guru's commands were obeyed and both Hindus and Muslims brought many flowers and put them down as the Guru had directed. Then they sat down to wait out the night. Some of them slept, others looked at the Guru's face by the fluttering light of the oil lamps that burned near his head, afraid of what they saw in that sleeping face. The breathing became softer and softer. It was now only a little while before dawn. It was the time that the Guru described as *amrit vela*, the time of nectar, the Guru's favourite time of the day.

The Guru came awake one last time. In a very faint voice, he asked his followers to pray. He himself said one last prayer, then drawing his sheet over his face he went into eternal sleep.

All through the morning the disciples sat beside their Guru in silence. Then in the afternoon when it was time for the funeral ceremonies the Hindus and Muslims both carefully examined the flowers they had brought. The Muslims looked at their flowers and found they were still as fresh as when they had brought them. When the Hindus looked at their flowers they too found that they were as fresh as when they had been plucked. Both sides looked at each other in wonder. Even in his death the Guru had underscored the lesson he had taught all through his life. All men are equal. There is no Hindu. There is no Musalman. There are only decent men, like the Guru, who have made their lives as beautiful and fresh and sweet-smelling as flowers with the good deeds that they have performed.

PART 2

Guru Angad Dev
to
Guru Tegh Bahadur
(1504 – 1675)

Guru Angad Dev
(1504-1552)

*I*t was five O'clock in the morning, Lehna had got out of bed, bathed and now sat down under the tamarind tree in his courtyard to meditate and to pray. This had been his habit for so long that Khivi, his wife, no longer knew when he stole out of bed.

Usually Lehna was so lost in his prayers that he did not notice when the birds began to twitter in the tree above his head. But now he was not able to concentrate and was aware of the beginning of the day and the first flutter of birds' wings. This had happened often in the recent past and at first he had ascribed it to the restlessness that he always felt at the approach of the *Navratras*. He was an ardent devotee of the Goddess Durga and during the *Navratras* he led a pilgrimage to her temple at Jawalamukhi. The excitement of the impending pilgrimage had always made him restless. But then he remembered that the previous year when the head priest of Jawalamukhi had finally brought him into the presence of the goddess, he did not feel the deep happiness that he had always felt. There was a feeling of inadequacy, a feeling that there should have been something more at the end of the pilgrimage.

Now, sitting under the tree in his courtyard, he felt the same sense of inadequacy and knew that his inability to concentrate on his prayers was caused by something more deep-rooted than by the excitement of the pilgrimage. This realisation made him uneasy and afraid. Then from his neighbour's courtyard he heard a soft clear voice raised in song. It was a strange hymn but the words gave him peace and strength and when the singer finished his song he was not afraid or restless any more.

All through the morning he helped his father. His father, Pheru, was a rich trader and there was a lot of work for Lehna to do. But as he worked his mind kept going back to the hymn and he wondered who had composed it. But mid-morning he could not bear it any more; he knew he had to find the answer to this question. He excused himself from his father and went to his neighbour's house.

"Tell me Jodha," he said coming straight to the point. "Tell me the name of the hymn you sang this morning and the name of the poet who wrote it." Jodha had just sat down to his mid-day meal and he looked up at his neighbour and smiled. "It is the *mool mantra*," he said. "It is written by my Guru, Guru Nanak of Kartarpur. Come, come and join me in my meal."

"Thank you," Lehna said, "but I must go. I have work to do."

Lehna's work was to persuade the members of his party to stop at Kartarpur on their way to Jawalamukhi. But his friends did not agree. If Lehna had not been the leader of the group he would have broken from them and gone to Kartarpur on his own. But as the leader he had certain duties and responsibilities which he could not give up, and so his visit to Guru Nanak would have to wait.

Two days later, he, like the other pilgrims, tied bells to his wrists and his ankles and they went on their way to the Devi singing and dancing. But each time he clapped his hands and stamped his feet and sang *Jai mata di* a soft, sweet voice would rise between the chants and say: *"Ek onkar, sat naam, karta purkh..."* Even when he came to the temple and went into the presence of the Goddess, it was Jodha's voice that kept humming in his ears.

It was a strange emaciated Lehna who returned to Khadur. The other pilgrims reported that he had eaten very little, only nibbled at his food when they had forced him to eat. He had behaved in a strange, uncharacteristic manner by keeping very much to himself all through the pilgrimage.

For two days after his return Lehna stayed in Khadur, two days and two nights. Then while everyone was asleep he mounted his horse and rode to Kartarpur. He came to the Guru's place (the *dera*) just before dawn. This was his favourite time of the day. It was also the favourite time of the day for Guru Nanak, who called it the *amrit vela*. As Lehna rode into the *dera* he noticed a strange silence, everything was still and quiet. He got off his horse and tied cloth around the horse's hooves so that their sound would not break the silence. He came as quietly as he could to the centre of the *dera* and as he did so he heard a strong beautiful voice break into the same hymn that Jodha had sung.

"*Ek onkar, sat naam, karta purkh...*"

He was overcome by the beauty of the voice and of the hymn. He let go the horse's bridle and fell on his knees. He lowered his forehead to the ground and wept and knew at last that this is what we have been searching for, he knew that he had come home.

After the morning prayers Lehna went up to a Sikh disciple who seemed to be some kind of a leader because so many of the other disciples showed deference to him.

"I am Lehna from Khadur," Lehna introduced himself. "I have come to have *darshan* of the Guru and to serve him."

"You are more than welcome, Lehna of Khadur. I am Bura Singh but people call me Baba Budha." He smiled as he said this and Lehna smiled too.

"Come. You must be tired. Let me show you where you will stay and where you may stable your horse."

Within a few days it was as if Lehna had always been in Kartarpur. Wherever there was work to be done Lehna was the first to reach out and attempt to do it. No task was too lowly, too menial for him.

He was in the fields at the break of dawn. When any construction work was to be done, he worked as a labourer from morning till night. In the summer he would sit fanning the people who ate in the *langar* and after the evening meal, while others had gone to a well-earned rest, Lehna toiled on in the *langar*, washing and stacking the utensils. And all the time he worked, his mind was on the Guru's words, the words he heard during the morning and evening prayers. He tried always to follow what the words told him to do, to live by these words. He was quite content to live in the Guru's shadow, to sit quietly on the fringe of the crowd and take in the beauty of his Guru's teaching. He had no desire to seek his Guru out, to be noticed by him.

But with Lehna's unstinting and devoted service it was only a matter of time before the Guru noticed him. Lehna had always been very fond of children. Even before he had his own children he loved to spend an hour or two every evening with the children of his village. He drew them as a magnet draws pieces of iron and they surrounded him begging him to tell them stories, asking him to teach them new games and he was always ready to oblige.

In Kartarpur, too, Lehna found great pleasure in being with the children. For a little while before the evening prayers he would join the children in their play and the whole *dera* would echo with the children's laughter and people would stop and smile and shake their heads and say: "What a child this stranger is!"

The Guru had noticed the stranger's presence, had seen with what dedication and sincerity he applied himself to every kind of task. One evening as he left his home to go out for the evening prayers he was greeted by the loud laughter of a group of children, laughter that was so joyous that it made him smile.

"Bhai Budha," he said turning to his trusted disciple, "what is it that makes our children so loud in their happiness?"

"Master, they have found a new playmate."

The Guru nodded: "Yes, so I hear."

The little group walked towards the central prayer area. By the time they came to where the children had been playing, the children had all gone, Lehna stood there by himself and as he saw the Guru approach he bowed low, waiting for him to pass. But the Guru did not pass by. He stood near Lehna and put his hand on Lehna's head.

"Who are you?" he asked in a gentle voice, "and from where do you come?"

For a moment Lehna stood there not daring to speak. The Guru had put his hand on his head, the Guru had addressed him. He felt such a deep joy that he was afraid to speak and thus break the spell. But the Guru waited and Lehna knew that he waited for his answer.

"I come from Khadur," he said, his voice so low it could hardly be heard. "My name is Lehna."

"Lehna," the Guru said, running the name softly off his tongue.

"Whose Lehna?" Lehna did not understand.

"Your Lehna, your debt, was here with me and that is why God had brought you to Kartarpur."

The days slid quietly into months and the months into years and Lehna worked each day to pay his debt to the Guru by working with tireless devotion in the service of the *sangat*, the assembly of devotees and disciples. Each night he went to bed happy in the thought that he had done the most that he could do, the best that he could do. He sought no reward, no special mark of affection from the Guru. Soon everyone in the community knew that he was special because of the special quality of his service and in small ways the Guru also showed a special mark of favour for his devoted follower.

Lehna had always shown consideration and love for his parents, his wife and his children. Now that he was away from them, he did not forget them. He wrote to his father as often as he could. Pheru had always known that his son was different from the sons of the other traders, because he had always found greater pleasure in giving than in getting. So it did not come as a great surprise to him that his son now spent all his time in the service of others with no thought for himself. Khivi, too, knew that there was something special about her husband. She missed him and when his letters were read out to her, tears would come to her eyes. He was a good man, her husband, and what he was doing must be good. So like Sulakhni, Guru Nanak's wife, before her, she prepared herself to wait out the time till her husband's return.

Sometimes Pheru would accompany Jodha on his visits to Kartarpur to see how his son was faring. On these visits Pheru listened to the Guru and was influenced by his teachings. Occasionally he invited his daughter-in-law to go with him and even though their stay in Kartarpur was limited to a few days, Khivi was happy to be with her husband again.

Lehna had been in Kartarpur for three years now, and it was an established fact that he was one of the Guru's chosen disciples. One day, after the morning prayers, the Guru sent for Lehna.

"You have paid your debt to me well," the Guru said, referring to their first conversation three years ago. "But there are other debts you still have to pay: the debt to your father, the debt to your wife and children. You must return to Khadur to settle your affairs."

The story of Lehna's service and of the favour he had received from the Guru had travelled to Khadur before him. When the news spread that Lehna had returned, all the people came out to greet him. There was love and affection, for a good, kind man who had been away for three long years, but there was also respect for the man who had come so close to the master.

People came to him for advice and they came to listen to his teachings, Guru Nanak's teachings, and they joined him when he sang Guru Nanak's hymns. Lehna spent this time in arranging his affairs and when he was sure that he had made sufficient provisions for his father, his wife and his children, he said goodbye and returned to Kartarpur.

He reached Kartarpur in the late evening. He had been delayed on the way because of a sudden sharp downpour of rain and had sheltered in a village while the rain fell, pacing up and down the farmer's house, impatient at this forced delay in his meeting with his Guru. The moment the rain stopped he rode out again, spurring his horse to greater speed to make up for the lost time. He had arrived at last in Kartarpur, in the evening, to find that the Guru was still out in the field. He stabled his horse and ran to the fields. As he went to touch the Guru's feet the Guru drew him into a silent embrace.

There were three bundles of freshly cut fodder that still lay in the field, waiting to be carried home. "I'll send a servant to carry this as soon as I get home," Lakhmi Chand said, Lehna lifted the bundles onto his head, one upon the other, and made his way back through the fields. The fodder was wet, dripping wet, and the muddy water flowed from his head down over his neck to his shirt and soon the shirt was covered with smudges. It was a beautiful shirt made of 'boski', soft Chinese silk that Khivi had bought from a trader who passed through the village. It was very expensive silk because it had been carried all the way from China along the old silk route. Khivi had bought this for her husband and saved it carefully, and when he had come home she made a shirt for him. No one in the village had a shirt like this and she was proud that she had given her husband something so beautiful. He, who cared nothing for worldly things, had teased her about it.

"When will I need to wear something so grand?" he had said and she had replied:

"When you go to meet your Guru," and his teasing had been stilled. Yes, he must wear something special for that special occasion. So on the day of his return he had worn this special shirt. And here it was now, sticking to his back, soiled and dirty. But he did not notice this. He was happy to be performing a service for his Guru. It was Sulakhni who noticed this. The moment she saw Lehna approaching the house with the loads of fodder on his head she took Guru Nanak aside.

"How could you do this?" she asked. "How could you allow Lehna to carry this load and dirty his clothes with mud?"

"When the mud comes from such willing and selfless service," Guru Nanak said quietly, smiling at his wife, "it does not remain mud — it becomes saffron. And when the load of fodder is carried by Lehna it is no longer a load but the halo of God's blessing." Sulkahni looked at Lehna, so humble and meek, and then she looked at her proud and arrogant son and she knew the truth of Guru Nanak's statement. She took Lehna into her home and gave him water for a bath and a set of clean clothes to wear, and when he had bathed and changed, she took his soiled clothes and washed them for him.

The rain played an important part in another incident in Lehna's life. A few months later the monsoon broke in a strong, heavy rain. For hours on end the rain came down, heavy and strong. A report was brought to the Guru that one of the newly built walls in the *dharamshala* had given way and the Guru hurried to see the extent of the damage. Part of a wall had indeed given way.

The Guru saw that if it was not attended to immediately there was danger of the entire wall coming down, danger of the roof caving in.

"Son," he said addressing Lakhmi Chand, "this must be attended to immediately."

"Yes, father," Lakhmi Chand said stifling a yawn because it was late and he was sleepy.

"I will send for the mason and have it attended to first thing in the morning." The Guru did not say anything more and returned home. Lehna slipped away quietly into the darkness and brought two labourers back with him. The mason was away on a visit to a neighbouring village and would not be back till the next morning. Lehna organised all the material — the bricks and the lime and the sand for the mortar. Hour after hour he struggled through the night rebuilding the wall as best as he could.

By the time the Guru stopped at the site on his way to morning prayers, the damaged part of the wall had been sufficiently rebuilt to avert any more danger to the building. Word of this incident spread through the community and it was clear to everyone that Lehna was the chosen one and most people knew without anything being said that he would be the next Guru. But there were some who felt that Sri Chand, Nanak's elder son, who was a very pious man, should be the next Guru. Sri Chand was not an ambitious man but these people tried to poison his mind against Lehna.

Guru Nanak in his wisdom saw that he must act to keep the peace in Kartarpur. He called Lehna, Sri Chand, Lakhmi Chand, Baba Budha and his other favourite disciples to him.

He addressed Lehna.

"Bhai Lehna," he said in his beautiful voice. "You have shown over these long years that you are flesh of my flesh and blood of my blood. You are my *angad*, part of my *ang*, my body." Lehna caught Baba Budha's eye and Baba Budha smiled. "Because you are my *angad*," Guru Nanak continued, "you must continue the work that I have begun. Come Bhai Budha, come forward and apply saffron paste to Angad's forehead." Then he put five copper coins and a coconut at Lehna's feet and bowed to him. Guru Nanak bowed to Lehna, and he was ordained as the second Guru of the Sikhs — Guru Angad Dev.

The Guru had appointed his successor during his lifetime to make sure that there would be no opposition to him later.

Gurdwara Charn Kamal Sahib, Machhiwara

Grudwara Sri Hazoor Sahib, Nanded

To avoid any trouble between Guru Angad and his son, Guru
Nanak decided that Guru Angad should go back to Khadur.
Without his physical presence the opposition to Guru Angad
would slowly melt away.

As always Guru Angad bowed to his Master's wishes and
returned to Khadur. Guru Angad laid great importance on a
proper education for children. Apart from studies, Guru
Angad realised that children should also be physically strong
and insisted that they should take part in sports. He asked
their teachers to organise competitions and he himself gave
away prizes to the winners. He said that physical fitness was
necessary because you could only have a healthy mind if you
had a healthy body.

Guru Angad was happy in Khadur, happy that he was
able to bring the teachings of his Guru to the people. At the
same time he missed his Guru very much and his deepest
wish was that the Guru should send for him. Then at last
the Guru did send for him and he returned to Kartarpur with
joy in his heart. But the joy turned to sadness when he
realised that his Guru was dying. He was with Guru Nanak
when Guru Nanak breathed his last. Then he took leave of
Mata Sulakhni and of Sri Chand and returned to Khadur. This
is what his Guru had wanted him to do and he knew that
this was the only way he could avoid any differences coming
up between him and the Guru's family.

At Khadur he continued the Guru's work. Some of Guru
Nanak's chief disciples like Baba Budha now came to Khadur
to follow Guru Angad and they saw that the lamp Nanak had
lit in Kartarpur now shed its light in Khadur. Khadur now
became the centre of the world for the Sikhs. Guru Angad
realised that what held his followers together were the
teachings of his Guru and these teachings had come to them
in the form of Guru Nanak's hymns. He now began to collect
all these hymns and to set them down on paper. These
hymns had all been composed in the language of the people,
in Punjabi. Guru Angad felt that they could not be written in

the Arabic script which was the script of the Koran, or in the Devnagri script which was the Sanskrit script, the script in which the holy books of the Hindus were written. Some historians say that he chose thirty-five suitable letters from different scripts and developed the Gurmukhi script in which he wrote Guru Nanak's hymns. Other historians are of the opinion that the script was already in existence and Guru Angad improved upon it. Guru Angad collected all his Master's hymns and wrote them down in the new script which was different from the script of the religious books of the Hindus and the Muslims. He made copies of this collection and gave them to each of the centres of the Sikhs, so that his followers could read these hymns and learn them by heart.

The Guru himself did not write as many hymns as Nanak, but the few *slokas* he wrote are now a part of the Guru Granth Sahib.

At this time an old man by the name of Amar Das came and joined the *sangat* at Khadur. He had been a Vaishnav but now he was in search of a Guru. He joined the community in Khadur and spent his life in the service of others.

Guru Angad took care to give all respect to Mata Sulakhni and to Sri Chand. He made frequent trips to Kartarpur to pay his respects and he greeted Sri Chand exactly as he had greeted Guru Nanak. He did everything in his power for Sulakhni and for Sri Chand and in this way they too came to love and respect him. They refused to listen to the people who tried to poison their minds against Guru Angad and Guru Angad was able to avoid a division among Nanak's followers.

Guru Angad had a very rich follower named Gobind who was involved in a property dispute with his relatives. It was a very valuable piece of property and Gobind prayed silently to his Guru for help and promised that if he won the case, he would build a new town for his Guru. As luck would have it Gobind did win the case and all the property became his. He was a true disciple and did not go back on his word. He came to the Guru for his blessings and asked for the Guru's help to build the new township. The Guru could not leave Khadur, so he asked his favourite disciple, Amar Das, to go and supervise the building of the new township. So the town of Goindwal was built. Gobind built a beautiful *haveli* and once again came to his Guru and begged him to come and live in Goindwal. The Guru was not in a position to leave Khadur but in order to keep his disciple happy he asked Amar Das to take up residence at Goindwal.

When Guru Angad had first brought the teachings of Guru Nanak to Khadur he had run into opposition from a group of *tapas* (ascetics) who had set up a *dera* in Khadur. The chief of these was Shiv Nath. Shiv Nath had opposed Guru Angad in every way but Guru Angad had quietly gone about his work and had soon gathered a large following. This made the *tapas* angry because they had been very powerful in the village and now their followers had left them and become followers of Guru Angad. One year there was a severe drought in Khadur and the surrounding area. The hot dry days became hot dry weeks and then hot dry months, but no rain fell. The newly planted crop dried in the fields and the fields were parched and the earth became hard and cracked. The trees lost their leaves and died. The wells dried up and people and animals began to die of thirst. The people came to their Guru and begged for his help.

"You are a man of God, master," they said, "and if you pray, God will grant your prayers."

"It is the will of God," he said, quietly suffering because his people suffered. "The rain will fall only when God decides that it must fall."

The villagers felt that the Guru could make the rain fall if he so wished and they were not happy with the Guru's answer. Some of the older villagers remembered that when they had been the followers of the *tapas*, Shiv Nath had sometimes worked miracles for them. Women who had no children and women who wanted sons had often gone to seek

Shivnath's help. He had said special prayers for them and sometimes the women got what they desired. Because of this people thought there was something magical about these prayers. Now the villagers felt that Shiv Nath might be able to work a miracle and bring rain to quench their thirst. When he heard what they wanted he taunted them.

"So now that you are in trouble you have remembered me. Go back to your Guru, whom you follow, and ask him to help you. Ask him to make the rain fall. Go, go."

The villagers returned sadly to their homes. But the hot dry days continued. Those who could leave left the village and went to live with friends and relatives in other cities and villages. But most had nowhere to go. Soon it was clear that unless the rain came they would all die and they went again to Shiv Nath and fell at his feet and cried.

"We are sorry, O Tapa. Forgive us. We will never desert you again." The Tapa smiled to himself, now he would have his revenge on Angad.

"All right, I will help you. But there is one condition. You must turn this so-called Guru out of your village."

It was a difficult condition. They had all been followers of the Guru and they all knew in their hearts that he was a great and pious man. How could they tell him to leave the village? But their suffering was great. They knew they would all die if the rain did not come and they believed that Shiv Nath could make the rain fall. So after a great deal of discussion it was decided that a group of five would go and request the Guru to leave the village. But when they reached the *dera* they came to know that the Guru had learnt of their difficulty and had left Khadur on his own and set up camp in a forest a few miles away.

The villagers went back to Shiv Nath. He organised a great *yagna* and recited many special *mantras*. He took generous offerings from the villagers and performed all kinds of rites. He promised that the rain would fall the next day, but the next day came and went and there was no rain. The days stretched into weeks and still there was no rain and the villagers realised that Shiv Nath could not make the rain fall. They realised that their Guru had been right, no man could interfere with the will of God. They were all very ashamed of what they had done and they went to the Guru and begged forgiveness. As was to be expected he forgave them readily and returned to Khadur. A few days later the rain came and the people, old men and women, and little children all ran out into the streets and sang and danced with joy.

Like Guru Nanak, Guru Angad knew that he must appoint his successor during his lifetime so that there would be no trouble after his death. So shortly before his death he appointed his successor. He announced that Amar Das would succeed him. Once again Baba Budha anointed the new Guru. Like Guru Nanak, Guru Angad also realised that his family was not happy with his choice. Specially his son Datu who had hoped that he would be the next Guru. To avoid any conflict between his family and Amar Das he asked Amar Das to set up his *dera* in 'Goindwal'. A few months later, surrounded by his devoted followers, Guru Angad breathed his last. The year was 1552 and Guru Angad was forty-eight years old at the time.

Guru Angad was Guru of the Sikhs for thirteen years. During his tenure he set up many centres. He organised a system of collecting the offerings from each centre and distributing them to the centres according to their needs. In this way the expenses of running the *langar* and the schools could be met. His special interest was the children. He knew that if the children were given a good education and made sound of body and mind, they would have good all-round personalities and grow up to be very useful members of society. This is why he persuaded all Sikhs to send their children to school. In the schools he made sure that the children were taught well. He insisted that education must be in the children's mother tongue, so that the children would have a sense of identity and would be proud of their mother tongue. He also insisted that the schools should have regular sports and should organise competitions from time to time.

He insisted that all the young men in his *deras* should be physically fit and made them all join the 'Akharas' and learn to defend themselves.

Guru Angad wrote down Guru Nanak's hymns in Gurmukhi and had them distributed to all centres. The collection of hymns later became a nucleus of the Sikhs' sacred book, the Granth Sahib.

Guru Angad carried on the tradition which had been started by Guru Nanak. He appointed his successor during his lifetime and chose the most deserving of his disciples, and in so doing bypassed his own son.

If we think of the Sikh religion as a building then we can say that Guru Nanak laid the strong foundation and built the frame. Guru Angad built the walls. If we think of Guru Nanak's teachings as a lamp we can say that Guru Nanak lit the lamp and Guru Angad protected the flame and made sure that the light from the lamp spread far and wide.

Guru Amar Das
(1479-1574)

*I*t was still an hour before dawn but Amar Das could lie in bed no longer. He was restless and his mind would not be still. For the major part of his sixty years he had always woken up at dawn and joined his father in prayer. Then over the years, as he grew older, he went often to the holy towns of Hardwar and Kurukshetra, sometimes once a year, sometimes even twice. He spent a lot of his time and money in helping the poor, the sick and the needy. He was respected by all the village-folks because he never spoke loudly, never lost his temper and always worked for the good of others. But in the last few years his visits to the holy towns, his bathing in the holy waters of the Ganga and even his acts of charity had not brought him much peace. On his last trip to the Ganga he had met a monk, a *brahmachari*. They talked of many things, about life and religion, and the monk was impressed by Amar Das's knowledge and learning. They spent a lot of time together. So when they were returning from Hardwar it was only natural that Amar Das should invite the monk to stop for a night in his home in Basarke.

After the evening meal, they climbed up the steps to the terrace where their cots had been laid. They talked late into the night and just as they were about to go to sleep the monk said: "You are so wise and know so much about religion. Who is your Guru?"

"I do not have a Guru."

"What?" the monk said in surprise. "You do not have a Guru? Then all my trips to the Ganga and all my fasts have come to naught because I have lived with you and eaten food with you." The monk left the house at once and hurried back to Hardwar to bathe again in the holy Ganga. He had committed a 'sin' by being with a man who had no Guru and he must wash away this sin!

Amar Das was very upset over this. It had been three nights since the monk had left in anger and all the three nights he had not been able to sleep. Perhaps this was the reason why he had not found peace even after twenty years of bathing in the Ganga. Without a Guru his search had been a failure. Now unable to stay in bed any longer he got up and very carefully, one step at a time, he felt his way down the staircase. He was halfway down when he heard the voice of Bibi Amro, his brother Manak Chand's daughter-in-law. She was the daughter of Guru Angad Dev of Khadur. The first light had now broken and he could see the dim outline of the girl's figure as she swept the courtyard of his brother's house. She was afraid of disturbing the other members of her family so she sang her hymn in a soft voice. But in the

stillness before dawn, Amar Das could hear each word clearly.
He stood where he was, moved by the sweetness of the voice
and the beauty of the words. But this was not the first time
that Amar Das had heard Bibi Amro singing this hymn. He
knew that by her patience, her love for the new family and
her sense of service, she had won the hearts of everyone.
She brought to her new home the Sikh way of life and the
teachings of both Guru Nanak and Guru Angad Dev. He had
been secure in his beliefs and had not wished to change and
so he had not listened to her words. But now, after the
monk's rebuke, he was full of doubt. Now he listened to her
words. In the beauty of Bibi Amro's song he saw a path along
which he could continue his search.

The song finished. It was now light. Amar Das hurried
into his brother's courtyard and fell at Amro's feet. She
covered her face and head and quickly drew back.

"What are you doing Babaji?" she asked.

"I bow before the voice that spoke through you. I bow
before the truth and wisdom of these words. Bibi take me to
your Guru, now, at once." Perhaps both Amro and Manak
Chand knew in their hearts that this was a very special
moment and they gave in to Amar Das's wish. In a short
while Amro and Amar Das set out on the journey from
Basarke to Khadur Sahib. They came at last to Khadur, to
the Guru's presence. Amro went in to bring to her father
the news of Amar Das's arrival and the Guru, out of respect
to a man who was almost twice his age, rose to his feet and
went forward to embrace him. But Amar Das would have
none of this. He fell at the Guru's feet and said: "I came as
a humble disciple of Guruji. Give me a place at your feet."

He was true to his word. During the following twelve
years all he sought was a place at the Guru's feet. He worked
like any other humble servant of the *sangat*. In spite of his
advancing years he worked wherever work was to be done,
and watching him, the Guru would often smile. In Amar Das's
humility and spirit of devotion he saw himself, the young

Lehna who had worked selflessly in the service of the Guru at Kartarpur. He saw the same spirit, the same light, a spirit and a light which he had not seen in any one else, not even in his own sons.

It was pretty difficult for Amar Das to accept the new way of life. One by one he had to give up beliefs that he had held dear for so long. The Guru said there was only one formless God but like all true Hindus he had believed there were many deities each of whom was a form of God. He himself had chosen to worship one of these deities, Lord Vishnu. The Guru taught that because God was without form it was wrong to worship idols. Amar Das had worshipped idols all his life. Wherever he had gone he had looked first for the idol so that he could offer his prayers. The Guru taught that there was no merit to be earned by going on pilgrimages and bathing in holy waters. He himself had spent a lifetime going to Hardwar and bathing in the waters of the Ganga.

And yet, painful as it was to give up all his beliefs, Amar Das did not hesitate. He did as the Guru taught because the Guru was above everyone. He filled his mind with the Guru's words, his days with the Guru's service, and there was no place for anything else.

When Choudhry Gobind built the Guru Mahal in Goindwal and asked Guru Angad to come and live in it the Guru told Amar Das to go in his place. He also told Amar Das to bring his family to Goindwal. In this way Amar Das could now also perform the duty which Guru Nanak had asked all his followers to perform, the duty of the householder, the responsibility of being a son, husband and father.

Though he lived in Goindwal Amar Das would get up very early in the morning, go to Khadur and spend the whole day in the service of his Guru and of the *sangat*. There was one service that he found special pleasure in. Every morning he carried fresh water from the river for the Guru's bath. For years he never failed in this service; nothing could stop him, nothing could deter him from his resolve; not rain, not storm, not the cold of the early winter mornings. His Guru had to be at the prayer meeting at dawn and before that he must have the water for his bath. So Amar Das woke up three hours earlier to bring the water to his Guru in time.

Then one morning, a dawn that was darker than any other, Amar Das or Amru, as he was called by some, missed his way in the dark, lost his footing and stumbled into a pit that a weaver had made for his loom. Somehow he was able to save the precious water from spilling. The rain had made the ground slippery and he could not step out of the pit without upsetting his *gāgar* (water pitcher) and he called out for help.

The first light had broken in the sky and the Guru waited for Amar Das and because Amar Das had never been late before, the Guru was sure that something had happened. He walked quickly towards the river. He came to the weavers' huts and picked his way through them and then he stopped. Very clearly he heard Amar Das's cries for help. Then from the hut near him he heard the weaver say to his wife: "Someone is calling for help."

"It must be Amru the homeless, wandering around in the dark. Go back to sleep."

The Guru reached the pit, drew the pitcher of water from his disciple's head and set it on the ground. Then he rescued Amar Das from the pit and held him in his embrace for long. He sent for Baba Budha. Then with his own hands the Guru bathed Amar Das with the water that had been so carefully brought for him. He dressed him in new clothes and asked Baba Budha to anoint him. He himself bowed before him and addressed him: "Home of the Homeless, the honour of the unhonoured, the support of those without support."

Thus was Guru Amar Das ordained as the third Guru of the Sikhs at the age of seventy-three years. He set up his centre at Goindwal. A few months later Guru Angad breathed his last and all the Sikhs now looked to Guru Amar Das for guidance and came to Goindwal to seek his blessings. Two rules the Guru laid down at the very outset were: All those who came to see him must first eat food in his *langar*, the rich along with the poor, the high-caste with the low-caste. The second rule was that no woman was to cover her face with *purdah* (veil).

Once Goindwal became the headquarters of the new Guru, the town began to grow very quickly. People came to meet the Guru and seek his blessings and decided to stay on in the town. Goindwal was located at an important point on the road from Lahore to Delhi. Because of this there were many travellers on the road and the town became an important trading centre. So many buildings were constructed that there was not enough wood and the Guru sent his nephew Sawan Mal to Haripur to get wood which could be floated down the Beas. Sawan Mal brought the teachings of the Gurus to the people of the area around Haripur. Eventually the Raja of Haripur and his queen became the Guru's disciples.

One day a band of devotees came from Lahore and among them was a very handsome young man. His name was Ram Das but people called him Jetha. Jetha impressed everyone not only by his good looks but also by his pleasing manners. He stayed in Goindwal and spent his days in the service of the *sangat*. He worked so hard that everyone noticed it; the Guru noticed it too but made no comment.

At about this time the Guru ordered the building of a *baoli* — a large well at Goindwal. This could be reached by climbing down eighty-four steps. These steps corresponded to the Hindu belief that each soul went through eighty-four hundred thousand births before it gained *moksha*. The Guru said, "He who goes down the steps and bathes in the *baoli* will gain freedom from the cycle of birth and death." In this way his followers no longer needed to go to bathe in the Ganga. The Guru also named Baisakhi (April 13), Maghi, the first day of the Indian month of Magh, and Diwali as the three days on which his followers should come from far and near to the Guru's place.

The Guru had taken personal interest in the building of the *baoli* and would spend hours in supervising the work. He saw Jetha working from morning till night, sometimes carrying the mud away like a common labourer, sometimes carrying the mortar to the bricklayers. Always there was a smile of joy on the young man's face, and still the Guru did not say anything.

By now there were hundreds of disciples who came to Goindwal everyday and the Guru realised that the number of his followers had become very large and there was need to set up a proper organisation.

He divided the northern region into twenty-two units, each unit was called a *manji*. The name was used because Gurus sat on a *manji* or cot when they met their visitors. Each *manji* was headed by a faithful disciple who gave guidance to all the Sikhs in the area of his *manji*? The Guru also trained a band of one hundred and forty-six followers of whom fifty-two were women. to attend to the spiritual needs of his followers. These apostles or *masands,* as they were called, could organise worship, spread the teachings of the Guru and collect offerings. As a result the Guru's teachings were spread far and wide and this increased the number of the Guru's followers.

Ever since Sawan Mal had brought the Guru's teachings to the hill people and the Raja of Haripur had become his disciple, many Rajputs joined the ranks of the Guru's followers. One day the Guru received a message that one of his followers, a young Rajput, had died from snake bite. As was his habit, he put everything aside and went to the youth's home to try and comfort the family. He gave all the comfort and solace he could to the boy's mother and father.

Then he looked around and saw the boy's wife. She was dressed as a bride. She wore a red suit and her bridal jewellery and on her hands and feet were the marks of fresh *mehndi*. When she finally looked up at the Guru there was fear in her eyes. He recognised her now, and remembered the time she had come to Goindwal three years ago, as a new bride, she had come, with her husband's family, to his house to seek his blessing. She had been dressed the way she was dressed now, in a red *dupatta* and all her bridal jewellery and he remembered the very fine patterns of *mehndi* on the palms of her hands and on her feet. When she had bent down to touch his feet he had stopped her and drawn her up and looked into her face. She had met his eyes briefly and then looked down again. In that brief moment he had seen fear in her eyes, fear of being in a new place, being among strangers. He remembered clearly what had happened next. He had given her the silver coin that he gave all new brides and new-born children as a token of his blessings. Then as she had turned to go he had stopped her. "Do not be afraid. You may be a daughter-in-law in the home that you are going to but in my home you will always be my daughter." She had looked quickly into his eyes again and this time the fear was gone. Then she had turned and followed her husband out of the house. Now here she was, a young widow, being compelled by her family to commit *sati*, burning herself on her husband's pyre.

No, the Guru decided, this could not be, not here in his *dera*. He took the girl's hand and raised her to her feet and led her out of the house. The family members, too surprised to react, parted and made way for the Guru. As he walked past the father the Guru stopped and addressed him.

"Remember," he said, "you brought the young girl to my house as a new bride three years ago?" The father-in-law did not look up.

"I said then that though she was your daughter-in-law, she was my daughter. With the death of your son she is no longer your daughter-in-law. That tie has been broken. She remains my daughter and I have come to take my daughter back to my house."

Even though a terrible tragedy had been averted there was still a great sadness that hung over the girl's life. Widows were looked down upon, they were regarded as unlucky and not allowed to take part in any function. They had to dress in white and eat the simplest of food. The Guru felt that this was cruelty that society inflicted on the unfortunate women. When he found a suitable man amongst his followers he encouraged him to marry the young widow. So word went forth in the community about the marriage that was to be held. All preparations were made but no pandit could be found to perform the ceremony. It was against their religion, they said, no one had ever heard of a widow being remarried. The time came for the wedding and still no pandit would come forward. Finally the wedding was performed by the Guru himself. Instead of Sanskrit *shlokas* and *mantras* the Punjabi hymns of the Guru were recited and the two became man and wife. Happiness returned once more to the girl's life.

The Guru gave instructions that none of his followers was to commit *sati*, and to marry a widow was an act of virtue. He said that pandits were no longer required for ceremonies, for births, marriages and deaths and any Sikh could perform these ceremonies. The ceremonies themselves were no longer made up of reciting Sanskrit prayers, which no one understood, but the singing of the Guru's hymns which everyone knew and understood.

The Brahmins were angry with the Guru because he had broken the caste barriers by insisting that everyone eat together. He had also done away with *sati* and encouraged widow-remarriage. Now he had taken away their importance by saying that religious ceremonies could be performed without them. They put their heads together and sent a deputation to Emperor Akbar's court. The Brahmins complained that the Sikhs under their Guru were destroying the Hindu religion and doing everything against the rules of the religion. Akbar gave the Brahmins a patient hearing.

"I cannot take any action," he told the Brahmins, "till I have heard what the Guru has to say in answer to these." He sent a message to the Guru asking him to come to his court at Lahore. Guru Amar Das was too old to make the journey and sent Bhai Jetha as his envoy. The only advice the Guru gave Jetha was that he must answer all questions carefully, honestly and without fear.

When Bhai Jetha reached the Emperor's court he was treated with great respect and given a very special welcome. He was told of the complaint that the Brahmins had made and he gave satisfactory answers to all the charges that had been made against his Guru and his teachings.

Birth and caste are not important, Jetha told the Emperor. It is our deeds that are important. A low-caste *shudra* can be a very good man because of his good deeds, just as high-born Brahmin can be a sinner because of his evil deeds. God is without form. It is wrong to make idols of him and to worship these idols. If it gives comfort to visit holy places and bathe in holy waters, we may do so. But we must remember that the best way to wash our sins is to understand our own deeds, to see where we have done evil and vow to be good and kind in the future. We must insist on good thoughts and good actions and not on empty rituals and the observance of strict rules regarding our food or our ceremonies. Any practice which reduces other human beings, specially women, to the level of sub-humans and does not allow them even the right to read the holy books, cannot be a religious practice and is not sanctified by any religion.

Akbar was very impressed by what Bhai Jetha had said and dismissed all the charges against the Guru and the Sikhs. He sent Jetha back to Goindwal with presents for the Guru and a promise that he would come to the Guru to seek his blessings.

When the Emperor reached the *dera* he was asked, like all other visitors, to partake of food in the *langar*. All kinds of food were put before him, as they were put before all those who came to the *langar*.

"Is this what the Guru eats?" he asked one of the attendants.

"No, your majesty. The Guru eats only *ogra*." (*Ogra* is coarse rice or bread.)

"Then I must eat only *ogra*. What is good enough for the Guru is good enough for me," said Akbar.

So a small helping of coarse unseasoned rice was put before the Emperor. As he ate, he noticed hundreds of pilgrims who were being fed in the *langar* and was greatly impressed by the organisation and by the Guru's generosity. After he had eaten, the Emperor was brought to the Guru who greeted him with affection. They talked together for a long time about religion and about spiritual matters. At last it was time for the Emperor to leave. He thanked the Guru for his blessings.

"I would like to do something for you to show my gratitude," he said before he left.

"The Almighty gives me all that is needed," the Guru replied.

"The need is not yours, O Guru," Akbar said in all humility, adding: "The need is mine. I need to do something for you and for the *dera*. I would like to give you a *jagir* and the income from this *jagir* could be used to help meet the expenses of the *langar*."

"The *langar* looks after itself," the Guru replied. "The faithful bring what they have to offer and what they bring is cooked and distributed. Nothing is kept for the next day, each day we start afresh."

The Emperor was confused. As he had said, the need to give was really his need. Then he saw Bhai Jetha and Bibi Bhani sitting a little away from them. He remembered Bhai

Jetha well and he also knew that he was married to the Guru's daughter, Bibi Bhani.

"Your daughter is my daughter," he said feeling happy that he had found a way out of the dilemma.

"I would like to give a present to my daughter."

"So be it," the Guru said smiling, "that I cannot forbid."

A few days later a band of officials from the Moghul Court came to the *dera* with the registration papers of a piece of land as a gift for Bhai Jetha and Bibi Bhani.

For long it had been in the Guru's mind that the Sikhs should have a permanent centre of their own. Tradition too demanded that before the new Guru was anointed he should have set up his own centre. The Guru knew that Jetha, when he became Guru, would have to move out of Goindwal, just as he himself had to move out of Khadur, and Guru Angad Dev had to move out of Kartarpur. So he called Jetha to him and asked him to set up a new township, on the land that had been gifted to him.

At about this time Guru Amar Das, feeling that his end was near, called Bhai Budha and other prominent Sikhs, including his sons, Mohan and Mohri, to him. He declared that Jetha, who would now be called by his original name 'Ram Das', would be the next Guru. Bhai Budha applied the saffron *tilak* as an act of anointment and Guru Amar Das placed the coconut and the copper coins at his feet and bowed to him. Everyone present bowed their heads in respect, and on September 1, 1574 Guru Ram Das was recognised as the fourth Guru of the Sikhs.

Guru Amar Das died in 1574 at the ripe old age of ninety-five. With his typical humility, just before his death he said that his followers should not observe the rites and customs of mourning that are meant for the dead. They should only recite God's name and as true Sikhs submit to the will of God.

He became the Guru at the age of seventy-three, an age at which most men say they have done with life and are happy to live in retirement. But in the twenty-two years that remained to him, he achieved a great deal.

His teachings were simple.

"Do good to others by giving good advice, by setting a good example and always having the welfare of mankind in your heart."

He reorganised the administration of the Sikh community so that the word of the Guru could reach more people. He set up twenty-two centres for the Sikhs so that they could get immediate help for all their problems from the nearest centre and not have to wait till they came to him.

He championed the causes of women. He took them out of *purdah*, forbade the practice of *sati* and encouraged widow remarriage. He said that women were in every way equal to men and fifty-five of his apostles were women.

The Guru was a great poet; he composed nine hundred and seven hymns and he reached out to his followers with his poetry and the poetry of the first two Gurus. These are great achievements and we remember the Guru for all these achievements. But we must also remember Guru Amar Das, the third Guru of the Sikhs, as a model of kindness. Whenever there was any pain or sorrow in the house of one of his followers it was as if there was pain and sorrow in his own house and he would abandon everything and go to comfort the one who was suffering. He fulfilled Guru Angad Dev's prophecy in more than ample measure. He was:

"The home of the homeless, the honour of the unhonoured, the support of those without support."

Guru Ram Das
(1534-1581)

*I*n Lahore in 1534, there was a well-known locality called Chuna Mandi. Lahore was a flourishing city and there were always new buildings coming up and because in those days *chuna* was used in the mortar for making buildings, the *chuna-mandi* also flourished. There were hundreds of shops and hundreds of godowns. But there were also hundreds of little houses on both sides of the narrow lanes: houses that were built one against the other like rows of match boxes. In these houses lived many lower middle-class people: many of them connected with the *chuna* trade and others because they could not afford to pay the rents in better localities.

In one such house lived Hari Das, a khatri of the Sodhi sub-caste and his wife Anup Devi. They were both very simple people who led simple lives and always worked for the good of others. They were quite content and happy with their lot in life. But as the years passed there was a shadow on their lives which caused them pain and unhappiness: they had not been blessed with a child. At first they thought it was only a matter of time but as the years passed they felt that God did not want them to have a child. They tried to accept the will of God with good grace. Anup learned to live with the taunts that her mother-in-law heaped on her and with the fun that her neighbours made of her childless state. She lavished her love on all the children of the area and Hari Das too found comfort in giving to others' children the love that he would have given his own child.

But in their heart of hearts, however, neither Hari Das nor Anup Devi ever gave up hope. On quiet evenings when, after the day's work and the evening meal, they sat side by side, the same thought would pass through both their minds. Some day they would sit there imagining their child playing in the courtyard. They prayed continuously that this dream would come true. At last by God's grace, twelve years after they were married, a son was born to them. He was a very handsome baby, fair and healthy, with sharp features and big clear eyes. He was named Ram Das (Servant of God), though they called him Jetha: the first born.

Everyone loved Jetha. All the women, who had made fun of Anup's childlessness, now looked for a chance to play with this happy, cheerful baby. They looked for excuses to come to Anup's house so that they could hold this baby for a little while. Jetha grew into a handsome boy, unspoilt by all the attention that he was given. Though he always answered everyone with a smile and spent time with anyone who stopped him or spoke to him, he was happiest when he was in the company of holy men. Long before he could even understand what they were saying he would sit in their company and listen to their discussions with interest. It became a joke in his family and among his friends. Everytime he was missing or someone was looking for him, a friend or a family member would call out: "Go to the banks of the Ravi where the holy men camp, you are sure to find him there." Before he was in his teens he was familiar with most of the Hindu religious texts, the Vedas and the Upanishads and knew most of the *shlokas* and *mantras* by heart. But knowledge of the holy texts alone does not fill your stomach, specially if you are from a middle class family like that of Hari Das.

Hari Das and Anup would sit side by side at the end of the day, waiting for their son to return from his visits to the holy men. While they waited they would worry about his future. It would have been all right if he was going to school. But after the first few years of formal education, once he had learnt to read and write, Jetha had stopped going to school. Instead he spent all his time listening to holy men the way Guru Nanak had done years ago. And like Kalu, Guru Nanak's father, Hari Das too worried about his son's future. But when

Ram Das did return at last from his visit with the holy men it was impossible to be angry with him. He showed great care and concern for his parents and everyone around. Young as he was he found pleasure in helping other people and taking upon himself work that others were not willing to do. When they saw this the parents would smile with affection and with pride. Yet, at other times their worry for his future would return and they often talked about this to their friends and relatives.

It was their neighbour who suggested a possible solution. He too was a simple man and earned his living by selling roasted gram (chana). "Give Jetha some roasted gram to sell," he told Hari Das and Anup Devi. "It is the simplest thing for which no special skills are required. He is very hardworking and once he understands that work can be turned into money everything will be all right. He will stop spending his time with holy men."

So Anup Devi prepared a big bag of roasted gram and gave him a small metal container with which to measure the gram when he sold it. Ram Das went with his neighbour who showed him a busy corner in the market, where he would find many customers. Jetha did, indeed, find many customers. His gram was sold out and for the next few days he came home to his parents every evening with the money that he had earned.

Hari Das was happy because he knew that this was only a beginning. As his son grew older he would apply his mind to other trades and would do well. Then a few days later while he was selling his gram, Ram Das heard that there was a group of holy men camped on the banks of the Ravi and he felt he must go to meet them. When he reached the camp he saw that the sanyasis had not eaten anything the whole day. Without a second thought he gave all his gram to the hungry sanyasis and came back even happier than when he had made money by selling his gram. He had no way of knowing that years ago another boy had felt this happiness too. Guru Nanak had also made a good investment by feeding a group of hungry *sadhus*.

Guru Amar Das had many followers in Lahore. With each passing year the number of his followers kept increasing and Ram Das often heard people talking about the Guru. He heard them talking about his teachings and about the great *dera* in Goindwal, and he wanted to go and visit the Guru. With his parents' permission he joined a group of devotees who were going to Goindwal.

Ram Das at once won the hearts of everyone around him with his polite behaviour and his great spirit of service. He worked from morning till night and he worked always with a smile. People around him became very fond of him and it seemed that Jetha had always been in Goindwal. When it was time for the band of devotees to return to Lahore, Jetha stayed on. He sent a message to his parents that he was well and asked for permission to stay on in Goindwal.

Bibi Bhani, the Guru's youngest daughter, had now reached marriageable age and her mother Mansa Devi was worried about finding a suitable boy.

"What kind of boy do you want for our daughter?" the Guru asked, when she voiced her concern.

Mata Mansa Devi looked up and saw Jetha standing at the door. She saw his good looks and remembered his pleasant manners and his selfless devotion to the Guru and his kindness and his humility.

"Someone like him," she said pointing to Jetha.

"Why someone like him?" the Guru asked. "There can be no one like him. So if you like Jetha so much, why not Jetha himself?"

"Yes," Mansa Devi said. " I know our daughter will be happy with him."

For Jetha his Guru's wish was his command. The Guru sent him home to Lahore to seek his parents' permission. Hari Das was proud that the great Guru had found his son

Gurdwara Sri Patna Sahib, Patna

Gurdwara Dukh Niwaran Sahib, Patiala

worthy to be his son-in-law; he readily gave his consent. So Jetha and Bhani were married.

Even after his marriage there was no difference in the life that Jetha led. He still worked with the same spirit. All day he would work and at night when he was sure the Guru was asleep he would slip quietly into the courtyard of the Guru's house where the Guru slept. Jetha would press the Guru's tired legs and massage the soles of his tired feet. The Guru would smile to himself in the dark and think of the very great love that this disciple had for him. At last the Guru did give an indication that he recognised Jetha as being a special devotee by sending him as his envoy to Akbar's court.

But it was only a short while before his death that Guru Amar Das formally announced that Jetha would be his successor. Jetha was anointed by Bhai Budha in 1574 and he became the fourth Guru of the Sikhs. In keeping with Guru Amar Das's wishes Guru Ram Das started the building of a centre of the Sikh religion. He had already started work on a tank while Guru Amar Das lived and after the latter's death he came to live there and a town was built around the tank.

The construction of the tank was a very big project and it took many years to complete the excavation. Sikhs, moved by love for their Guru and for their religion, came from far and near to help with the work. Bhai Budha, too old now to work himself, would sit in the shade of a *beri* near the tank from where he would supervise the work that was being done. A great deal of money was required to buy building material and to run the *langar* for the large number of devotees who had come to work on the project. The Guru's treasury had been exhausted and the Guru wondered what he could do to keep the work going.

He invited his most faithful devotees to a meeting. Through his *masands* he made a direct appeal to his devotees in each *manji* (sub-centre). There was an overwhelming response to this appeal. Money now came in regularly and never again did the Guru have to worry on this account. The

holy tank which later came to be known as Amritsar, the pool
of nectar, began to take shape and nearby its banks the
devotees built a house for their Guru which was called Guru
Mahal.

As the township grew the Guru encouraged traders to
settle there. This suited the traders because of the town's
proximity to Lahore. With the revenue from this trade the
Guru was able to send his missionaries to all parts of India.
Gradually the town of Ramdaspur (or Amritsar as it came
to be called later), became an important commercial centre
and soon it rivalled Lahore in importance. More than its
commercial importance Amritsar became, in later years, the
centre of the Sikh world and Guru Amar Das's dream was
fulfilled.

Guru Ram Das had many followers but the most
important disciple was Bhai Gurdas.

Bhai Gurdas was the son of Guru Amar Das's younger
brother, Datar Chand. Guru Amar Das had taken on the
responsibility of his education and the boy had come to live
in Goindwal. He was a very intelligent and devoted disciple
and did much to spread the Gurus' teachings. Guru Ram
Das recognised this and sent him to Agra to set up a centre
there.

Like the first three Gurus, Guru Ram Das was also a
poet. He wrote many hymns and prayers which were later
included in the collection of sacred writings. One of his
poems *Var Gauri* gives some details of the life of Guru Amar
Das.

The Guru had three sons: Prithi, Mahadev, and Arjun.
Prithi proved to be greedy and selfish while Mahadev was
an ascetic and had cut himself off from worldly matters. Over
the years Arjun showed total obedience to the Guru's
wishes. He proved through his spirit of service that the light
of Nanak's lamp had passed to him. So when the time came
the Guru declared that Arjun would be the next Guru. The
aged Bhai Budha applied the *tilak* and Guru Ram Das put

five copper coins and a coconut at Arjun's feet and bowed to him.

Shortly afterwards, in 1581, Guru Ram Das passed away at Goindwal. The fourth Guru died at the age of forty-seven; he had been Guru for seven years. He knew that the most important task before him was to strengthen the practices that Guru Amar Das had begun. Like Guru Amar Das, Guru Ram Das made sure that everyone who came to him, first ate at the common *langar*. By doing this he made the *langar* an accepted and essential part of the Sikh religion.

He made sure that all religious ceremonies were performed in Punjabi, the language of the people and that no pandit or priest was needed for this. Perhaps he remembered the wedding ceremony of the Rajput widow that Guru Amar Das had performed, because he wrote a very beautiful hymn specially for weddings and this hymn is used at all Sikh weddings even today.

Guru Ram Das strengthened the organisation of the Sikh religion. He was in regular touch with the *manjis* and because of this *manjis* functioned efficiently and many more followers joined the *sangat*.

He was a very quiet and humble man and his dealings with people were always mild and gentle. This is why during his time there was no trouble with the Muslims or the Brahmins. There was also no trouble with the sons of the Guru who had been passed over for the guruship.

Once Sri Chand, son of Guru Nanak, came to Amritsar. He was now an old man. Guru Ram Das treated him with great respect and stepped down from his *gaddi* to greet him. Sri Chand was happy to see how well the Sikh religion had grown. Any bitterness he may have had at not being made the second Guru was now forgotten. Yet before he left he could not help making a joke at the Guru's expense.

"Everything is well," he said. "And I am truly happy to see your wonderful work. But tell me, Ram Das, why do you keep such a long beard?" He indicated the Guru's long flowing beard which reached up to his waist. The Guru folded his hands and bowed to the Sant. "It is so long Babaji, so that I can clean your feet with it."

He bent down and removed the dust from Sri Chand's feet with his flowing beard. Sri Chand was moved to tears, he drew the Guru up and held him in a tight embrace. Then he drew away and held Ram Das at arm's length and looked closely at his face and then into his eyes.

"The light of my father shines in your face and in your eyes," he said in a quiet, steady voice. "Such humility is a very special gift from God. I can see, now, why you are the Guru and not I." He put his hand on Guru Ram Das's head in blessing, then turned and strode away from the dera.

Guru Arjun Dev
(1563-1606)

*I*n Guru Amar Das's house in Goindwal there was always the sound of children at play. The Guru had many grandchildren and they filled the house with their noise. The children shouted to each other while at play and they laughed at each other's jokes. Most beautiful of all these was the sound of little bare feet pattering across the brick floors.

The Guru loved all his grandchildren dearly and always found time to play with them and listen to their stories.

One day the Guru had some important visitors, a group of religious leaders who had come to discuss certain matters with the Guru. While they were all involved with serious talk, Arjun, Bibi Bhani's youngest son, came crawling into the room. He was only a baby but already he was very fond of his grandfather. He stopped near the door and looked around. When he saw his grandfather, he made a happy gurgling sound and came crawling towards him. The Guru picked him up, kissed him on the forehead and held him on his lap. Arjun lay in his grandfather's lap, happily sucking his thumb. Here Bibi Bhani found him when she came looking for him. But when she reached out to take him away, the Guru shook his head and Bhani understood that she must leave the baby there. She turned and went back to her work. After this it became a common sight to see the baby Arjun in his grandfather's lap.

The Guru ate very simply. He usually ate only *ogra*, a dish made from rice and dal. Since he did not want any of his disciples to feel compelled to follow his example, he usually ate his food alone in his room. One day his food was brought to him while he was busy writing, and Bibi Bhani left the covered *thali* near him and went quietly away. When the Guru did, at last, turn to have his meal, he was surprised and amused to see that Arjun had already uncovered the *thali* and was eating the *ogra*. The Guru sat back and smiled and watched the child while he ate the food. When his little stomach was full he looked towards his grandfather and saw the Guru smiling at him. He too smiled and toddled out of the room. The Guru smiled again and ate the rest of the food.

Arjun was very devoted to his parents. When his father became Guru he spent as much time in the Guru's presence as he could. For him the Guru had become his Guru too. Young as he was he knew that the first rule of his religion was complete obedience to his Guru. He found great happiness in being with the Guru, in carrying out the Guru's wishes. He helped with the building of the holy tank and understood how important it was to his father. He listened while his father talked to Bhai Budha and Bhai Gurdas and understood that his father had great plans for the future of the Sikhs. Like all the earlier Gurus, Guru Ram Das composed beautiful hymns. From him, as from his grandfather, Guru Amar Das, Arjun got the inspiration to compose poems and hymns himself.

Arjun's life, as we have seen, centered around the Guru. As he grew from being a boy to a young man, his fondness to be with the Guru grew as well.

Guru Ram Das's time and energy were spent completely in building the holy tank and making plans for the temple. He was never able to go anywhere. Whenever there was work to be done outside the *dera* he always asked one of his senior disciples or one of his elder sons to attend to it. He understood Arjun's need to be always with him and very rarely asked Arjun to go on these errands and this was resented by Arjun's eldest brother Prithi Chand.

Prithi Chand had seen the wonderful work that was being done on the holy tank and the large offerings brought to the treasury by the *masands* and had met the important people who came to greet the Guru. He realised that the Guru's position was one of great power and authority. Quite early in his life he began to imagine that this position would one day be his. As he grew older he began to think that since he was the Guru's eldest son he must be the next Guru. Now he saw that his father kept Arjun close to him and he became jealous of Arjun. He felt that Arjun was trying to win his father's love in order to usurp Prithi's rightful place as the next Guru.

One day the Guru's cousin Sahari Mal came to visit him, with an invitation for his son's wedding. The Guru was too busy in his work to be able to attend and he looked for someone to go in his place. Since it was a family affair it would be best if one of his sons attended. Since Prithi was the eldest he sent for him and asked him to go.

Prithi stood for a moment in silence, his eyes fixed on the ground near his feet. Because he was already jealous of his brother Arjun, he was suspicious of everything. He thought that while he was away at the wedding Arjun would come even closer to the Guru.

"Father, I cannot go." Everyone was shocked by his words.

"I will stay here and work for you here."

"This is also my work," the Guru said softly, "By going to the wedding you will be serving me." Prithi shook his head.

"No," he said, still not looking his father in the eyes. "I will not go to the wedding."

The Guru knew what was in Prithi's heart. He smiled, thinking how stupid his eldest son was. Succession to the Guruship had never been automatic and merely by staying on in the *dera*, Prithi would not be made the next Guru. In fact by his refusal he had broken the basic tenent of the Guru-*shishya* relationship — the tenet that demands implicit obedience on the part of the disciple.

"Please yourself," he said gently. "It does not matter."

He turned then to his second son.

"Mahadev, my son, will you go in my place?" Here too the Guru knew what the answer would be even before he put the question.

Mahadev was a recluse and did not enjoy taking part in functions like weddings. He would not make this sacrifice even to please his father.

"Father, you know I do not enjoy taking part in such functions. Why don't you send Arjun?" The Guru turned to his youngest son. The boy's eyes filled with tears at the thought of being separated from his Guru even for a few days. But he had learnt his lesson well; no matter what the personal pain, he must carry out the Guru's wishes. He came forward and touched his father's feet and turned away.

"And stay for all the ceremonies," the Guru called after him.

"Don't come rushing back after a day or two," the Guru said in an affectionate tone.

The boy turned back to face the Guru. This time there was no sparkle of tears in his eyes, no fear of the pain that he would have to bear in the coming days.

"I will not return till you send for me." Once more he bowed to the Guru and then turned and went away.

The story goes that Arjun was very unhappy being away from his Guru and he wrote two letters to his father giving expression to his pain. Both these letters were received by Prithi who hid them from his father. The Guru worried about Arjun. It was strange that Arjun should have stayed away for so long without sending any news. At last, Arjun wrote a third letter to his father and the messenger was instructed to deliver the letter only to the Guru. The Guru immediately wrote back to say that his son should return and, true to his word, it was only after getting this letter that Arjun did return. By going away willingly even when he suffered so much pain, Arjun showed his devotion to the Guru.

The years passed and with each passing year Arjun gave further proof of his unselfish devotion to the Guru and his dedicated service to the *sangat*. It was clear to all that he, more than any other disciple, had understood so well the teachings of the Gurus. So it was no surprise that when the Guru realised his end was near he proclaimed Arjun as the next Guru. Again it was Baba Budha who applied the *tilak* (saffron-mark) on his forehead. On September 1, 1581, at the age of eighteen, Guru Arjun Dev became the fifth Guru of the Sikhs.

For the first time the Sikhs had a Guru who had been born and brought up in the Guru's household. He had listened to the teachings of two Gurus — his father and his grandfather, and seen how they looked after the running of what was now a huge organisation. He also understood the tasks that lay ahead of him.

The foremost task was to complete the holy tank and the sacred temple which had been the dream of both his father and his grandfather. He knew that he had to give to the Sikhs a centre that was as important as Banaras and Hardwar were to the Hindus or as Mecca and Medina were to the Muslims.

Guru Arjun began by making the tank bigger. He wanted to pave the tank and line it with masonry and to build side-walls. For this he needed special bricks. Bhai Bhalo, a Sikh from Malwa, was sure that he could give the Guru the bricks that were needed and set up the first of many brick-kilns. Wood was required for these kilns. Once again Sikh disciples were sent to the neighbouring hill states to get the wood, and word of the Guru and his teachings spread further and further into the hills, and many of the Rajas came down to visit Ramdaspur and got the Guru's blessing.

Prithi Chand had still not accepted Arjun as the Guru. He tried to turn the Sikhs against his brother by telling them false stories against the Guru. The Guru heard of this but he was too busy with the new project to pay attention.

While the tank was enlarged and paved, work on the design of the temple had been started. The Guru kept an open mind and discussed all the details with his disciples. At first it was felt that the temple should be built on a great height like the mountain shrines of the Hindus. In this way the temple would be seen from miles around and would inspire people everytime they looked up to it. But the Guru convinced everyone that the temple they were going to build was not like any other temple. He said that the temple should be built at a lower level than the land around it. The Guru was a very humble man and felt that the temple should inspire humility and reverence. If the temple was built lower everyone who came to visit it would have to go down to it and in doing this they would feel humble the way one should feel humble in a place of worship.

There was also a great deal of discussion as to the number of doors the building should have. Many different ideas were presented. Finally, the Guru voiced his opinion.

"There should be no doors," he said. "The temple should be open from all four sides so that it is always open to those who wish to enter."

The designs were completed and work was started in 1588. Guru Arjun Dev asked Hazrat Mian Mir, a great Muslim saint, to lay the foundation-stone.

Hindus, Muslims and Sikhs worked side by side on the building of the temple. As the temple took shape people saw that it was a mixture of the styles of both Hindu and Muslim buildings.

Though the Guru's followers gave generously of their money and their labour, the project was so big and grand that at one stage work slowed down. Hired labour was needed and with this more funds. Guru Arjun Dev realised that the Sikhs should have a fund from which money could be taken whenever it was needed. This would help not only the construction of the temple but any other community work that the Sikhs might take up in future. He gave instructions that all true Sikhs should contribute one-tenth of their income for the service of the community. This was called *Daswandh.* The *masands* were instructed to collect this money and bring it with them to Ramdaspur on the first day of the month of Baisakh.

The temple was at last completed. The holy tank was filled with water and given the name of Amritsar, and in course of time the town around it also came to be called Amritsar.

After the temple was completed the Guru decided to go on a tour of the Punjab. This tour lasted for five years, and during this tour he built three new townships, Tarn Taran, Kartarpur (not the one that was Guru Nanak's Kartarpur), and Hargobindpur. Of these Tarn Taran became a very important pilgrimage centre in its own right. During these five years Guru Arjun Dev brought thousands of people into the Sikh fold.

Guru Arjun Dev returned to Ramdaspur in 1595. Immediately on his return he was faced with a fresh crisis, caused by his elder brother Prithi Chand. Prithi Chand had composed a hymn and used Nanak's name at the end, the way all the Gurus did. Guru Arjun Dev realised that if Prithi could do this, anyone could do it. In times to come no one would be able to tell which hymns had been composed by the Gurus and which by other people. There could also be a time when other people using Guru Nanak's name could compose hymns which would go against the Gurus' teachings. This could cause confusion in the minds of the Gurus' followers.

The Guru knew that this could mean very serious trouble for the Sikhs and the only way to avoid this was to make a collection of all the hymns composed by the first five Gurus. This would be the authentic collection of the hymns and teachings of the Gurus and people like Prithi would not be able to fool the Sikhs and cause trouble for them.

The Guru realised that this task was of the greatest importance and placed it above everything else. He discussed this with Bhai Budha and Bhai Gurdas and it was decided that Bhai Gurdas would help him in this great project.

On Guru Ram Das's death, Bhai Gurdas had returned from Agra. During the construction of the great temple he had made himself useful in every possible way — specially in writing letters and keeping accounts. He had impressed the Guru with his intelligence, his scholarship and his ability to work hard, and had come to be recognised as a prominent member of the community, next only to Bhai Budha.

The first task was to collect all the compositions of the first four Gurus. Guru Arjun Dev had his father's compositions with him and knew that he could get the compositions of the first three Gurus from Bhai Mohan at Goindwal. As a child he had been present when Guru Amar Das had asked his son Mohan to make a collection and if he could get this collection it would make his task easier.

He sent Bhai Gurdas with a request to Bhai Mohan. Bhai Mohan, even though he lived in Goindwal, lived the life of a total recluse. He did not meet anyone or see anyone and rarely spent time even with his wife and son. Bhai Gurdas was lucky to find him. Bhai Mohan considered the Guru's request for a few moments and then shook his head.

"No," he said, "these hymns were given to me by my father. My son Sahas Ram has written them down in two *pothis* (volumes) and these *pothis* are the most valuable and sacred possession I have. I will not part with them."

When Bhai Gurdas returned with this message Guru Arjun Dev smiled.

"Baba Mohan is not one to deny a sincere request. I will go to him myself."

By the time the Guru reached Goindwal, Baba Mohan had again retreated to the upper room of his house, on the river Beas and was lost in meditation. The Guru sent all his attendants away and took up his position in the street below Baba Mohan's window. Day after day he sat there waiting for the moment when his uncle would notice him, and day after day there was no response. While waiting, the Guru composed a beautiful hymn in the *Rag Gauri* and sang it in his beautiful, clear voice. The hymn was addressed to Mohan, which is one of the names that is given to God. Baba heard the hymn and his heart softened at the sweet humility of Guru Arjun Dev. He came down to the street, bowed to the Guru and handed over the *pothis* to him.

Apart from the Goindwal *pothis*, there were, at that time, other collections of the Gurus' hymns which had been collected and preserved by devoted Sikhs. Guru Arjun Dev tried to collect as many of these as possible. One of the most important of these was a volume presented to the Guru by a Sikh, Bakht Arora of the Hassan Abdal area. Guru Arjun Dev also went to Kartarpur and Khadur and got collections of the works of the earlier Gurus from Sri Datu. Then the Guru sent messengers and important disciples like Bhai Piara to far-off places to collect the compositions of the saints whose teachings were similar to the teachings of the Gurus.

When the Guru had collected all the material possible, he went with Bhai Gurdas to Ramsar, a mile away from Hari Mandir, the temple built by him in the holy tank. Here on a clean vacant patch in the centre of a thick grove of *ber* trees, tents were put up and the Guru and Bhai Gurdas began their monumental work. All the hymns that the Gurus composed were composed for singing by the *sangat* and each Guru had indicated in which *Raag* the composition was to be sung. Guru Arjun Dev took this as a starting point. There were altogether thirty *Ragas* that had been used for the different compositions. So he arranged his compositions according to the *Ragas*. The *Japuji* was kept at the beginning, at the head, and all the other compositions were arranged in thirty groups according to the *Ragas* to which they were to be sung.

All the Gurus took the title of Nanak when they became Guru and wrote their hymns under the pen-name of 'Nanak'. This meant that there was no way of knowing which Guru had composed a particular hymn. Guru Arjun Dev felt that there should be some indication as to the authorship of the hymn. So he gave each Guru the title Mahala or 'Home of God' and a number. So Guru Nanak was designated as Mahala Pehla or first home of God. Guru Angad Dev as Mahala Dooja or second home of God and so on. The hymns in each *Raag*-group were arranged in the chronological order of the Gurus. At the end of the book Guru Arjun Dev included the compositions of the *bhaktas* like Kabir, Ravidas, Namdev, Farid and others.

Bhai Gurdas, a great poet in his own right, worked as the scribe for the original Granth. For a year the Guru and Bhai Gurdas worked at their task and the holy book of the Sikhs was at last completed. When we look at the original copy we see that the Guru studied every page again and again even after Bhai Gurdas had set it all down. The compositions of some *bhaktas* were considered unsuitable and were excluded. The original *Granth*, in rich leather binding, is preserved at Kartarpur. It is in the custody of the Sodhis, the descendants of Dhirmal, Guru Arjun Dev's grandson.

The Granth was installed with great ceremony in the Hari Mandir. At the installation ceremony the Guru asked Bhai Gurdas to make some recitations from the book. Later he appointed Bhai Budha, now an old man, as the first *granthi* or custodian of the book, and it was Bhai Budha who read from the book at the morning and evening prayer-meetings.

Bhai Budha was one of the first Sikhs to listen to Guru Nanak's teachings. He had been invited to apply *sandal-wood* paste to the foreheads of all the Gurus from Guru Angad to Guru Arjun Dev and had been by the side of all the Gurus.

Because the *granth* contained all the teachings of the Gurus, it soon became a symbol of the Gurus. This fact was emphasised by the instruction given by Guru Gobind Singh to the Sikhs. After him there would be no Guru in flesh and blood. All the teachings that the Sikhs needed could be got from the *Granth* and they must regard it as their Guru. This instruction of the Tenth Guru is repeated after prayers when the Sikhs recite together.

"Sabh Sikhan kau hukam hai, Guru manyo Granth."

(We command all Sikhs to hold the Granth to be the Guru).

Since the Granth is now the Guru the text has remained exactly the same as when Guru Arjun Dev wrote it down, except for the addition of Guru Tegh Bahadur's hymns by Guru Gobind Singh.

Thus we see that by compiling the *Guru Granth Sahib*, Guru Arjun Dev produced much more than what he set out to do. He gave the Sikhs a holy text which finally became a focal point for all Sikh communities, no matter where they were based. The Granth is now given the same respect that would be given to a living Guru. The Sikhs bow to it when they come into its presence and make offerings to it.

All major religious ceremonies of the Sikhs consist in making a complete reading of the Granth Sahib either in forty-eight hours of non-stop recitation, or in small parts spread over a week or ten days. At the close of this ceremony sacred hymns are sung and *prasad* is distributed. No event in a Sikh's life, such as naming ceremony for a new-born child, marriage, and prayers for a departed soul, can take place without the presence of the Granth.

Prithi's hostility towards his brother remained unabated. He used the Granth to try and create more trouble for the Guru. Through some influential officials he complained to Emperor Akbar about the holy book. The officials complained that the book contained passages which were decidedly anti-Muslim and anti-Islam in tone. Akbar did not at first believe this. His own experience of Guru Amar Das and of Sikhism had shown him that Sikhism was a very tolerant religion and that Sikhism taught respect for all religions. It was unlikely that the fifth Guru would preach against Islam or write things against the Muslims. But the complaints were repeated again and again and at last Akbar decided to make an inquiry.

As it happened Akbar had to make a trip to the North. He stopped outside Amritsar and sent a message to the Guru asking to see a copy of the Granth Sahib. Bhai Budha and Bhai Gurdas read out a few of the hymns. Then Akbar asked other learned men like Sahib Dyal to make random readings from the Granth.

Akbar found that apart from the writings of the Guru, the Granth also contained the writings of poet-saints, both Muslims and Hindus, from all parts of Northern India. He found that all the hymns were very beautiful and expressed his own beliefs that each religion should respect all other religions and that the practice of religion should be simplified. Akbar was delighted with the Guru's work. He followed the

Sikh practice, bowed before the holy book and made an offering of fifty-one gold mohurs. He also gave robes of honour to Bhai Budha and Bhai Gurdas and sent presents for the Guru. In spite of Prithi's hostility Guru Arjun Dev bore him no grudge and invited him to come and take charge of the *langar* at the Hari Mandir.

The death of Emperor Akbar and the coming of Jahangir to the throne of Delhi marked a radical change in the attitude of the Mughals towards the Sikhs.

Many Muslims had become followers of the Gurus and this had made the Muslim religious leaders angry. While Akbar was alive they had not dared set up an opposition to the Sikhs. But on Akbar's death these religious leaders came out openly against the Sikhs. Jahangir did not have the spirit of religious tolerance that his father had. He was keen to win favour with the Muslim religious leaders and was ready to support their viewpoint. Most of all he himself was jealous of the growing influence of the Guru and the Sikh religion. He wrote in his diary that he was aware that many Hindus and Muslims were following the teachings of the Guru.

From this it was clear that he was only looking for an opportunity to suppress the religion and this opportunity came a few months after he became Emperor. His son Khusrau had been Akbar's favourite and many people at the court had felt that Khusrau would make a better Emperor than Jahangir. Shortly after Jahangir's accession to the throne Khusrau revolted against him. While he was trying to collect an army he visited Guru Arjun Dev in Amritsar and asked for the Guru's blessing. The Guru was a man of peace and could not help the prince in war effort. The Guru gave him his blessing just as he would have given his blessings to anyone who came to his *dera*. But this innocent and harmless act was to lead to trouble between the Sikhs and the Mughals. Khusrau was not able to build up a strong army and was defeated and arrested by his father. Jahangir decided to punish all those who had helped his son and to crush the Guru as well. Jahangir wrote in his diary: "I fully knew his (the Guru's) heresies and ordered that he (the Guru) should be brought into my presence, that his houses and children be made over to Murtaza Khan, the Governor, that his property should be confiscated and that he should be put to death with torture."

The Guru received the Emperor's summons with complete equanimity. He had no illusions about the fate that awaited him and was quite reconciled to it. Before he left in answer to the Emperor's summons he sent for Baba Budha and gave instruction that his son Hargobind should be made the next Guru of the Sikhs.

Mian Mir tried to help the Guru by speaking to the Emperor and the Governor. But they both turned a deaf ear. Many of the Guru's disciples wished to accompany the Guru to Lahore because they knew that this could be the Guru's last journey and wanted to be with him. The Guru dissuaded them from going with him. Accompanied by a handful of attendants Guru Arjun Dev made the short journey from Amritsar to Lahore and presented himself at the court of Murtaza Khan, the Governor. Murtaza Khan ordered that the Guru should be chained and taken to a dark, airless dungeon in the fort where he was treated like a common criminal. His fine clothes were taken away and he was given a coarse robe to wear. His only food was dry *rotis* and water. But he did not notice these things as his mind was occupied all the time in prayers.

Next day the Governor ordered that the Guru be brought into his presence.

"Do you deny," the Governor asked, "that the traitor Khusrau came to your *dera* to ask for help?"

"No," the Guru replied in a strong clear voice. "I do not deny it."

"Do you deny that you applied *tilak* to the traitor's forehead and treated him with every mark of respect?"

"No," said the Guru once more. "No, I do not deny it."

"The Emperor Jahangir has ordered that for your role in the mutiny you must make a public apology and pay a fine."

The Guru shook his head.

"I had no role to play in the rebellion. The prince came to me like so many other people come to me. I gave him my blessings in the same way that I give my blessings to all the people who come to my *dera*. I did not give him any assistance. So I cannot apologise or pay a fine."

"The Emperor's orders are clear," Murtaza Khan said. "If you do not apologise and pay the fine you will be put to death."

The Guru knew what Jahangir was trying to do. By making him apologise and pay a fine the Emperor was trying to bring the Guru and the Sikhs under his rule. If the Guru gave in, the Sikhs would always be at the mercy of the Emperor. If he apologised for something he had not done, or paid a fine, he would be recognising the authority of the Emperor over the Sikhs.

"No," he said, "I cannot apologise or pay a fine, not even if you put me through death."

Murtaza Khan looked down at the Guru from his throne. The Guru met his gaze without flinching and it was the Governor who had to look away. He knew that the Guru had not helped Khusrau and he also knew that the Guru would not give in. He would have to carry out the second part of the Emperor's orders.

"Take him back to the dungeon," he ordered.

Murtaza Khan sent for his chief executioner, who was a specialist in torture. He was able to invent newer and more horrible means of torture every time he had to deal with a victim. It was said that he could make people say whatever he wanted them to say after just five minutes of torture.

Now he came into his master's presence, bowed low and waited for his master's orders.

"You have heard of the so-called Guru who is in our prison?"

"Yes, Master, I have heard of him."

"The Emperor has a special interest in this man. He wants him to die a horrible death. But before he does he must apologise for what he has done and beg forgiveness."

"I will do my best, my lord. I have not failed you as yet, I do not think I will fail you now."

"I know that," Murtaza Khan said, "I only stress that this work is of the greatest importance. Here!" He threw a bag of gold coins to the executioner. "There will be more if the work is completed to my satisfaction." The executioner put his mind to the task and came up with an ingeneous solution. It was the hottest time of the year, so the torture would be through heat. Out in the burning sun, on a high piece of land he dug a pit which was covered by a plate of iron. He lit a huge fire under the plate. Once the plate became red hot the Guru would be made to sit on it.

Town criers were sent around the city to make announcements about the torture. The people were told that it was the Emperor's wish that they should come to see how a traitor was punished. Long before the sun rose on May 30, 1606, huge crowds had collected around the place. Every rampart of the fort, the roof of every house outside the fort and every tree-top was occupied by the people who had come to see the torture. All around the little hill there was a sea of people. There were soldiers everywhere to keep the people under control and to see that no one interfered with the proceedings. The hours stretched on. The sun had risen and was beating down on earth with all its fury. The heat became unbearable and many people in the crowd fainted and had to be carried away.

Then when the day was at its hottest the Guru was brought from the dungeon. His hands and legs were in chains and he had difficulty in walking. Yet he walked straight and tall and there was no fear on his face. There was only peace and a soft glow and it was as if he was going to address his *sangat* and to lead them in prayers. A way had been cleared for him in the crowd and he came at last to the base of the little hill. He paused for a moment and then climbed up the steps that had been made for him. When he reached the top, the jailers unlocked the chains. The Guru looked briefly at the iron-plate and then down at the people swarming around and smiled. A murmur went up from the crowd and then a group of women began to wail. The Guru held up his hand and the wailing stopped. The executioner threw a few drops of water on the plate. The water hissed and evaporated instantly. He signalled to the guards. Two of the guards came forward. One last time he looked around at the people. A hush descended on the crowd. There was complete silence, the silence of people waiting in fear. Then he took the few steps that were needed to get him to the iron-plate. He sat down cross-legged on the plate and closed his eyes and his lips moved in prayer.

There was a change in the attitude of the crowd. There was still total silence. But now it was the silence of respect and admiration for the great courage of the Guru.

The Guru showed no pain. There was a joy singing in his heart. What he was doing was for his God and for his people. The more his tormentors made him suffer the greater would be his sacrifice. The more he suffered the stronger his people would become.

The executioner was angry. He had been sure that his victim would scream with pain and beg for mercy, admit his sins and ask for forgiveness. But this had not happened. Instead this strange Guru sat through the pain without a cry.

The executioner looked up at the fort. He knew that Murtaza Khan was up there in the highest chamber of the fort. He also knew that if he failed, instead of the promised reward, his own life would be in danger. He looked again at the crowd. He could see that many of the people were crying openly, many of them had folded their hands in prayer and many were now kneeling down, their foreheads touching the ground in homage to the great man. He knew he had to act quickly. If he allowed this to continue more people would express open sympathy for the Guru and some of them might decide to free the Guru and Murtaza Khan would have a revolt on his hands.

The pit had been filled with sand over which the wood was burning. One side of the pit was open and it was through this that more and more wood was being added to keep the iron-plate hot. He called two of the guards. They used shovels and drew up the hot sand which they poured over the upper part of the Guru's body. A loud cry went up from the crowd. A few even ran to the base of the steps where they were stopped by the guards.

There was no change on the Guru's face. His lips still moved in prayer and there was such peace and calm that it touched the hearts of all the people who watched. The executioner became more and more frustrated. He ordered more wood to be put into the pit, more sand to be poured over the Guru's body. Yet there was no cry from the Guru, no protest, no expression of pain. On and on the torture went. For the crowd who watched, the Guru's great strength became a superhuman force. They knew that this could only have come from God and from complete faith in God.

As the torture continued, even the executioner began to have doubts. He was sure now that the Guru was a saint because only a saint could have lived through so much, only a saint could have borne such great pain without a cry. Had he been right to torture a man of God? God would be angry with him. He had orders to carry out. His master Murtaza Khan would have been angry with him for not carrying out his orders. But was Murtaza Khan's anger a more terrible thing than God's anger?

At last the day of agony came to an end. The sun sank low on the horizon and the breeze that blew up from the river brought a marginal relief from the heat of the day. The torture was called to a halt. The Guru put on his robe and covered his bruised body. Preparations were made to take the Guru back to his prison. Before he came down from the hill he turned to his tormentors.

"My body is covered with blood and sand and secretions from my blisters," he said quietly. "Give me permission to wash it all clean in the waters of the river."

They had all seen the agony he had been put through. They had all been touched by his great strength. Now they were touched by the humility of his request. There could be no harm in letting him bathe in the river. The Guru was led to the river bank, the crowd following at his heels.

The guards stopped at the top of the flight of steps which went down to the water. The Guru drew off his robe. The crowd gasped as one man. Even in the fading light they saw that his body was covered with blisters and burns and wounds. The Guru went down the short flight of steps and lowered his bruised and battered body into the waters of the Ravi and swam a few strokes. In spite of his great courage and forbearance the torture had been too much for him. Even the effort to swim became too great. The waters closed over his head and he was drowned. His soul surrendered its earthly frame.

The sun had sunk over the horizon leaving only a soft orange glow. The darkness gathered over the land. Lights were lit in the fort and the homes outside the fort, and still the guards and the crowd waited for the Guru to return. The minutes stretched into hours. An alarm was raised. Boats with lights were sent out up and down the river and professional divers dived from the boats to look for the Guru. But it was no use, his body was never found by his tormentors.

Guru Arjun Dev was the head of the Sikhs for twenty-five years. During this time he continued with the work that the Gurus before him had started. All five Gurus tried to combine the best features of Hinduism and Islam. They

Gurdwara Sri Harmandir Sahib, Amritsar

Gurdwara Sri Fathegarh Sahib, Sirhind

respected all religions and tried to build up an understanding among them. They were all peace-loving and spent their lives in prayers, meditation and the service of others. They preached that the focus of good life was one of love of God and service of humanity. They set up new centres of worship and new townships and collected money for projects that would benefit the community. They were all great poets; Guru Arjun too gave the Sikhs many psalms, including *Sukhmani* or the song of peace, which is one of the most popular hymns in the Punjab.

Two of Guru Arjun Dev's greatest achievements were the building of the Harimandir and the compiling of the Guru Granth Sahib. Both these gave the Sikhs a distinct identity. The Muslims had their Mecca, the Hindus their Haridwar and the Sikhs now had their Harimandir in Amritsar. The Muslims looked for an answer to all their problems in the Koran, the Hindus had their own holy books. For the Sikhs the Guru Granth Sahib now had all the teachings they needed to learn.

But it is with his death and the manner of his dying that Guru Arjun Dev gave a new and important lesson to his followers. His followers learnt from their Guru that they must resist evil even if they had to give up their lives for it. They must fight evil and injustice with all the force at their command.

The last message that he sent to his son was to arm himself fully and to prepare himself for the struggle ahead — a struggle against the cruelty and oppression of the Moghul rule. Through his martyrdom Guru Arjun provided the strength which was to keep the Sikh religion alive in the difficult years ahead.

Sikhs all over the world remember Guru Arjun Dev's pain and suffering even today. His death anniversary comes during the hottest time of the year. On this day Sikhs put up stalls along all roads. They request all buses and cars, scooters and bicycles, and pedestrians that go by to stop, and serve them cold water and *sherbat*. By quenching the thirst of thousands of travellers, the Sikhs hope to quench a little of the memory of the terrible thirst their Guru must have felt as he sat on that hot iron-plate about four hundred years ago.

Guru Hargobind
(1595-1644)

There was always a period of time between the evening prayers and the evening meal when Guru Arjun Dev and Mata Ganga, his wife, were alone together. This had become a very special time for them. Ganga looked forward to this time as her very own. She had the Guru to herself and could share all her thoughts and her feelings with him and during this time he was not only her Guru but also her husband. There was always a warmth in being together and happiness. But one evening when the Guru was thirty-one years old there was no happiness in being together. The Guru sensed an uneasiness in his wife's manner. "What is it Ganga?" he asked coming straight to the point as he always did. "What is it that is troubling you?" "Do you need to ask?" she replied and for the first time that evening she looked straight into her husband's eyes. "You are not only my husband, you are my Guru too. You know what is troubling me." The Guru did indeed know what was troubling his wife.

"It is the will of God," he said in a gentle voice. "We must accept his will and live with it."

"But in this matter the blessings of holy men are also important. Many women who are childless have been blessed by holy men and have received the gift of children."

The Guru knew that this was true.

"Who can be more holy than you? Why do you not give me your blessings?" Mata Ganga put the edge of her dupatta over her mouth and wept. The Guru put his hand on her head.

"I am not holy," he said with all humility. "I am a servant of God and of my people and I try to serve them to the best of my ability. That is all. Besides, even if I was holy it would not be right for me to bless myself or my own family."

Mata Ganga began to weep again.

"Do not weep," the Guru said.

"There is a holy man who can give you the blessings you want. Bhai Budha is a man of God. Go to him and seek his blessings. They will bear fruit."

Mata Ganga saw the sense of this. Bhai Budha was indeed a man of God who was greatly respected for his holiness. Surely his blessings would bear fruit. She wiped the tears from her eyes, smiled at the Guru, then hurried into the house to supervise the serving of evening meals.

The next day Mata Ganga went to visit the saint. She had woken up early and dressed herself in her best clothes. She took with her baskets of food and sweets and many rich presents. She rode in a horse-drawn carriage and was escorted by a troop of servants.

Bhai Budha at that time lived in a little forest just outside Amritsar. He heard the approach of horses and came out of his hut to see who was coming. He saw the group of people and then the carriage. Before the leading rider could announce Mata Ganga's arrival, Bhai Budha asked:

"What commotion is this in the Guru's household?"

The rider bowed low to the saint.

"Mata Ganga has come to seek your blessings."

"Tell her I will not see her," Bhai Budha said. He turned abruptly and went back into his hut. The rider went up to the carriage and repeated what Bhai Budha had said. Mata Ganga was hurt and upset and ordered her party to return to the Guru's house.

That evening when they were alone together she would not look at the Guru at all.

"What is the matter?" he asked. "I hear you went to Bhai Budha's house today. Did he not give you his blessings?" Mata Ganga could not control herself and broke into wild cries. The Guru waited. When the weeping stopped he asked again: "What did the saint say?"

"He would not see me. He just locked himself in his hut and would not see me." For a moment it seemed that she would break into tears again, but she controlled herself.

"Tell me more," the Guru said.

Mata Ganga told him the details of all the preparations she had made. As he listened, he smiled.

"You made a big mistake," he said.

"You must go to him in humility. You are seeking a favour from him and you must appear before him in the simplest manner."

The next day Mata Ganga set out to see the saint again. This time she was dressed in very simple clothes made of homespun cotton. She wore no jewellery and her feet were bare. She took no presents or rich food. On a simple brass *thali* she took the food that the saint ate: four *rotis* made of *bajra* and some onions. The *thali* was covered with a simple cotton cloth. She had no attendants or maid-servants and carried the *thali* herself. She did not ride in a carriage but walked barefoot to the saint's hut.

It took longer for her to reach and she was afraid that he might already have eaten his food. But when she reached the hut she found him sitting outside. "Come, come little mother," he said, "I have been waiting for my food and I am hungry." He took the tray from her and she bowed in greeting. "Sit down." She just sat on the ground at his feet. He drew the cover off the *thali*. Then he squashed an onion with his fist.

"You will have a son," he said as he began to eat. "He will be a very handsome man. He will also be a brave man, a very brave man, and will crush his enemies the way I have crushed this onion."

Mata Ganga felt her heart fill with happiness. She was sure now that with the saint's blessing her wish would be fulfilled. She waited till the saint had finished eating. Then she bowed to him and picking up the *thali* hurried home.

That evening the Guru saw his wife in a different mood. She sat with a faraway look in her eyes. Everytime someone spoke to her, she would smile and nod her head. Then she would be lost in her thoughts again. But there was no sadness in her face and in her eyes there were shining stars and the Guru knew that she had received the saint's blessings. When they were alone together he said: "You look very happy. I can see that the saint has given you his blessings."

She smiled with pleasure, "Yes," she said quietly. "The saint has given me his blessings. He has said that we will have a son, a son who will be both handsome and brave."

Nine months later a son was born to her and they named him Hargobind. As soon as the child Hargobind could walk he was put in the charge of special teachers who taught him riding, sword fencing, wrestling, boxing. The Guru himself would supervise this instruction. Bhai Budha and Bhai Gurdas were confused by this. They did not understand why there was need to learn the martial arts.

"What is this strange education that you are giving your son? You were not given such an education by your father and your grandfather," Bhai Budha asked the Guru.

"It is not strange education," the Guru explained. "He is being taught the scriptures and everything that he needs to know. But we are living in troubled times and things are going to become very difficult for the Sikhs. So it is important that every Sikh must know how to defend himself. This he can do only if he is strong and learns all the skills that a soldier learns." The Guru knew that the education he imparted to his son would become the model for all Sikh children and from this point of time all Sikh boys did indeed learn how to defend themselves.

By the time Hargobind was ten years old he was well on his way to mastering all the skills that his father wanted him to learn. He was a very handsome young boy, tall and well-built and wherever he went people turned to look at him. He was sure of himself and had the confidence of a man very much older.

A year later Guru Arjun Dev was arrested and led away to prison in Lahore. He sent a message to Bhai Budha that in an eventuality Hargobind should be anointed as the Guru. The last message that his father sent him was that he must fight evil with all the strength at his command. The son took this message to heart and it was the message that he taught all his followers.

At his anointing Bhai Budha brought the *seli* or the sacred headgear which had been worn by all the Gurus from Guru Nanak downwards. This headgear was a symbol of renunciation. The Gurus continued to live in the world of men but by wearing this headgear they showed that they had no attachment to material things. Guru Hargobind pushed the *seli* away and would not wear it. Instead he wore a *kalgi* (aigrette) in his turban. At his waist-belt he wore two swords, one for *Miri* which stood for temporal power and the other for *Piri* or spiritual power.

The Guru established a regular routine for himself. This routine was a mixture of the way of life of the previous Gurus and the way of life that Guru Hargobind felt was needed at the time. He would wake up long before dawn while the world was still in darkness, and bathe in the holy tank. Then he would join his followers in prayer and in meditation. The rest of the day was spent in military activity. He raised an army and would watch the soldiers as they practised. He engaged experienced generals to teach his soldiers the principles of battle and different movements they should make while in battle. These movements were practised over and over again till they had been perfected. The Guru himself took an active part in these exercises. He also spent a lot of time in hunting and encouraged his disciples to do likewise. This taught the Sikhs to ride fast over difficult countryside and to be able to live off the land. Many brave disciples proved their strength and fearlessness and were appointed as commanders by the Guru. Among these were Bidhi Chand, Pairana, Piara and Lehngi.

The Moghuls had hoped that by putting Guru Arjun Dev to such horrible torture they would frighten the people. No one would want to become a follower of the Guru and the Sikhs would be crushed. Guru Arjun Dev's martyrdom had the opposite effect. The Guru's great courage encouraged more and more people to turn to Sikhism. The Sikhs were now ready to lay down their lives to protect their religion. The Guru now adopted the lifestyle of a ruler. He held court, listened to complaints and settled disputes. He received agents and ambassadors from rulers and princes and exchanged presents with them.

Bhai Budha was upset by the amount of time the Guru spent in physical activity. He had been with five Gurus and so he felt it was his duty to point this out to Guru Hargobind. The Guru reassured him: "You must understand that never before has a Guru had to face circumstances like the ones that I am facing. I want to make sure that never again will they be able to do what they did to our Guru. Besides didn't you say I would crush my enemies the way you crushed the onion that my mother brought for you? How can I do this if I am not strong?"

Jahangir had ordered that Guru Arjun Dev's children should be arrested along with him. He had also ordered that all the Guru's properties should be confiscated.

The Governor in Lahore felt that Guru Arjun Dev's death was such a terrible one that the Sikhs would be crushed and did not feel there was need to do anything more. He felt the Guru was only a boy and there was little that he could do.

As a result he did not notice that the young Guru had completely changed the nature of the Sikh organisation. But as reports of the growing strength of the Sikhs and of the Guru's army were brought to him he realised that he had underestimated the young boy and was greatly alarmed. He sent an urgent message to Jahangir requesting him to take action. Jahangir knew that he must act firmly and decisively against the Guru but he needed an excuse to do this, an excuse he could not find. It was the Empress Nur Jahan who came to his rescue. By now she controlled all her husband's decisions.

"Did you not ask this Guru's father to pay a fine for helping Khusrau?" The Emperor nodded.

"And did he not refuse to pay the fine?"

"Yes, that is why he was tortured and killed."

"Well, then your problem is solved. Legally, as his father's successor, the Guru is liable to pay his father's fine. Ask him to pay it. He will refuse, like his father did before him and you will then have your excuse to punish him. You can put him into a prison far away from Punjab. Without the Guru's presence this movement will soon die out."

A messenger was sent to Guru Hargobind's court asking him to pay the fine. As was expected the Guru refused to pay.

Jahangir issued orders to the Governor of Lahore for the Guru's arrest and the Guru was arrested and brought to Gwalior where he was imprisoned in the fort. There were some other political prisoners, including some princes who were held as prisoners in this fort. In a very short time the Guru had won the hearts of all these princes with his cheerful and helpful ways. They were also impressed by his knowledge and understanding of religious and spiritual matters.

Groups of Sikhs came to Gwalior to catch a glimpse of their beloved Guru. They would wait under the walls of the fort for hours on end and when he appeared on the ramparts for a moment they would bow to him and shout their greetings. This became a daily ritual. Everyday large groups of Sikhs would gather near the fort and as the days went by the number of pilgrims increased.

The Governor of the fort was a kind man who was very impressed by the Guru and admired him greatly. But he was afraid of the ever increasing number of Sikhs who came to the fort every day. He stopped the Guru from coming on the ramparts and showing himself to his followers. Again this move backfired. In spite of the Guru's absence the number of Sikhs visiting Gwalior kept increasing. They would go around the fort exactly in the way they go around their temple and then they would stop at a particular spot which was thought to be close to where their Guru lived. They would bow to the ground, silently ask for the Guru's blessings and then return home.

The Governor of the fort became alarmed. He sent a detailed report to the Emperor and once again the Emperor turned to Nur Jahan for advice.

"The only way to stop this is to release this Guru from prison. At the same time you cannot let him go back to Amritsar because, once in Amritsar, he will again become a threat to you. Release him from Gwalior and invite him to come and be your guest here in Delhi. He will not be able to refuse your invitation. Once he is here do not let him go back home. You can keep an eye on everything he does."

It is said that the Guru refused his freedom unless the other prisoners were freed along with him. This was done and to mark this event there is a Gurdwara called *Bandi Chhor* in the Gwalior fort. The Guru was released after he had been in prison for a little more than a year. He was asked to come to the Emperor's palace where he was treated like a royal guest. He went everywhere with the Emperor.

"I have heard that you are very fond of sports," Jahangir said to the Guru one day. "I am going out on a tiger hunt and wish you to come with me."

"That I will gradly do," the Guru replied.

The royal party waited on a piece of high ground which was shielded from all sides by tall trees and bushes. The beaters had spread out on the other three sides to ensure that the tiger would come close to where the royal party was. The Emperor and the Guru looked down at the spot below them because it was expected that the tiger would first appear there. Suddenly there was a sound behind them and the Guru saw the tiger leaping from a hillock just above them. The tiger landed on the Emperor's back and pulled him off his horse. The whole party panicked and horses and elephants ran around in confusion. Some of the hunters tried to shoot at the tiger but missed. The Guru urged his horse forward and riding towards the tiger slashed at the animal with his sword. Seeing a new enemy the tiger turned away from the Emperor and its attention was now fixed on the Guru. There was a single-handed battle between the tiger and the Guru and finally the tiger was killed. Both the Emperor and his queen were touched because the Guru had risked his life to save Jahangir.

Nur Jahan came in person to thank the Guru. She was pleased by his great charm and when she talked to him she was pleasantly surprised to find that he respected all religions. When she commented on this the Guru told her that the holy book of the Sikhs contained the teachings of Hindu and Muslim saints. She was convinced that such a man could not be an enemy of her husband and she persuaded Jahangir to let the Guru return to Amritsar.

Everyone thought that now the conflict between the Muslims and the Sikhs was over though the Guru himself thought otherwise. He knew that it was only a temporary phase and so very quietly and discreetly he began to build up his army again. He selected the strongest and bravest among his followers to become his soldiers. He also hired professional soldiers, mainly Pathans, the most famous of whom was Painda Khan. Once again he began to train his army for war.

He heard that the Governor of Lahore was sending reports of his activities and his growing strength to Delhi. He did not wish to come into open conflict with the Mughal Emperor and decided that one way of avoiding this conflict was to fulfil his long cherished wish of visiting his followers in the different centres and of setting up new centres. One of his disciples, Almast, looked after the temple of Nanakmata near Pilibhit. He wrote to the Guru to say that a band of *yogis* was troubling him and were trying to take over control of the temple. The Guru decided to go to his disciple's aid.

He travelled to Pilibhit and restored the temple to Almast. He stopped at many places on the way and spread the message of the Gurus. He also visited Nankana Sahib and other places that were sacred to the memory of Guru Nanak. During this time, in 1613, a son was born to his wife, Damodri. The boy was named Gurditta. It is said that Gurditta looked exactly like Guru Nanak. In 1617 a second son Suraj Mal was born to the Guru's second wife Mahadevi. The Guru's third wife Nanaki bore him three sons, Ani Rai in 1618, Atal Rai in 1620 and Tegh Bahadur in 1622.

Guru Hargobind then went to Kashmir and met his followers there. He also visited the Hindu holy shrines in Garhwal. Everywhere the Guru went, he had temples built. He appointed missionaries to go out to preach the teachings of the Gurus. They also explained why the peaceful ways of Guru Nanak had been changed to a military mission by Guru Hargobind. On his way back to Amritsar he met the Raja of Bilaspur. The Raja was very pleased with the Guru and gave him the gift of a large plot of land in the foothills of the Himalayas on the banks of the Satluj. Here the Guru built a small retreat called Kiratpur.

For more than fifteen years the Guru was left alone by the Mughals. This was partly because he had won the goodwill of Jahangir and Nur Jahan and partly because he was very discreet and did not openly do anything that would annoy the Mughals.

In his heart the Guru always knew that this period of peace was a temporary phase. Jahangir and Nur Jahan had, for various reasons, been tolerant of the Sikhs. But during the short period that he had spent at Jahangir's court the Guru knew that none of Jahangir's sons would be so tolerant. This is why the Guru made every effort to prepare for what was to come.

Jahangir died in A.D. 1627 and was succeeded to the throne by Shah Jahan. Shah Jahan was to earn a name as one of the greatest Moghul Emperors. He built many buildings which even today are among the most beautiful ones of the world. But though he showed so much feeling for beauty in lifeless things like brick and stone he showed no feeling in his relationship with human beings. He was a very intolerant king — specially as far as religion was concerned. The moment he came to the throne he ordered that no more Hindu and Sikh temples were to be built. Even the temples that were half complete were not to be completed and no repairs on temples were allowed. Whenever he could lay claim to places that were sacred to other religions he did so. For example, he claimed the *baoli* built by Guru Arjun Dev in Lahore, filled it up and built a mosque over it. He also passed an order that all marriages between Muslim women and non-Muslim men were illegal. Over the years many Muslim women had married Hindu and Sikh men. Now they were separated from their husbands and children and returned to their parents. He passed an order that no Muslims were to be allowed to change their religion. This was considered to be a direct attack on the Guru and on the Sikhs because many Muslims came to Amritsar and after listening to the Guru became Sikhs.

Naturally all these actions created tension and fear in the minds of non-Muslims. This tension became so great that it was only a matter of time before there was an open conflict between the Muslims and non-Muslims, specially the Sikhs. It only required a small excuse to blow up the whole situation.

This excuse was provided in A.D. 1628. Both Shah Jahan and the Guru were hunting in the same forest outside Amritsar. Both their hawks attacked the same duck. The Guru's followers captured the Emperor's hawk and refused to give it back. Hot words were exchanged and the Emperor's soldiers were beaten up. After a few days Shah Jahan ordered his general Mukhlis Khan to attack the Guru's camp. At this time preparations were being made for the wedding of the Guru's daughter. When news came of the advancing army the women and children were quickly shifted out of the camp.

The Guru collected soldiers and took up position in the fort of Lohgarh which he had built outside Amritsar. The forces of the Mughal Emperor reached Amritsar in the middle of night and a fierce battle took place between the two armies. The air was thick with arrows and spears and the smoke of match locks. Battle cries ran through the air and there was the strong smell of blood and of rotting bodies. The battle raged for many days and many brave and famous warriors were killed on both sides and yet the result remained inconclusive. In order to spare further loss of life it was decided that the Guru and Mukhlis Khan, commander of the Moghul forces, would engage in single combat. The result of this duel would decide the outcome of the battle.

The Guru galloped into the field and asked Mukhlis Khan to strike first. He said this was the rule of the Sikhs: they did not seek war nor did they strike the first blow, but when a blow was struck against them they faced it with courage. Mukhlis Khan was a much older and more experienced soldier than the Guru and was also thought to be more skilled. He took great care and aimed a blow with his sword at the Guru which the Guru received on his own sword and pushed aside. The Guru's skill with the sword was a surprise to Mukhlis Khan but he was still sure of success. He raised his sword and tried to strike a second blow which the Guru received on his shield.

"You have had two turns," he said. "It is my turn now." He swung his sword down and even before Mukhlis Khan knew what was happening the sword had slashed across his neck and his head fell on the battlefield. A loud cheer from the Sikh forces greeted the success of the Guru. The Moghul forces were silent and gloom descended upon them. A saint had defeated a skilled and experienced soldier. According to the rules of the battle they accepted defeat and left the field. There is a shrine called *Sanghrana Sahib* in memory of the Guru's first great victory against the Moghul army.

Shah Jahan wanted to send in another army to avenge this defeat at the hands of Guru Hargobind, but one of his admirers, Wazir Khan, convinced him that he should not do this. Wazir Khan said that the Guru was a man of peace who did not seek to control any territory and only wished to be left alone. He was a saint, a man of God, and wished only to pursue matters of religion and matters concerned with the welfare of his followers. For the time being Shah Jahan listened to Wazir Khan's advice and decided to leave the Guru alone. The Guru took advantage of this period of peace and consolidated his position further. The people now said that the Guru was more powerful than the Moghul Emperor. Stories of his great courage were repeated again and again and they inspired brave young men to come forward to join his army which became stronger. Those who could not join his army sent him gifts of horses, weapons and gold. People who were tired of the cruelty of the Moghuls felt that the Guru could save them from this cruelty: he had been able to defeat the Emperor's army once, he would be able to defeat it again.

The Guru retreated from Amritsar to Kartarpur and then to Hargobindpur, a small town which his father had built. There was not enough place for the Guru and his large number of followers and as a result the town had to be made bigger. The building activity attracted the attention of the Moghuls who felt that the Guru was again becoming strong and should be crushed.

Abdullah Khan, the subedar of Jalandhar, decided that this was a good chance to win the Emperor's favour. He collected all his forces and marched towards Hargobindpur. He sent a message to the Guru that he should leave the town so that bloodshed could be avoided. The Guru ignored this message.

He spoke to his followers and explained his position. He said that the fight was being forced upon him. He told them that they should not fire the first shot, but at the same time, when the enemy attacked, they should face the attack and not turn their backs upon the enemy. He told his army that they should not kill an enemy-soldier who had surrendered or who was running away from the battle-field; they should not harm women and children and should not indulge in looting civilian property. The Sikhs were fighting for the right to live in honour and peace, not for any kind of gain.

Abdullah Khan's soldiers swooped upon the Guru's force. The Moghul forces were far greater in number than the Guru's army, but the Guru's army fought with greater courage. Finally the Guru's warriors won the day. So in 1630, two years after the first battle, the Guru won another major battle against the Moghuls.

He now completed the expansion of Hargobindpur. To everyone's surprise and wonder one of the greatest buildings in Hargobindpur was the mosque which the Guru built. Many of his soldiers and workers were Muslims and he wanted to make sure that they had a place where they could worship. So even while he was fighting against the Moghul army and its great Muslim generals, he showed respect and tolerance for their religion.

It was during this time that Bhai Budha, who had served six Gurus with complete devotion, passed away. Bhai Budha had lived a full life and seen the Sikh religion through all its stages of growth.

"My Guru," he said with his dying breath, "my only regret is that I am going at such a difficult time. You of all the Gurus have had to face the most difficult time. I would have liked to go with the knowledge that you have crushed your enemies."

The Guru put his hand on the saint's shoulder. "You gave me this blessing before I was born. I will crush my enemies. It may take time but I will overcome all my enemies. Do not worry about me. You have served me as you have served all the Gurus with complete devotion. You have been fearless and strong and you have not hesitated to speak to me when you have had doubts about my conduct. God will reward you for this, so go in peace. Go with the knowledge that all your work has borne fruit. Your son Bhai Bhana, who is one of my favourite disciples, will take your place and continue all the good work that you have done."

Bhai Budha was reassured, and folding his hands one last time in greeting to his Guru, he left this world.

Guru Hargobind built a new town at Kiratpur. The work of building this town was taken up by his son Gurditta who planned the buildings and organised the construction. Gurditta did a wonderful job in the building of the new township and everyone who came to see the new town admired its beauty.

In 1629 another great follower of the Guru, Bhai Gurdas, passed away. Bhai Gurdas had been the scribe who wrote the Guru Granth Sahib. He had been one of the great disciples of Guru Ram Das and of Guru Arjun Dev, and Guru Hargobind had always regarded him with great respect. But differences had come up between Bhai Gurdas and the Guru because Bhai Gurdas could not understand the way of life adopted by the Guru. He could not understand why the Guru had taken to a military way of life. In his poems he had compared the way of life of the sixth Guru with the way of life of the earlier Gurus and expressed his unhappiness with the change. But when he saw the two battles with the Mughals he understood why the Guru had made the change. He died with the knowledge that the Guru had forgiven him for his doubts. He knew that Guru Hargobind had for him as strong a love as he had received from Guru Arjun Dev.

Horses were the immediate cause of the third battle between the Guru and the Moghul forces. Sikhs of Afghanistan sent many presents for the Guru, including two wonderful horses, Dilbagh and Gulbah. It was said that they ran so fast that their hooves did not appear to touch the ground. Their fame had spread far and wide and when they passed through Lahore, an official captured them and gave them as a gift to the Governor.

The Sikhs were incensed by this and wanted to use force to regain the horses. The Guru was against precipitating another war. Bhai Bidhi Chand disguised himself and went to the Governor's stables where he met Sondha Khan, the stable-keeper, and gained employment as a groom. He proved to be so good with horses that he was soon given charge of the two prized horses. When he was sure that he had won the confidence of the Moghul officials, Bidhi Chand made his move. He bought wine for the guards and grooms and when they were drunk he escaped with the two horses. The Moghul army led by Lal Beg was sent to recover the horses. The Guru, on the advice of Rai Jodh, had retired into the wild countryside near Bhatinda as this would be a more favourable battleground for him. In 1631 a fierce battle, which lasted eighteen hours, was fought. All the important Moghul warriors were killed and the Guru's side suffered twelve hundred casualties and wounded. Bidhi Chand and Rai Jodh were both amongst the wounded. This is called the battle of Nathana Tank. What remained of the Moghul army fled from the battlefield. This was the third decisive victory for the Guru and his Sikhs. After this battle the Guru returned to Kartarpur.

At this point Guru Hargobind fell out with his famous general Painde Khan. The relationship became so bad that Painde Khan and his son-in-law, Asman Khan, were both dismissed from the Guru's service.

Painde Khan went to the Moghul court and offered his services against the Guru.

"I have been with the Guru for many years," he said. "I know all his strengths and all his weaknesses. If you send a strong army with me I am sure I can help to defeat the Guru."

The Mughals decided to take advantage of this offer. So in 1634 a large force under Kale Khan, brother of Mukhlis Khan, along with Painde Khan and Asman Khan, was sent out against the Guru. It is said that on the eve of the battle, Dhir Mal, Guru Hargobind's grandson, wrote a secret letter to Painde Khan promising to help the invading forces with secret information about the Guru's army.

The Guru had taken up position in Kartarpur and the Moghul forces surrounded him from all sides. His generals Bidhi Chand, Jati Mal, Lakhi and Rai Jodh had divided the defence of the town among them. The Mughal army attacked the town and a fierce and bloody battle followed.

The Guru's sons, Tegh Bahadur and Gurditta, fought with great skill and courage. In fact Tegh Bahadur wielded his sword so well that he caused great harm to the Moghul army and it seemed that the battle would go in favour of the Guru's forces. Some of the remaining Moghul generals now called upon Painde Khan.

"Where is your secret knowledge of the Guru's forces?" they asked him. "If you really have such knowledge you must use it now." Painde Khan had no choice but to lead a fresh attack against the Guru. He came face to face with the Guru and tried to strike him but he only managed to cut the Guru's stirrup. A single blow from the Guru and Painde Khan fell to the ground mortally wounded. The Guru dismounted from his horse and held Painde Khan's head in his lap. "I have always regarded you as my child," he said with great sadness. "You came to me as an orphan and I gave you all my love and built you into a great warrior. I find no joy in your defeat. Your time is near. Read the Kalma so that you can be at peace with God." Painde Khan moved his lips silently and then breathed his last. The Guru sat there in the thick of battle with Painde Khan's head cradled in his lap. When the sun shone down on Painde Khan's face, he put up his shield to give him shade.

In another part of the field Bhai Gurditta's arrow killed Asman Khan. Like the Guru, Bhai Gurditta too gained no joy in this victory. Asman Khan and he had grown up together and had been playmates and now the Pathan had died at his hands. He turned to his father and surrendered his arms. "Let me go home," he said, "and die in peace." He left the battlefield.

The battle raged on. Kale Khan and Qutab Khan, great Mughal generals, were among the many Moghul soldiers who died. The loss on the Sikh side had been heavy too. The Guru had lost seven hundred brave generals and soldiers. Finally the Moghul forces were left without any leaders and abandoned the battle. So in 1634 the Guru defeated the imperial forces for the fourth time.

In these four battles Guru Hargobind had suffered great losses. He knew that he needed time to strengthen his army, before he could face the Moghuls again in open battle. So he withdrew to his mountain retreat in Kiratpur where there could be no open battle, only skirmishes. Even if the Moghuls attacked, the terrain was such that his smaller army could face them. But after four major defeats the Moghuls decided to leave him alone.

The Guru's fame spread far and wide and people called him *Miri Piri Da Malik* (master of the temporal and spiritual power.) He had shown that he carried the torch of Guru Nanak. He had travelled over large areas teaching people and bringing the word of the Gurus to them and he had also worked hard for the welfare of his people. He was a great spiritual leader. By defeating the Moghuls he had shown that he was also a great military leader who had the strength to defend his followers even against the might of the Moghul Empire. The number of his followers increased greatly. In spite of the laws passed by Shah Jahan people embraced Sikhism by the thousand. Mohsin Fani, a Muslim historian, who lived at the time, has written:

"From this time the disciples of the Guru increased considerably and in this mountainous country, as far as the frontiers of Tibet and Kahota, the name of the Musalman was not heard of."

Gradually as the danger of another Moghul attack receded, Guru Hargobind reduced the strength of his army. He now had only a personal bodyguard of three hundred horsemen and sixty artillery soldiers.

The Guru's last years in Kiratpur were marked by great personal tragedy. In the course of a few years he lost five members of his family in quick succession. These included three of his sons. The saddest of these losses was that of his son Gurditta in 1638. Gurditta had earned a name for himself not only as a brave and intelligent young man but also as a great follower of the Gurus' teachings. Added to this was the burden of his grandson Dhir Mal turning against him.

In the Punjab when a man dies, part of the funeral ceremonies is the ceremony of the turban. In this ceremony the eldest son of the deceased is recognised as his successor. On Gurditta's death the Guru sent for Dhirmal to come for the turban ceremony. In this way Dhirmal would be recognised as the legal heir to Gurditta. He would at least inherit Gurditta's personal property. Dhirmal was also asked to bring the copy of the Granth Sahib that was with him. The Guru wished that portions of the holy book should be read on the solemn occasion of his son's funeral. Dhirmal refused to come to Kartarpur. He had done terrible things and was afraid that the Sikhs would object to his being given a turban and might even take the Granth Sahib away from him. So the turban ceremony was performed by his younger brother Har Rai.

The Guru kept his grandson Har Rai always with him and came to love him dearly. He gave him all the instruction both spiritual and secular that he had given to Gurditta. Har Rai was also trained in the use of arms. The Guru spent the last ten years of his life in Kiratpur in prayer and meditation. It was a peaceful life in contrast to all the years of war and bloodshed that he had been through.

As his end drew near he was not sure as to who should succeed him. He watched his two surviving sons and grandson closely. Suraj Mal, his eldest surviving son, showed no interest at all in Sikh affairs. His other surviving son, Tegh Bahadur, had withdrawn into himself and detached himself from the world and from other men.

The Sikh community was growing rapidly. The need was for a Guru who would be actively involved in the affairs of the community and would show a keen interest in its members. Guru Hargobind decided in favour of his grandson Har Rai. In March 1644 Har Rai, who was then fourteen years old, was consecrated as the seventh Guru of the Sikhs. Guru Hargobind had invited all his friends and relatives and a very large gathering was held. Prayers were said. Then Har Rai was led by the Guru to Guru Nanak's seat and Bhai Bhana, Bhai Budha's son, applied the saffron *tilak*. Guru Hargobind bowed before the seventh Guru and offered him five copper coins, a coconut and flowers. All those present bowed before the new Guru and made their offerings.

A few days later Guru Hargobind passed away. Before his end he advised his son Tegh Bahadur to go and settle in the village of Bakala in Amritsar district. He also gave instructions that there should be no mourning on his death. There should only be the recitation of hymns from the Granth Sahib.

It is easy to understand how Guru Hargobind inspired devotion in his followers. He was tall and handsome. He had a very keen sense of humour and had a very pleasing manner of speech. He showed concern and regard for everyone and always worked for the welfare of his followers. His father's torture had steeled his will. He was a young boy at the time, but he determined that he would make his followers strong enough to stand up against the strength of the Moghuls. Before him the Gurus had all been pacifists. Guru Hargobind was a very practical man and understood that the times had changed. He believed in peace but he also emphasised that the Sikhs had the right to defend their faith. If they were threatened they would take up arms and fight wars to protect themselves. The Punjabis are by nature strong, self-confident and unafraid, and do not like to bow before tyranny and oppression. As a result Guru Hargobind's teachings appealed to them and became very popular. The Guru himself led his army to victory against the Moghul forces in four battles.

By the time the Guru died the Sikhs had been transformed. They were still a peace-loving people and did not seek to conquer land. But at the same time they were ready to defend what was rightfully theirs. They would fight to protect their faith and their property to the point of death. The Guru had set an example and shown the way: a true Sikh was now not only a saint but also a warrior.

Guru Har Rai
(1630-1661)

The child Har Rai was a great favourite with everyone in Kiratpur. He was a handsome, intelligent child, very friendly with everyone and always smiling. If he was aware of his importance as the Guru's grandson, he never showed it. Even as a child he cared for the pain of others. Both his grandfather and grandmother loved him dearly and this love became stronger when he lost his father Gurditta. The Guru kept him always by his side and the boy's grandmother made him the centre of her life.

The Guru made sure that his grandson got the best training in riding, in swordsmanship and in archery. By the time he was in his teens Har Rai was an excellent rider and a skilled swordsman. At the same time Har Rai watched his grandfather closely and learnt a great deal about his religion and its special ways. He soon knew most of the Sikh prayers and hymns by heart. He would also go hunting with his grandfather but unlike his grandfather he did not kill animals. Instead he captured animals and brought them back to the little zoo he had built in Kiratpur.

In March 1644, a few days before the death of Guru Hargobind, Har Rai was ordained as the seventh Guru of the Sikhs. Within a year of becoming the Guru, Guru Har Rai had to face the first crisis of his stewardship. Kiratpur was situated within the territory of the Raja of Bilaspur. The Raja had trouble with the Mughal rulers and it seemed that there would be war between the two sides. If the Guru stayed on in Kiratpur he would have to take sides with the Raja and the Sikh soldiers would have to fight alongside the Raja's army. The Guru considered his position very carefully and realised that he was too young and inexperienced to lead his soldiers into battle with success. He also realised that the Sikh community had just recovered from the effects of the battles that his grandfather had fought. It was true that all the battles had been won by the Sikhs, but the Sikhs had lost many brave soldiers. If they went into battle again there would be more losses. The Sikhs were a young community and at this stage could not waste their energies in more wars. Then the Guru's elder brother Dhir Mal, who was working against the Guru, had already formed an alliance with the Guru's enemies. If the Guru came into open conflict with the Moghuls it would give Dhir Mal the chance he needed. But more than anything else the Guru was not sure that the Raja's cause was a just cause, because he was not sure that the Raja himself was not to blame for the position he was in. As such he decided against the risk of taking part in a war and decided to move out of Kiratpur and go further into the hills. So with his family, servants and a bodyguard of three thousand two hundred armed men the Guru moved to Taksaal, a small village in Sirmour state. Here he was able to live a life of peace and of prayer and kept out of conflict, both with the Moghuls and with his brother Dhir Mal.

Days passed into months and months into years. Reports from the centres came to the Guru and he was worried by what he had heard. Without a Guru at Amritsar to look up to, the administration in the centres had begun to weaken, without the physical presence of the Guru to give them spiritual strength some of the Sikhs had begun to turn to the other claimants of the Guruship. People like Dhir Mal had become strong because the Guru was not present in Amritsar. The *masands* now did not report to the Guru and had stopped coming to Amritsar. Some of them kept the money they collected from the Sikhs for themselves and became rich and powerful.

Guru Har Rai decided that he would not return permanently to Kiratpur or Amritsar. The factors that had made him move out of Kiratpur still existed. At the same time he had to do something to counteract what was happening in his organisation. He decided to travel from Taksaal and visit all his centres one by one. He spent some time in each centre and checked the working of his missionaries. When they saw their Guru, they came and received his blessings and the Sikhs' devotion again became strong. The Guru's rivals found that their followers had begun to leave them and go back to the Guru. In the past the Sikhs used to go to their Guru. Now they found that the Guru was coming to them. As a result many people who would otherwise not have had a chance of listening to the teachings of the Guru, now came to listen to him and the number of Sikhs increased. Many important families in the Punjab like Patiala, Nabha, Jind, Kaithal and Bagrian, had been impressed by Guru Hargobind. Now the heads of these families met Guru Har Rai and listened to his teachings and joined Sikhism. Because of these important additions to their numbers the Sikhs became even stronger.

At the end of 1658 Guru Har Rai decided to return to Kiratpur. Once again Kiratpur became an important centre of the Sikh religion that it had been during Guru Hargobind's time.

Guru Har Rai was a man of peace who lived a life of prayer and meditation. His life was a great deal like the life of Guru Nanak. Every morning he would get up very early, bathe, and listen to the Gurbani together with his followers. Then he would speak to his followers about the teachings of the Gurus. During the day he would work for the welfare of his people. In the evening too there would be a prayer meeting and the singing of hymns. He travelled from centre to centre and remained very close to his people. He would stop at the huts of the poor people and eat their simple food. This would give them great happiness and it also gave them a chance to share their problems and difficulties with the Guru.

Guru Har Rai worked very hard to remove the differences of caste. He often came out openly in favour of people of low caste and also encouraged marriages between people of different castes and classes.

The Guru did everything possible to avoid conflict. But when he was attacked he did not hesitate to strike back. Once while he was returning to Kiratpur, the women of the Guru's household were left a little behind. A Moghul force headed by the grandson of Mukhlis Khan, who had been killed in a battle with Guru Hargobind, was going from Lahore to Delhi. Seeing the unattended ladies he felt it was his chance to take revenge for his grandfather's death, and attacked the party. The Guru and his soldiers heard the noise, rode back and attacked the Moghul soldiers. There was fierce fighting and the Moghul force fled before the courage and strength of the Guru and his soldiers.

There was, at this time, tension between Shah Jahan's sons because each of them wanted to be the Emperor after Shah Jahan's death. Dara Shikoh had no interest in wordly matters. But he was the eldest son and was also his father's favourite. So it was obvious that he would be the next Emperor.

Dara Shikoh became suddenly ill. It was a strange illness and none of the *vaids* and *hakims* in the Emperor's court could diagnose it. There were rumours that he had been poisoned by his brother Aurangzeb. But there was no proof of this. All medical treatment proved ineffective and it was feared that Dara Shikoh was going to die. Shah Jahan had special prayers said for his son's recovery and sent his messengers to all the holy men in his kingdom to ask them to offer special prayers for his son. One of the messengers came to Guru Har Rai. In spite of all the battles that had been fought between Guru Hargobind and Shah Jahan, Guru Har Rai treated the messenger with courtesy and listened patiently to what the messenger had to say.

Guru Har Rai was a practical man. He knew that life and death were in the hands of God. He also knew that God often acted through men. So he sent for his own *hakim*, who was a very skilled man.

"*Hakim* sahib," he said when the *hakim* had taken his seat. "Prince Dara Shikoh is very seriously ill. Can you prescribe a medicine for him?"

"I will do the best I can, Guruji."

The *hakim* turned to the messenger.

"Well you describe his illness to me?" he asked the messenger.

The messenger described the symptoms of the illness in detail.

Twice during the description the *hakim* asked more questions. When the messenger had finished the *hakim* sat silent for a little while thinking about what had been said. "Guruji," he said at last. "The prince has been poisoned. I think I know the poison that has been used. If I am right I know the herb that will cure him."

So the Guru sent this herb back to Shah Jahan. The *hakim's* diagnosis was right and Dara Shikoh was cured of his illness.

Much later, one of Guru Har Rai's disciples asked him: "Guruji, the Emperor Shah Jahan caused so much trouble for Guru Hargobind and for the Sikhs. Yet when his son was ill you sent a herb to cure him. Is this not strange?"

The Guru smiled and said, "When the axe cuts the sandal trees, the sandal tree perfumes its blade. When you break a flower the flower perfumes your hand. We must learn a lesson from this. We must return good for evil."

Shah Jahan was grateful to the Guru for saving his son's life. For some time there were friendly relations between the Sikhs and the Moghuls. But then Aurangzeb, impatient to become the Emperor, rebelled against his father, captured him and made him a prisoner. He then turned towards his brother Dara Shikoh. When his brother's soldiers came to look for him, Dara Shikoh fled to Punjab. He came to Guru Har Rai for help and Guru Har Rai gave him shelter.

There was no clash between the Moghul army and the Guru's soldiers but the Guru did help Dara Shikoh to escape to safety. Finally Dara Shikoh was captured and brought back to Delhi, condemned by the *qazi* and beheaded. Aurangzeb was angry with the Guru for having helped Dara Shikoh and he sent a message to the Guru asking him to come to Delhi.

When this message was received the Guru called an assembly of his Sikhs to decide what should be done.

"No Guruji," one of the senior disciples advised, "you should not go to Delhi. Look at this Emperor. He put his own father in prison and beheaded his own brother. How can such a man be trusted?"

"There is no harm in going," said another Sikh. "After all the message is in the form of an invitation. For many years now we have had a good relationship with the Moghuls and they have left us alone. Now if we refuse the invitation it will make the Emperor angry and he will seek revenge."

"No, no Guruji," said a younger Sikh. "We cannot let you put your life in danger. We know that Aurangzeb does not like non-Muslims and looks for every chance either to destroy them or to convert them to Islam. He has destroyed many Hindu temples in Mathura, Ajmer and Varanasi. No good can come from this meeting."

The debate went on and the Guru saw that there was a lot of truth on both sides. At this point Guru Har Rai's son Ram Rai spoke up.

"This is the first move by the new Emperor towards us. He has held out the hand of friendship towards us and we should not turn this hand away. Instead we should also reach out to him with friendship. Through this meeting we can make him see that we only wish to follow our religion and to live in peace. Since there is fear of danger to the Guru let me go in the Guru's place. I will be his envoy."

Ram Rai was only eleven years old at that time and everyone was surprised by the wisdom of his words. A small group of senior disciples, who were known for their wisdom, were selected to accompany Ram Rai. They would remain with him throughout the trip and advise him on what he would say or do. Before he left he had one last meeting with his father.

"Remember, my son," the Guru said in warning, "our Granth Sahib is our holy and sacred book and we are not permitted to adapt or change even one word that is written in the Granth. In your discussion with the Emperor you must be sure that you quote the Granth exactly as it is."

"Do not worry Guruji. I respect the Granth Sahib more than I respect anything else in the world."

Aurangzeb greeted the Guru's party with great respect and they were treated as very special guests. Ram Rai was singled out for special attention. The Emperor spent a lot of time with the boy and asked many questions about the Sikh religion. A very cordial relationship was established between the two and the Sikhs began to feel that it was good they had come.

One day the Emperor spoke to Ram Rai. "There is one line in your Granth that I do not understand. Everywhere else your Gurus have spoken about other religions with respect. But in this one line they have criticised the Muslims and this had hurt the Muslims very much."

The line the Emperor was referring to was:

"The Musalman's body when reduced to dust is used by the potter to make pots. When these pots are put in the kiln the dust cries out as it burns." This is part of one of Guru Nanak's hymns. The context is that the end is the same for everybody. A Hindu's body, when he dies, is cremated. The Muslim's body is buried. But this too finally goes into the fire. So it is not our religious practices which make us different from each other, but our actions.

Ram Rai had shown great confidence when he had suggested that the Emperor's invitation should be accepted. He knew large parts of the Gurbani by heart, but he was not old enough or learned yet to discuss the finer points of meaning. The Emperor's question left him confused and he did not know what to say. Prakash, one of his admirers, suggested that they should give a simple, easy answer and not get involved in any discussion or arguments. In this way not only would they save their skins but they would protect the friendly relations that seemed to have been built up with the Emperor. Probably on this Sikh's prompting Ram Rai prepared his answer. "There was a mistake made by the scribe while writing down that line. The original word is *beiman* (faithless) and not Musalman."

The report of Ram Rai's explanation was brought to the Guru. He had feared this might happen and had warned Ram Rai against this danger and yet Ram Rai had fallen into the trap. He was aware that Ram Rai was only a young boy. He was also aware that Ram Rai had probably only repeated what one of his advisers had told him to say. But his mind was turned against his son. "The milk of the tigress is only kept in a cup of gold. The Guruship is like this milk. Ram Rai has shown by this action that he is not made of pure gold and so he is not a fit vessel for holding the Guruship. Ram Rai shall never see my face again. My younger son Har Krishan will be the next Guru."

Ram Rai tried to make up with his father. He sent many messages, made many apologies. He requested again and again that he should be allowed to meet the Guru in order to explain his position. But the Guru turned a deaf ear. Even though it had hurt him greatly to do so he had turned completely away from his son and never saw him again.

Guru Har Rai passed away in 1661 at the age of thirty. It is probable that he died because of some fatal illness and that the end came suddenly and unexpectedly. But before he died his younger son Har Krishan, then only five years old, was ordained as the next Guru. Once again Bhai Bhana applied the saffron *tilak*. Guru Har Rai put five copper coins and a coconut at the young boy's feet and went around him four times and Guru Har Krishan became the eighth Guru of the Sikhs.

Guru Har Rai was the Guru of the Sikhs for seventeen years. He gave the Sikhs seventeen years of much needed peace, during which they were able to build up their strength. He travelled from centre to centre and made sure that these centres became as strong as Amritsar and Kiratpur. He came very close to his people and worked for their welfare. He protected the sanctity of the Guru Granth Sahib even when he had to disown his own son. Guru Arjun Dev had compiled the Granth to ensure that the teachings of the Gurus remain in their original form. If anyone changed even one word in the Granth Sahib he would be tampering with the teachings of the Gurus. Guru Har Rai made sure that no one would ever make such a change, by disowning his own son for changing just one word in the text.

Guru Har Rai was a simple man of God who lived a simple life. He was kind and compassionate. His message to the world was:

"When a temple or a mosque is damaged you can repair it. When a temple or a mosque is broken you can rebuild it. But you can never repair or rebuild a broken heart."

Guru Har Krishan
(1656-1664)

*R*am Rai must have been hurt and upset by what his father had done. But he respected and loved his father. By himself he would have accepted his father's wishes and would not have claimed the succession. But a group of very senior and powerful *masands* who wanted a puppet Guru whom they could manipulate persuaded Ram Rai to send a petition to the Emperor, claiming that he had been deprived of his birthright.

The petition asked the Emperor to use his influence to settle the matter and ensure that the Guruship was restored to Ram Rai as he was the Guru's elder son.

Aurangzeb decided to send a message to Kiratpur asking Guru Har Krishan to come to Delhi so that the Emperor could decide about this matter.

Mirza Raja Jai Singh was a very important officer in Aurangzeb's court. He was an admirer of the Gurus and their teachings and he was not happy at what was happening. He was afraid that Guru Har Krishan would refuse to come to Delhi and this would give Aurangzeb the excuse he was looking for. He would declare Ram Rai as the new Guru and also make war on the Sikhs. Raja Jai Singh asked Aurangzeb if he could take the message to Kiratpur personally and escort the Guru back to Delhi, an offer which Aurangzeb was to accept.

Raja Jai Singh arrived on the outskirts of Kiratpur in the late evening. It was the time of the evening prayers and a huge crowd has collected on the river bank. On a raised platform sat a small group of people. Raja Jai Singh was attracted at once to the little boy, who sat straight and erect in the middle of this group. He was a very handsome boy, with a fair complexion and sharp features. Even from a distance he could see the glow on the boy's face. The prayers were being conducted by one of the Sikh elders, but from time to time the little boy would recite a few hymns. His voice was strong and clear and it had that very special sweetness that only a child's voice can have. He looked around and saw in the faces around him devotion and admiration for the Guru.

It was a beautiful place. As a background to the prayers there was the sound of the river and the sound of the wind in the trees. The prayers themselves were so beautiful that Raja Jai Singh sat on for many hours listening to them.

The prayers finished and the *sangat* was at last aware of the strangers in their midst. The Raja was escorted up to the platform where the Guru sat. He greeted the Guru, the Guru's mother Mata Krishan Kaur and the other Sikh elders. The Sikhs had heard good things about the Raja, but they were suspicious of his sudden arrival in their midst. In spite of this the Raja was greeted warmly and made comfortable.

The discussion took place the next day after the morning prayers.

"As you are aware Guruji, your brother Ram Rai has presented a petition to the Emperor. Before he takes any decision he would like to hear your side of the case and has asked me to escort you to Delhi." The Guru did not say anything, only looked straight into the Raja's eyes.

"As far as we are concerned," Mata Krishan Kaur said, "there is no case, there are no sides." The Guru looked quickly once at his mother as she began to speak and then back again at their visitor.

"Guru Har Rai anointed Guru Har Krishan as his successor; for the Sikhs that is final. There can be no argument, no conflict, no doubt in this matter; he is the inheritor of Guru Nanak's light. There is no need for him to go to Delhi to settle this."

There was a pause and Raja Jai Singh realised how difficult his task was going to be.

"I agree with you mother," he said, lowering his eyes in respect as he spoke to the Guru's mother. "This fact is beyond doubt. But if he does not go to Delhi there are those who will think that he is afraid because he is not sure of his position, and this will strengthen the lies that Ram Rai's admirers are spreading."

Still the little Guru did not say anything. His eyes were fixed on the Raja's face. After a pause Mata Krishan Kaur spoke again.

"We do not trust the Moghul. Nothing good has ever come for the Sikhs from him. We cannot even be sure of the Guru's safety while he is in Delhi."

"I will take personal responsibility of that, mother. The Guru will be my guest. You know how Rajputs treat their guests — I will give my life before I allow a hair of his head to be touched. I will be by his side always."

"Consider also," he went on: "This will be a chance for the Sikhs to meet their Guru. All the way to Delhi and in Delhi itself hundreds of thousands of Sikhs will get a chance to have *darshan* of their Guru. Many of these Sikhs will never be able to come to Kiratpur and this is something they will talk about for years. 'We saw the Guru,' they will tell their children and their grand-children and the Guru's blessings and their memory of these blessings will make their lives richer. Would you deprive them of this?"

Mata Krishan Kaur turned to the other senior *masands* sitting behind her. They had a short discussion in low voices and then she lowered her head and spoke to the Guru. The Guru listened to her words and nodded his head. Then he turned back to the Raja.

"My mother and my *masands* advise me that I should go to Delhi." His voice was strong and unafraid. He added: "I bow to their advice. I will go to Delhi with you, but I will not see the Emperor."

There was a gasp of surprise from the people around and the Raja knew that this was a decision the Guru had made on his own. Again there was a discussion between the Guru's mother and his advisers. Again she whispered to him. Again he shook his head but this time negatively.

"My mind is made up. My father, my Guru, made me promise that I would never see the Emperor's face. I gave him this promise. I will not break this promise."

The Raja recognised the strength of steel in the Guru's voice and knew that there was nothing that would change this decision. He realised that he was in a difficult position. If Guru Har Krishan was not going to appear before the Emperor it would make the Emperor angry. At the same time if he did not accept the Guru's decision the Guru would refuse to go to Delhi.

"I respect your decision, Guruji," and as he spoke he realised that he did indeed respect the Guru from the bottom of his heart. He respected the fact that one so young could have made this decision and stuck by it. "I promise you that you will not have to see the face of the Emperor. I myself will act as your ambassador. I will see the Emperor on your behalf and tell him whatever you wish to say to him." There was silence for a while. Doubts and suspicions and misgivings seemed to have all been cleared.

"Come," the Guru said getting to his feet. "We have only today and there is much that I want to show you."

The Raja had been right. As they moved towards Delhi, word of their passing had gone before them. Large crowds collected even before the first light broke in the sky and when the Guru arrived there were hundreds and thousands of men and women, infants and children and the aged, pushing and jostling for a glimpse of their beloved Guru. Sometimes they would arrive at a place late in the evening to be told that the crowd of devotees had been waiting since early dawn, waiting patiently in the burning sun, waiting without food and water, for a brief glimpse of their Guru.

All through the journey the Guru behaved with such confidence that Raja Jai Singh found it easy to forget that he was only five years old. It was as if it was Guru Har Rai walked amongst his people, as if Guru Hargobind walked amongst his people. The Raja saw how the light from Guru Nanak's lamp had passed from one Guru to the next, becoming stronger and brighter with each passing.

In Delhi the Guru and his party were escorted to Raja Jai Singh's house in the village of Raisina. He was treated with great respect by the Raja's household and given every comfort. A beautiful Gurdwara, Bangla Sahib, now stands at this site.

In his private quarters the Raja could talk of nothing except the Guru. The Rani found it difficult to believe everything that her husband said because she could not forget that the Guru was only five years old and she was curious to meet the Guru. The next day she disguised herself as a servant and went to the Guru's apartment where a small group of people had already formed to meet the Guru. The Guru listened to each of his visitors and at last it was the turn of the Rani. Before she could speak he smiled and said: "You are no servant woman."

The Rani was surprised. She had drawn her veil across her face so that the Guru would not see her. Now she let it fall. "Do not be surprised," the Guru said gently. "If you were a servant woman your hands would be hard and rough with the work that they had done. Your bare feet would not cringe, from the heat of the stone floor as they do now." The Rani bowed before the Guru and asked for his blessings.

Word of the Guru's arrival travelled quickly. Ever-increasing crowds gathered each day at Raja Jai Singh's house. The Emperor did not seem to be in a hurry to take a decision. Raja Jai Singh sensing the conflict in the Emperor's mind spoke on behalf of the Guru.

"Do not decide in favour of Ram Rai, your Majesty," he advised at one of their private meetings.

"You have seen what a large following the Guru has here in Delhi. I have seen the people who came to meet him all along the way. I can assure you that his following is far, far greater in the Punjab. If you support Ram Rai you will earn the enmity of all the Sikh people. There will be unrest among the people which might lead to an open revolt."

This was a strong argument because Aurangzeb could not afford unrest so soon after he had become the king.

"Besides, think of the insult if the Sikhs do not respect your decision. They have already made their decision. You have seen for yourself the hundreds and thousands of people who have accepted him as their Guru. Do you think you can force them to change this?"

Aurangzeb knew that he could not.

"Extend your support to the Guru," Raja Jai Singh advised. "The Sikhs will be happy that you have respected their wishes. They will think well of you and will not do anything against you and the Guru will be your friend."

The Raja was, of course, right and Aurangzeb understood this. He sent his son to meet the Guru to show his friendliness towards the Guru. At the same time he gave Ram Rai a large piece of land in the Doon Valley to set up his *dera*. By doing this he indicated that Ram Rai would not be going back to Kiratpur. Ram Rai founded his own *gaddi* in Dehradun which continues to this day. In fact Dehradun got its name from Ram Rai's *dera*.

At this time small-pox broke out in Delhi and within a few days thousands of people had fallen prey to this disease. Some of the Guru's advisers felt that the Guru should not risk his life by staying in Delhi and should return at once to Kiratpur. Others said that even if he did not return to Kiratpur he should remain in his apartment and not meet anyone. If he continued to meet his disciples there was the risk of his contacting the disease. The Guru ignored both these groups: perhaps he felt it would be cowardly to turn his back on danger, perhaps he felt that he could not turn away from his people when they needed him the most. He continued to meet all his devotees and tried to help those who were sick.

What his admirers feared did happen: the Guru was struck by small-pox. At that time there was no proper treatment to this disease and soon it was clear that their Guru was close to his end. Before he died his mother and his *masands* collected around him. They put five copper coins and a coconut on a *thali* and asked the Guru to name his successor.

With Ram Rai and Dhirmal both claiming the Guruship, it was important that the dying Guru settle the issue of succession before he breathed his last. The end was very near. The words he spoke came slowly, one at a time. But they were spoken clearly and everyone present heard them and understood them. He put his hand on the *thali* "BABA BAKALA," he said and having performed his final duty as the Guru, Guru Har Krishan found eternal peace.

Guru Har Krishan was about eight years old when he died and he had been the Guru for nearly three years. He was a friendly, cheerful boy who won the hearts of all he met. He respected the age and wisdom of his mother and the *masands* and listened to their advice. But he was capable of making up his own mind. He was sensitive to the world around him and was a keen observer of men. He showed great concern for his people and was aware of his duties as their Guru and did not let anything come in the way of performing these duties. He was unafraid of death. He showed flashes of great maturity and wisdom, most notably in the choice of his successor.

Guru Tegh Bahadur
(1621-1675)

"*B*aba Bakala". These were the two words by which Guru Har Krishan indicated who would be the next Guru. But from these two words his trusted followers, Diwan Dargah Mal, Mati Das, Sati Das, Guruditta and Dyal Das, knew at once who the Guru meant. When Guru Har Krishan used the term *Baba* he meant somebody who had the relationship of a grandfather to him. The only living person who bore such a relationship to the Guru was his granduncle, Tegh Bahadur, who did, indeed, live in Bakala at the time.

Tegh Bahadur, the youngest and the sixth child of Guru Hargobind, was born at Guru-ka-Mahal in Amritsar in 1621. His mother was Nanaki, daughter of Hari Chand Khatri, a prosperous trader from the village of Bakala. It is said that at his birth he was given the name of Tyag Mal.

In addition to reading, writing, arithmetic, religion and music, Tegh Bahadur also learnt to ride, hunt, shoot and use the sword. Guru Hargobind took an active interest in his children's education and he would often come to see them while they were practising. He always had an encouraging word for them and would praise them if they did well. In order to win this praise, Tegh Bahadur would work even harder. Because of all this physical activity, Tegh Bahadur grew into a strong, strapping lad.

When Tyag Mal was eleven years old, Lal Chand Khatri, one of the prominent citizens of Kartarpur, offered his daughter Gujri's hand in marriage to him. Guru Hargobind was very fond of Lal Chand and Mata Nanki liked the little girl Gujri very much. So even though both the parents did feel that their son was a little too young for marriage, they decided to accept the proposal.

Shortly after the wedding, Guru Hargobind's troubles with the Moghul forces began. From 1633 onwards a series of battles were fought between the Moghul forces and the Guru's army. At the time of the first of these battles, Tyag Mal was twelve years old.

The Guru kept Tyag Mal at his side and from the reports that came from the battlefield and the discussions that followed, the boy learnt a great deal about the strategies and manoeuvres of battle.

In 1638 on the eve of the battle of Kartarpur, the Guru knew that Tyag Mal was at last ready to go into battle and sent for his son.

Tyag Mal came into the Guru's presence and bowed before him. "Tomorrow we go into battle," the Guru said. Tyag Mal's heart quickened with excitement. He knew that this could mean only one thing. But he did not let the excitement show on his face.

"Yes, my lord, I know." But when he looked up at the Guru he could not hide what was in his eyes. The Guru smiled at his son's excitement.

"You have worked very hard and prepared yourself and you are now ready to go into battle. You will command one of the wings of the army." Tyag Mal bowed to the Guru again.

It was a fierce battle. The force from Lahore had been joined by the force of the Governor of Jalandhar, and the Moghul forces far outnumbered the Guru's forces. Yet the Sikhs fought with great courage. The Guru's sons Gurditta and Tyag Mal set a fine example for their soldiers by taking risks and leading their men personally. Gurditta was overcome with grief when he killed his childhood friend Asman Khan and withdrew from the battle. Tyag Mal fought with great courage to the very end.

At the end of the battle, Tyag Mal came to report to the Guru. He was tired and his face and clothes were covered with dust and stained with blood and smoke from musket fire. The Guru listened to him carefully.

"You talk of the courage and bravery of others, my son. You do not say anything of your own deeds."

"I only did what I had to do," Tyag Mal said, looking his Guru in the eye.

"If there was anything worthy of note that I did, it was because your light shone in me during the battle. I cannot take credit for it." The Guru was pleased by this humility. "You have fought so bravely," the Guru said, "shown so much courage with the sword and the gun that from now on you will be known as Tegh Bahadur (lord of the sword)".

Tegh Bahadur, as he was now called, was greatly respected by the Sikh community. Stories of his great courage were told and retold and he became a hero. But like his brother Gurditta, Tegh Bahadur could not put the bloodshed and the horrors of the battlefield out of his mind. He had seen hundreds of soldiers being killed and lying dead on the battlefield and as he went around the *dera* he saw hundreds of orphans and widows.

As the years went by he became more and more quiet and withdrawn and he turned to religion and to prayers for comfort.

The Guru saw the change in his son and was saddened by the signs that his youngest son showed of becoming an ascetic. But the Guru also understood what was troubling the young man's mind and left him alone to work it out for himself.

Then came the deaths of Tegh Bahadur's three brothers: Gurditta, Atal Rai and Ani Rai. This filled him with grief and he was sure that life was meaningless, a dream. He turned away completely from the world of men and spent all his time in reading the holy book. He withdrew to Bakala and in deference to his wishes left him alone.

Shortly before his death, Guru Hargobind decided that his grandson Har Rai would be the next Guru. He decided against Tegh Bahadur because Tegh Bahadur had cut himself off entirely from the world of men and was for all practical purposes an ascetic. Tegh Bahadur understood and respected his father's decision and felt no bitterness and came to the ceremony at Kiratpur when his newphew Har Rai was installed as the seventh Guru. He sat by his father's deathbed, serving him in every way he could.

"You have been a good son," the Guru said. "And you are a good man. Take your mother and go back to Bakala and stay there. There is some land in Hargobindpur which is in your name and the revenue from this will be enough to support your mother and you."

Tegh Bahadur did not want anything. His needs were few and his grandparents were only too happy to take care of these. He stayed long enough in Kiratpur to attend to all the funeral ceremonies and then, taking his leave from the new Guru and accompanied by his mother, went back to Bakala.

At Bakala Tegh Bahadur followed a set routine. He had a basement built in his house, a small cell below the floor of his room. Here he would meditate for hours on end. His fame as a holy man spread far and wide. Though he did not like meeting people, people still came to him for advice and comfort. So he fixed certain hours in the day for meeting his disciples.

The needs of his family were few, so he was able to use most of this money to help the poor and the needy. For twenty-six years he lived the life of a saint. The Sikhs remembered him as a brave young soldier but they also knew him as the holy man who gave help and comfort to people in need. This was the man whom Guru Har Krishan had nominated as the ninth Guru.

The five Sikh elders escorted Guru Har Krishan's mother, Sulakhni, to Kiratpur in 1664. They stayed there for a few months to help her to come to terms with her grief and to settle her affairs. Then, carrying the *thali* with the five copper coins and the coconut which Guru Har Krishan had touched, they went to Bakala.

News of Guru Har Krishan's last words had spread far and wide. It is said that by this time twenty members of the Sodhi families of Kiratpur, Kartarpur and other places had come to Bakala and had all set up their *deras*. They were all related in some way to the Guru and they all claimed that they were the Baba Guru Har Krishan had referred to in his last words.

The most serious claimant was Dhirmal, Guru Har Rai's elder brother. He claimed that the father's elder brother is also often referred to as Baba. He also said that since he had the original copy of the Guru Granth Sahib, he had the strongest claim to the Guruship.

The five Sikh elders came at last to Bakala in August, 1644, went straight to Mata Nanaki's house and told her everything that had happened. Then they called a meeting of all the prominent citizens of Bakala, both Sikhs and non-Sikhs, and repeated what they had told Mata Nanaki. Bhai Gurditta turned to Tegh Bahadur. He placed the *thali* with the sacred articles at Tegh Bahadur's feet and bowed to him. Tegh Bahadur accepted the charge that had been given to him and became the ninth Guru of the Sikhs.

Here, the story of Bhai Makhan Shah discovering the Guru at Bakala is often mentioned in the biographies.

Guru Tegh Bahadur's succession to the Guruship was not acceptable to Dhir Mal. He made one last effort to gain the Guruship. He incited his faithful *masand* Sihan to make a personal attack on the Guru. But Sihan only succeeded in wounding the Guru. The Guru recovered from his injuries, Sihan confessed to his misdeeds and Dhir Mal stood discredited. He went back to Delhi.

The Guru now decided to move to Amritsar. He bathed in the holy waters of the tank. Then he took a round of the holy tank as all pilgrims do. When he reached the door leading to the bridge it was shut on his face and locked from inside, he found that he could not have *darshan* of the temple. His followers, who had come with him, were very angry and wanted to break the door but he held them back and set up his camp a little away from the temple.

When Guru Hargobind had moved out of Amritsar, the control of the Golden Temple had passed completely into the hands of Prithi's grandson who was afraid that if Guru Tegh Bahadur came and lived in Amritsar, he would lose control of the Golden Temple. This is why he had shut the door in Guru Tegh Bahadur's face.

One of the Guru's disciples, a lady by the name of Hariyan, was most upset by the Guru's exclusion from the

Harimandir. She organised the other ladies of Amritsar and they decided to take action. They led the Guru back to the Golden Temple in a big procession and Harji was shamed into opening the doors and letting the Guru in.

The Guru did not want to create a conflict. So he stayed in Amritsar only long enough to have *darshan* of the Harimandir. Then he moved on to Khadur. He stayed for a few days in Khadur and then went on to Kiratpur. Here, too, he only stayed long enough to have *darshan* of the shrine and to meet all his disciples.

Guru Tegh Bahadur knew when he became the Guru that he must do what all the other Gurus had done before him. He must build his own centre. But he could not decide where he would build it.

Once he stopped to rest at a place about eight kilometres from Kiratpur. This place was at the foot of the Shivalik Hills. The sun was low over the horizon and everything was bathed in the warm glow of the setting sun. The sky was filled with birds flying home to their nests. The Guru looked up and saw the beautiful hill of Naina Devi with the ancient temple at the top just eight miles away. Further away he saw the Dhauladhar range covered with snow. At his feet was the river Satluj. The Guru felt complete peace. He felt a stillness in his heart and knew that he had found the place he was looking for.

The Guru bought the land from the Raja of Kahlur (Bilaspur). The place was named Nanaki Chak to honour the Guru's mother and the Guru asked Dewan Dargah Mal to take charge of the planning and the building of their centre. The Dewan consulted many master-builders and drew up a plan for a small township. The three most important buildings would be the temple, the rest-house and the Guru Mahal, and these three buildings would be built first. The foundation for the new centre was laid in June, 1665, by Bhai Gurditta. Most of the important Sikhs built houses here so that they could be close to their Guru. As more and more people began to live here, traders and shopkeepers also came and settled here.

While construction was still at an early stage the Guru decided to visit his followers outside Punjab. The Guru left Dewan Dargah Mal and Bhai Gurditta in charge of the construction work, and towards the end of the year set out on his travels to the East. He was accompanied by his mother, his wife, her brother Kirpal Chand, Dyal Das, Mati Das, Sati Das and some other devoted followers.

The Guru travelled through the south-east of Punjab and came to an area called Bagar, which is now part of Haryana. Here he was upset to see the sad condition of the people. They were very poor and many of them had taken to a life of crime and sin.

He spent a lot of time in this region and helped to improve the condition of the people and taught them how to lead useful lives. By the time he left this place and moved on towards Delhi he had brought great changes and development to this area.

The Guru came to the outskirts of Delhi and set up his camp and thousands of Sikhs came to meet their Guru. Ram Rai, who was in Delhi, heard reports of the Guru's large following and this made him very jealous. The Emperor was not in Delhi at the time, so he went to the Kotwali and complained to the Darogah that the Guru and his followers were creating a disturbance. They were forcing people to give them money and other presents and they were also speaking ill of Islam. The Darogah, fearing that there might be a riot, arrested the Guru.

All this happened so suddenly that the Guru's followers did not know what to do and they decided to turn to Raja Jai Singh, who had always been a great admirer of the Gurus, for help.

Raja Jai Singh was at this time away in the Deccan fighting a war against Shivaji. Raja Ram Singh, Raja Jai Singh's son, took up the Guru's cause. He spoke up for the

Guru and convinced everybody that the Guru was innocent. He also stood surety for the Guru and the Guru was freed from prison. Before moving on, he gave Raja Ram Singh his blessings and told him that if ever there was anything that the Sikhs or their Guru could do for him it would be done.

The party moved through Agra, Allahabad, Banaras and Gaya. From Gaya the Guru's party was taken to Patna by Bhai Jaita, one of Guru Hargobind's favourite Sikhs. Mata Gujri was now expecting a child, and it was not safe for her to travel in this condition. So the Guru made all arrangements for her in Patna and left her in the care of his mother and brother-in-law, Kirpal Chand, and travelled on towards Assam.

Many Sikh *sangats* had been set up by Guru Nanak when he had made his journey to the east and these *sangats* had increased during the time of the other Gurus, specially during the time of the Sixth Guru. *Masands* had been appointed to look after the day-to-day needs of the Sikhs and this had made the *sangats* even better organised and stronger. But none of these *sangats* had been visited by any Guru since Guru Nanak had come this way a hundred and fifty years ago. Guru Tegh Bahadur felt it was important for him to visit these *sangats*.

The other reason he travelled east at this time was to fulfil his promise to Raja Ram Singh. When Aurangzeb had imprisoned Shivaji and his son Sambhaji, he had placed them under Raja Ram Singh's charge. The prisoners had escaped and Aurangzeb felt that Raja Ram Singh had failed in his charge. The Raja was divested of his official position as punishment. He was also ordered to lead an army against the King of Ahom. The last Moghul general who had been sent into Assam, Mir Jumla, had died in the attempt. Raja Ram Singh felt that he was being sent to certain death and was reluctant to go. At the same time he was afraid of the Emperor's anger if he refused to obey his orders. He came to Guru Tegh Bahadur while the Guru was at Gaya and asked for the Guru's help and advice. The Guru remembered what the Raja had done for him in Delhi and felt a deep obligation to help the Raja.

"Do not worry," he said putting his hand on the Raja's shoulder. "When right is with you, God is with you, you must not be afraid of what the Moghul can do to you. I will come with you to Assam."

The Guru and the Raja crossed the Brahmaputra. The Guru visited the Sikh centres at Sylhet, Chittagong, Sondip and Dacca and he was happy to see flourishing *sangats* in each of these towns. On December 26, 1666, a son, Gobind Rai, was born to Guru Tegh Bahadur. This happy news reached the Guru while he was in Dacca.

Some new biographies of the Gurus put the year of Gobind Rai's birth as 1661, instead of 1666. Kartar Singh Duggal, in his *Sikh Gurus: Their Views and Teachings* (1993) supports the new date, that is, 1661 as the Tenth Guru's year of birth.

At Dacca Raja Ram Singh's personal bodyguard of 4,000 horsemen was joined by the army of 18,000 horsemen and 30,000 foot-soldiers left behind by Mir Jumla. He also recruited 15,000 local archers. With this army the Guru and the Raja moved into Assam. They camped at Dhuhari, where Guru Nanak had stayed. The Guru advised Raja Ram Singh not to attack the king but to come to an agreement. While the negotiations were going on he himself toured Assam. Through his teachings and his work for the people he won a lot of respect. Reports of his work reached the king who too began to respect the Guru. One of the princes, Raja Ram, came to the Guru for his blessings and became his follower.

The talks between Raja Ram Singh and the Ahom king went on but there did not seem to be any chance of a treaty being signed. In the meantime a few of the tribes showed signs of revolting against the king. The king was in an unhappy position, on the one hand, he had a large foreign army at his doorstep and on the other some of his own people were turning against him. He came to the Guru for help and advice.

"Make peace with Raja Ram Singh," the Guru advised, "sign a treaty with him. He will then take his army back to Delhi and you will be free to settle your own affairs."

"You know the Raja well," the king said. "Help me, O holy one, to make a treaty that will not bring me dishonour."

The Guru protected the interests of both sides and was able to work out a treaty which was accepted by both the king and Raja Ram Singh. In this way, war and bloodshed were avoided. Raja Ram Singh made an offering of a large sum of money to the Guru and the Raja of Assam also gave him many presents. The Guru had come to Assam for two reasons : to help his friend Ram Singh and to visit the Sikh *sangat*. Both these tasks had now been accomplished and he decided to return to Patna to rejoin his family.

For the next three years the Guru's greatest pleasure was to be with his little son Gobind Rai. Gobind was a very handsome boy who showed signs of great intelligence. But the Guru did not stay very long in Patna. He received the disturbing news from the Punjab of the forcible conversion of Hindus and Sikhs to Islam. The Guru decided to go back to Punjab to be with his people in their hour of need.

The Guru reached Nanaki Chak, later known as Anandpur, in 1672. What had been a collection of a few buildings when he left had now become a town. He was pleased at the way the town had grown. The Guru's followers, the residents of Anandpur, were very happy to see their Guru. They came out in large numbers to greet him and carried him back in a procession. There was great rejoicing in the town and at night the people lit oil lamps and put them on their walls in rows just as they do on Diwali. The Guru's family joined him in Anandpur a few months later.

The Guru found great joy in being back in Anandpur. He had a mother and a wife who both loved him dearly. They were contented and happy and he shared their contentment and happiness. He had a very gifted son and he spent a lot of time in taking care of his education.

The Guru made sure that Gobind got the best instructors for each subject that he learnt. He kept a close eye on his son's progress and found pleasure in seeing how well he was doing. Perhaps the happiest time for the Guru was the time he spent alone with his son. They would walk along the open high ground where there is now a group of buildings near the Gurdwara Sisganj. He would listen to his son telling him about his instructors, about his lessons and about his friends. He would talk to his son preparing him for the difficult times ahead. He would talk to him about the Gurus' teachings and tell him stories from their lives. It was here and now that Guru Tegh Bahadur composed many of his beautiful hymns which mark him out as a great poet. One hundred and fifteen of these poems were later included in the Guru Granth Sahib by Guru Gobind Singh. It was a perfect time, a perfect period in the Guru's life.

But perfect times and perfect periods last long only in story-books, in fairy tales; in life they are always short. In Guru Tegh Bahadur's life too this period was a little more than a brief pause.

Special orders were given against the Sikhs. Kafi Khan writes, "Aurangzeb ordered the temples of the Sikhs also to be destroyed and the Guru's agents (*masands*) for collecting the tithes and presents of the faithful to be expelled from the cities."

The local officials, in order to win favour with the Emperor, began to use very harsh measures to convert non-Muslims. People were tortured and killed without mercy and hundreds were thrown into prison. This filled the people with fear and hopelessness.

Guru Tegh Bahadur knew that something must be done to help the people and to give the non-Muslims encouragement and strength so that they could face

Aurangzeb's cruelty with courage. He decided to go from village to village to instil confidence in them and make them shed their fear.

Some people had tried to stand up against the Moghul. In 1669 the Jats of Agra and Mathura had rebelled against the Emperor, but the Moghul Army had crushed them. Thousands of Jats were killed in battle and thousands more were captured and tortured. The Jat houses were plundered and the Jat women were raped. Seeing this, 1000 Jats embraced Islam. In 1672 the *satnamis*, a Hindu sect of farmers and traders who carried arms, rebelled against the Emperor. They fought very bravely and won a few battles. But finally they were defeated and most of them were killed. The few survivors were forced to become Muslims.

Now it seemed that people had given up. This is why Guru Tegh Bahadur wanted to go from village to village to give them hope and courage. He chose first of all the land between the Ghaggar and Satluj, the area that is called Malwa. There had been no rain in this region and there were no canals to bring water from the rivers to the fields and the land was like a desert. The people were cowed down not only by the Muslim officials but also by their poverty. The Guru used the money he had brought from Assam to help the people to improve their lives. He dug wells so that they could get water both for drinking and for their fields and he built tanks so that rainwater could be collected and stored. He bought cows and buffaloes and gave them to the poor. He also had many kinds of trees planted so that the whole area would become rich and green.

Reports of the work that the Guru was doing travelled far and wide. The Hindus and Sikhs came to the area to see the development work that had been carried out. It was a time when everything seemed dark and bleak because of Aurangzeb's cruelty, but now, through the Guru's work, they felt there was hope: here was a Guru who could give them new life. Weak hearts were made strong again and people began to have faith in the future. They decided to stand up against the Moghuls. The Moghul officials were jealous of the Guru's work.

Aurangzeb's orders to convert all non-Muslims to Islam were being carried out with the greatest ferocity against the Kashmiri Brahmins. The Brahmins are the highest caste among the Hindus and the Kashmiri Brahmins were considered to be the most learned and intelligent of all Brahmins. So if the Kashmiri Brahmins were converted to Islam it would be easy to convert all the other non-Muslims.

The Emperor Aurangzeb had said that he did not want to see a single *tilak* or *janeiu* (sacred thread) in Kashmir. Iftikar Khan, the Governor of Kashmir, was determined to carry out his wishes. In the first few months he forced a large number of Pandits to become Muslims. Those who refused were killed. Soon the Pandits who did not want to become Muslims began to run away from Kashmir because they saw in this the only way they could escape death and keep their faith. All the crucial administrative posts in Kashmir were held by Kashmiri Pandits, many of whom fled from Kashmir. Iftikhar Khan realised that if this trend continued he would soon have no one to run the administration for him. He called a halt to the forcible conversions and sent for all the prominent Pandits in the State. He explained to them that there was no escape from the Emperor's orders. He tried to convince them that it was in their interest to embrace Islam of their own accord. He offered them all kinds of temptations and inducements to persuade them to convert. If they did not accept he would be forced to adopt his old policy of forcible conversion and they would not get anything out of it. Pandit Kirpa Ram of Mattan, who was the spokesman of the delegation, asked Iftikhar Khan for a six months' grace period so that they could convince their congregation that it was best to accept Islam. The Governor acceded to this request. It was the season of the annual pilgrimage to the holy cave at Amarnath and Kirpa Ram and his friends set

out on this pilgrimage. Perhaps God would provide a solution
to their problem. In spite of the terrible cruelty of the
Governor they met many other pilgrims on the way. Seeing
them Kirpa Ram felt a deep sadness in his heart. Would this
be the last time that the pilgrims would be going for *darshan*
of the shrine? Next year at this time would there be no one
going along this route? No, it couldn't be. For hundreds of
years, their hearts singing with faith, thousands and thousands
of pilgrims had come from the four corners of the country.
Surely their faith, their prayers would keep this pilgrimage
alive. The sadness left Kirpa Ram's heart. He knew that God
would give them an answer.

But even after he had completed his pilgrimage to the
sacred cave and returned to Pahalgam there was still no
answer. He was stronger, stronger to face the end, but the
end would be when the six months were over.

Then on that last night at Pahalgam, a fresh group of
pilgrims came in to share their room. Immediately there was
an exchange of greetings, a rush of introduction. Kirpa Ram's
group moved closer to make place for the new group. The
new group cooked a simple meal and invited Kirpa Ram and
his companions to join them, an invitation that was declined
because they had already eaten. Kirpa Ram watched them
in the flickering light of the cooking fire, in the dim light of
the oil lamps. They were simple people, simple rustic people.
But there was something special about them. It took him
some time to realise what it was — it was the absence of
fear in their eyes. Later, after the group had eaten and they
sat exchanging news, Kirpa Ram understood why there was
an absence of fear. They talked of a holy man, a Guru with
the strange name of Tegh Bahadur.

The pilgrims talked of his coming to their village and of
all that he had done for them. They talked of how he had
given a new life to them and with this the hope of a better
tomorrow. One by one they all dozed off and there was quiet
in the room. Kirpa Ram snuggled up in his blanket, glad that

there were so many people in the room, their body warmth kept out the cold. Just as he drifted off to sleep Kirpa Ram's thoughts turned again to the holy man. Strange how one man could affect the lives of so many men. The sleep left him, he came wide awake, his heart beat with excitement. Yes, yes, he thought, if he could bring hope to others he could bring hope to them, the hope of a better tomorrow. God had given them an answer. They would go and meet this Guru and seek his advice.

Kirpa Ram discussed his proposal with the other Kashmiri Brahmins the next morning and they all agreed that they should go to the Guru for help.

So from Pahalgam the sixteen Pandits went down to Anandpur as quickly as they could. Still it was almost a month before they reached Anandpur. The Guru was away with his son Gobind walking the high grounds and an attendant was sent to inform the Guru of the arrival of the Kashmiris. The attendant found the Guru and his son sitting side by side under a tree, lost in conversation. The Guru looked up and saw the attendant coming towards them. He stopped in mid-sentence. His heart told him that this was the end of the perfect period of his life. He waited for the attendant to catch his breath and to speak:

"Guruji," the attendant said, "there is a group of Pandits from Kashmir who have come to see you. They said it was urgent."

"Attend to their needs," the Guru said. "I will come soon." But even after the attendant had gone the Guru made no move to return to Anandpur. He sensed that this was the last time he would be alone with his son, the last time he would know such peace. Gobind sensed this too.

"The Pandits are waiting," he reminded his father. Together father and son walked back to Anandpur through the glow of the setting sun.

The Pandits met the Guru after the evening meal. Kirpa Ram told the Guru of their problem and of the six months' grace period that they had been given.

"We have come to you for advice, Guruji," he said. "For advice and for help."

The situation seemed hopeless and there was no help or advice that the Guru could give them at the moment. "You must be tired after your long journey," the Guru said. "Leave your problem with me and go and rest. I will think about it. Perhaps I will be able to find an answer." The Pandits went to their rest while the Guru sat on in the gathering darkness. He was lost in thought and his attendants did not want to disturb him. It was Gobind who broke into his father's thoughts.

"What is it father?" he asked. "You are lost in thought and look worried. What is it that is on your mind?"

The Guru told his son of the Pandits' problem. "I am sure that there is only one solution to their problem. If a holy man can give his life the Pandits can still be saved."

"Who can be more holy than you father?" the boy said without a moment's hesitation. The Guru was happy. He too had been thinking that it was he who should make the sacrifice. His son's words only confirmed this. He drew Gobind into his embrace.

"You are right my son. It is your father who must make the sacrifice." The next day the Guru sent for the Kashmiri Pandits.

"You must go back to your Governor," he said, "and tell him that you are all ready to become Muslims, each and everyone of you, but on one condition. The condition is that Tegh Bahadur must become a Muslim. If this condition is fulfilled all the Kashmiri Brahmins will become Muslims too."

The Kashmiri Pandits were happy. Kirpa Ram knew that this condition seemed a very easy condition and the Governor would accept it. He also knew that it was in fact an impossible condition because Guru Tegh Bahadur would never give up his faith. They bowed to the Guru and took their leave and almost at once they set out in their return journey to Kashmir.

They reached Srinagar long before the grace period of six months was over and asked for a meeting with the Governor.

"We have decided, my lord," Kirpa Ram said, when they were brought into the presence of the Governor. "The Kashmiri Pandits have all decided to become Muslims. But we have great respect for Guru Tegh Bahadur, the Guru of the Sikhs, and he must give us the lead. If he becomes a Musalman we will all become Musalmans."

Iftikhar Khan was very pleased. It would be easy to convert the so-called Guru of the Sikhs and with this one conversion the problem of the Kashmiri Pandits would be solved.

Aurangzeb was still camped at Hasan Abdal, close to the borders of Kashmir, and Iftikhar Khan brought the message of the Kashmir Pandits to him. The Emperor was very pleased.

The Emperor sent a strong force to Anandpur to arrest the Guru and bring him to Delhi. The Guru along with Bhai Jaita, Bhai Dyal Das, Bhai Sati Das and Bhai Mati Das and a few other faithful followers had left for Delhi to give himself up to the Emperor. The Moghul force set out from Anandpur and caught up with the Guru's party at a place near Ropar. The Guru advised his followers not to offer any resistance. The Guru and his four senior disciples were arrested. The Guru was locked up in an iron cage and the cage was put on a cart so that the Sikhs could see what had happened to their Guru. The four disciples were put in chains and the party moved back to Delhi. All along the way the Sikhs who came out to see their Guru were shocked to see him locked up in a cage like an animal. They knew they were seeing the Guru for the last time. Some of them just looked on, too dazed to do or say anything, others began to weep. There were still others who raised angry slogans against the Moghul soldiers. At a few places it seemed that the Sikhs were going to take the law into their own hands and attack the party and free their Guru.

But always the Guru smiled and counselled his Sikhs. "You must have patience," he told them, "patience and courage. Do not do anything rash. I am locked up in a cage but I go to Delhi of my own free will."

His words stilled the anger of the Sikhs, but they could not take away the sadness from their hearts.

"What will become of us?" they asked.

"God will take care of you," the Guru said, "as He has always done. Bow to his will — accept whatever He does to me. He will only do what is good for me and for you."

The party moved on and came at last to Delhi. The Guru and his disciples were brought to the *Kotwali* in Chandni Chowk.

The next day Khwaja Abdullah, the *darogah* of the *kotwali*, came to see the Guru in his cell. He offered all kinds of inducements to the Guru to tempt him to become a Muslim. When this failed he tried to frighten the Guru by saying that his young son would be left without a father, his wife and his old mother would be left without support.

The Guru smiled. "You do not know what you say, *darogah*. God will be a father of my son and will look after my mother and my wife. He will give strength to my followers and lead them along the right path as He has always done. Do not waste your time and your breath, do what you have to do." The *darogah* turned and left the cell. The Guru was once again lost in prayer.

The *darogah* had failed to convert the Guru to Islam. He now decided that he would make the punishment to the Guru and his followers so severe that it would be a lesson to everyone else and would deter people from becoming followers of the new religion.

The eleventh of November, 1675, dawned bright and clear. There was a cold, sharp wind to remind everyone that winter had come. But there was not a trace of cloud in the sky and the sun, when it came up, was bright and warm. It brought relief to the thousands of people who had formed up in row upon row around the square, in the early hours of the morning. They had been shivering in the cold. Now the warmth of the sun brought them some comfort. In the bright light they saw three objects arranged close to each other. There were two poles driven into the ground about three feet apart. Next to them was a stool with ropes and a saw lying on it. A few yards away an open fire-place had been made. A large quantity of wood and coal was already burning and over the fire was a huge cauldron, three quarters full of boiling water. Close by there was a third pole that had been driven into the ground. Next to it were bundles of cotton and ropes and a container with tar in it. They also saw a raised platform at one end of the square.

Everywhere, there were armed soldiers and policemen. The Guru and his four followers escorted by armed soldiers were led to the square and the Guru was led onto the platform. The Guru sat down crosslegged and almost at once he began to pray. A soldier removed Bhai Jaita's chains and a broom was handed to him.

"Go, Tegh Bahadur's Sikh," the *darogah* said, "Go and sweep the courtyard. Let the people see that this is all that a Sikh is fit to do." Bhai Jaita bowed to his Guru. Then he took the broom in his hand and began to sweep the courtyard. A few of the spectators laughed and jeered but most of them just watched in silence.

The *qazi*, in flowing black robes, walked into the square and the crowd fell silent.

"You, who call yourself Mati Das, step forward," the *darogah* ordered. Bhai Mati Das stepped forward.

"Mati Das you have been ordered by the Emperor to become a Muslim," the *darogah* spoke loud and clear and each word was heard by the crowd.

"I am a Sikh," Bhai Mati Das said in an equally loud, clear voice. "And I will always remain a Sikh."

"Do you then refuse to obey the Emperor's orders?"

"I do," said, Bhai Mati Das.

The *qazi* stepped forward.

"You are guilty of treason. For this I sentence you to death."

There was a murmur in the crowd. The *qazi* held up his hand and there was silence again. A soldier removed the chains on Bhai Mati Das's hands and legs. Bhai Mati Das bowed to his Guru and the Guru held up his hand in blessing. Bhai Mati Das's hands and feet were tied to the poles so that his body was stretched between the poles. Jalaludin the executioner picked up the saw and stood on the stool. A gasp went up from the crowd as they understood what was going to happen. They looked closely at Mati Das's face. He too had understood what was going to happen but he only smiled. Jalaludin placed the saw in the centre of Mati Das's head. With slow deliberate movements he began to saw. Mati Das did not cry, did not protest. Jalaluddin sawed through the body till the body was in two parts. The ground was covered with blood. All eyes turned to look at the Guru. He had watched the execution of his beloved disciple without blinking his eyes and without an expression on his face. His lips moved in silent prayer.

"You have seen what has happened to one of your faithful Sikhs," the *darogah* said when the executioner had finished. "Do you want your other followers to suffer the same fate? You can save them. All you have to do is to become a Muslim."

The Guru said nothing.

Bhai Dyala and Bhai Sati Das were called forward turn by turn. They refused to become Muslims and the *qazi* condemned them to death. Bhai Dyala was thrown into the boiling water whereas Bhai Sati Das was wrapped in cotton which had been soaked in coal-tar, tied to the pole and burnt alive.

The Guru did not turn away from the suffering of his followers. He watched it all from where he sat with a calm serene expression on his face.

By now the crowd was still, shocked into silence by this set of cruel deeds. There was not a sound save the rustling of the wind in the trees. At last the *darogah* turned to the Guru. Two soldiers stepped forward to help the Guru to his feet. He ignored their help and rose to his feet himself. The *darogah* and the *qazi* came onto the platform.

The crowd watched, unable to believe what had happened, or what was going to happen. The *darogah* addressed the Guru and repeated the question he had asked three times already.

"Do you refuse to become a Muslim?" the *darogah* asked.

"I do," said the Guru in a calm clear voice.

"The Emperor has ordered that you become a Muslim. Do you refuse to obey the Emperor's orders?"

"I do," said the Guru again. The *darogah* turned to the *qazi*. The *qazi* gave his *fatwa*.

"You Tegh Bahadur, the Guru of the Sikhs, have refused to obey the orders of the Emperor. You are guilty of treason. For this you are condemned to death."

The chains of the Guru were removed. Jalaluddin, the executioner, sharpened his sword. The moment seemed to stretch on endlessly. At last he tested his blade against his thumb — it was sharp enough.

"Do you have a last wish?"

"Yes," the Guru said, "give me five minutes to make my peace with my God," The Guru sat down again, his head bowed down, his eyes closed, his lips moved in prayer. But this time not silent prayer. The prayers flowed loud and clear and beautiful and filled the square with their music. They sounded on the ears of the crowd and stilled all pain and anger and sorrow. The hush remained. But it was a hush of acceptance, of peace and of strength. The Guru was lost in his prayers. He was already one with his God. Exactly five minutes later Jalaluddin lifted his sword high in the air. The sound of the sword as it cut through the air was drowned in the sound of prayer. The prayer stopped, cut off in mid-sentence. The severed head lay on the ground below the platform. The Guru still sat crosslegged, blood gushing from the neck.

Again the only sound was the sound of the wind in the trees and the echo of that beautiful prayer. The minutes stretched on and still the crowd did not move, did not utter a word.

At last Abdullah was sure that all those who were present had learnt a lesson. The soldiers hurried the crowd away.

The square was left to the bodies, the guards and the wind. All through the morning and into late afternoon the bodies lay in the sun and swarms of flies buzzed around attracted by the blood. Vultures began to collect on the trees. Groups of people formed on the rooftops and at street corners and looked at the bodies. They would have liked to go and claim them but everywhere there were soldiers.

Then in the late afternoon the sky began to darken. There were no clouds but the sky was covered with a blanket of red. The red turned to brown and the brown became darker till it was black. It was the coming of a sandstorm. The wind became stronger and lashed at the faces of all who were still in the square. It clawed at their clothes and blew sand into their eyes and their mouths.

Everyone hurried inside. The soldiers drew the end of their turbans across their faces but this was no real protection. It became so dark that they could not see their hands when they held them in front of their eyes. First one and then all the others, hurried to the shelter of the *kotwali*. No one would come to steal the bodies in this blinding sandstorm.

The square was deserted. The streets leading to the square were deserted. The wind blew strong and sand piled against the walls. There was not a soul around. Not a soul except Bhai Jaita. All through the afternoon he had stood there like a statue. The crowd and the guards, in the face of the terrible things that had happened, had forgotten him. Now he was sure that there was no one to stop him for what he did, he would not be seen.

He moved as quickly as the blinding storm would allow and collected the bodies of the three disciples. The Jamuna flowed nearby and as quickly as he could he cast the bodies into the water. Then he claimed the Guru's head. He hid it under his robe and under cover of the darkness and the storm he stole away with his precious possession.

Another person waited in the shadows near the square. Bhai Lakhi Shah, too, took advantage of the storm and the dark. He hid the body in his cart and drove quickly to his straw hut.

He drove the cart into his hut, untied the bullocks and led them to safety. Then he set fire to his hut so that the Guru's body could be cremated.

After two hours, when the storm at last abated, the guards stumbled back into the square. They saw that the bodies had disappeared and reported the matter to the *darogah*. The *darogah* was upset. He would have liked the bodies to rot in the sun and for the vultures and the dogs to feed on them. This would be a lesson to all those who refused to obey the Emperor's orders to embrace Islam. Now the bodies had disappeared. The *darogah* made inquiries everywhere and sent out search parties but he got no answers.

At the place where Guru Tegh Bahadur was executed there is a beautiful Gurdwara, Sisganj. Another beautiful Gurdwara, Rakabganj, marks the place where his body was cremated. A Gurdwara, also called Sisganj, in Anandpur marks the place where his head was cremated.

It is said that while Guru Tegh Bahadur was a prisoner in Delhi he was questioned by the officers of Aurangzeb's court. In answer to one of these questions he replied:

"Hinduism is not my religion. I do not believe in many things that the Hindus believe. I do not believe in caste, in idol-worship, in pilgrimages. Yet I would fight for the right of

Gurdwara Sis Ganj, Delhi

Gurdwara Srī Bangla Sahib, New Delhi

all Hindus to live according to their religion. I would fight for this right even if I had to give up my life in this fight."

We must remember how Guru Nanak refused to wear the sacred thread, the *janeiu*. Remembering this, it seems ironic that Guru Tegh Bahadur should have given up his life to protect the Hindus' right to wear the sacred thread. But through his death Guru Tegh Bahadur set an example for a very important part of the Guru's teachings. The Gurus taught that we must respect all religions the way we respect our own religion. The Gurus taught that we must always defend the weak and the oppressed.

Martyrs are people who give their lives for their beliefs, for their countries and for the religions and they are remembered with great respect in every country. Guru Tegh Bahadur was also a martyr. But he was different from other martyrs. Guru Tegh Bahadur gave his life to protect, not his own beliefs, but the beliefs of the Hindus. Through this sacrifice Guru Tegh Bahadur saved the Brahmins of Kashmir. He saved the country from a flood of religious intolerance and taught the people to respect the religion of others. He gave his life to defend the individual's right to follow the religion of his choosing.

By so doing he earned, in full measure, the name *Hind-di-Chadder* — the protector of Hindustan.

PART 3

Guru Gobind Singh
(1666-1708)

Early Years

(1666-1708)*

*T*he storm showed no sign of abating. For almost two hours now the wind had been blowing sand through the streets of Delhi as if in anger. Amongst the few people who walked the streets at the time was a thin, wiry man in his mid-forties. He was about five feet eight, dressed in a long flowing robe. There was a thick beard on his cheeks and chin and his long hair hung around his head in thick matted locks. He was like one of the hundreds of mendicants in Delhi who collected around temples and mosques and begged for alms. There was nothing about him that was worth taking note of, not even the cloth wrapped bundle that he carried slung over his shoulder.

He was familiar with the streets of Delhi; he had spent almost three years here once and he knew the way from the *Kotwali* to the Kashmiri Gate well enough. He was not worried about finding his way, not even in the dark and the blinding fury of the storm. He was worried about getting through the gate. He was afraid that the policeman at the gate might question him too closely and become suspicious, or, even worse, might ask to see the contents of his bundle.

---

*K.S. Duggal puts the dates as 1661-1708.

But the policeman only made a joke about his being out in the storm and let him out through the portcullis.

The wind blew from the north and drove the sand into his mouth, his nose and his eyes. He was helpless because he had nothing with which to cover his face. Someone else would have looked for shelter — a grove of trees, a house in a village or even a blind street somewhere where he could wait till the storm abated. But the traveller could not wait. He had to get as far away from Delhi as possible, as quickly as possible. He quickened his steps and hurried along Sher Shah road. In the dim light he discerned the dark silhouettes of the minars that marked each *kos* as he passed them and had a fair idea of how far he had come from Delhi. At last he saw to the left the lights of a dozen camp-fires and knew that he had found the caravan. He hurried up to the camp and obtained permission from the leader to join the caravan.

The next morning the caravan moved on. If the traveller did draw attention to himself it was because he never let go of his bundle. But there was nothing suspicious about this, some of the other travellers too had belongings which they did not permit out of their sight even for a moment.

From Sirhind a smaller group moved up into the hills and came at last to the gates of Anandpur.

"We have brought you to your destination safely," one of the guards said.

"Now that we move on, tell us what is in that bundle. You have guarded it with your life. Is it gold that you have wrapped up inside?"

The traveller smiled.

"It is something more valuable than all the gold in the world."

"May it bring you happiness," the guard said. *"Khuda hafiz!"*

The other travellers said their goodbye and moved on and our traveller turned to the gate.

"I come from Delhi," he told the gatekeeper, "and I bring a special message for the Guru."

It is not strange that he was not recognised. He had a flowing beard, his robe was in tatters and hung loosely on his body which was a little more than skin and bones.

The Guru was in conference with his mother and his senior disciples and the traveller was escorted into the Guru's presence. A hush fell upon the gathering at the appearance of this stranger.

"Yes," the Guru said, not recognising the traveller immediately.

"They say you have a special message for me."

The traveller nodded his head. He bowed again to the Guru, then he put his bundle on his head and, stepping forward, placed it on the empty seat next to the Guru.

Very carefully he untied his bundle and let the folds of the cloth fall away. There on the seat lay the head of Guru Tegh Bahadur. There was a loud gasp. Those who were sitting sprang to their feet, some of the women in the congregation began to weep.

"Who are you?" the Guru asked. The traveller had got down on his knees and with the corner of the cloth he was wiping the sand from Guru Tegh Bahadur's face and from his hair. "I am Jaita, the Rangretta," he said quietly. His work finished, he lowered his head. The Guru went down to him and drew him to his feet.

"Rangretta, Guru *ka beta*," the Guru said and embraced the traveller. Then he turned and looked at his father's head. He looked at each of those beloved features so still in death and his child's heart filled with grief. He felt that if he did not cry he would choke to death, his heart would break. "Remember," his father had said during one of their last walks together. "In all things you are the Guru. Everything that you say, everything that you do, is a model for your people." This memory came back so clearly and Guru Gobind knew that he could not cry. Even if his heart broke, even if he choked on his grief, he could not cry, for if he cried all his followers would cry. With that one decision the Guru left his childhood firmly behind and stepped into his life as an adult. He knelt before his father's head and touched the ground with his forehead. Then he sat down at the foot of the seat.

"Tell me," he said, his voice loud and clear, putting all signs of grief away. "If you know, Jaita, the manner of my father's death." "I was there, Guruji," Jaita said and went on to relate the manner of Guru Tegh Bahadur's death.

"You must rest now," the Guru said getting to his feet when Jaita had finished. He came to Jaita and put his hand on his head. "This was well done." Then the Guru turned to Dewan Dargah Mal. "Make sure that all Bhai Jaita's needs are taken care of." He turned to his mother. She sat too shocked by the news to react. She looked straight ahead of her, not aware anymore of what was happening around her.

"This is no time for grief, mother," he said gently caressing his mother's face. "This is a time for rejoicing. My father has made the supreme sacrifice. Let us not take away from his glory by giving way to tears." Mata Gujri buried her head in her son's chest, her son who was only nine years old. She felt the steel that had come into his heart and this feeling gave her strength. When she pulled herself away she sat up proud and straight with no hint of grief on her face, no sign of tears in her eyes.

The pyre of sandalwood was set on Guru Tegh Bahadur's favourite spot on the high ground. Everyone in Anandpur had collected to watch the funeral. The crowd was large. But there was pin-drop silence because of the deep sense of shock. It had all been so sudden, the *sangat* had not had a chance to react. In the silence Guru Gobind Rai walked up to the pyre, his father's head carried on top of his own head. The sand had been washed from the face, the hair had been washed and oiled and tied up and a turban had been wrapped around the head. The young Guru carried his father's head and placed it with respect and reverence on the funeral pyre. Then he knelt on the ground before the head and bowing low touched his forehead to the ground. Everyone followed his example. Then he got to his feet and recited the *Japji Sahib* and set the pyre aflame.

A cold winter wind sprang up and fanned the flames and soon the flames burnt in fury and licked at the wood. The dry wood burnt quickly and along with it burnt the remains of the ninth Guru. Guru Gobind stood on, watching the flames. But his face showed no emotion. His followers joined him in the singing of hymns from the Granth Sahib. And when at last the mortal remains of Guru Tegh Bahadur were consumed by the flames it was a deep stillness that went with him in the silence of acceptance of God's will — the same silence that had filled Chandni Chowk when the Guru had begun to pray. Nanak's light had indeed passed from Tegh Bahadur to Gobind. The *Sohila*, the last of the Sikh's five daily prayers, was then read and food distributed to all.

Young as he was Guru Gobind realised that the Sikhs must remain strong in the face of this tragedy. They could only do this if life continued without a break and in his own life he made sure that there was no break. Guru Tegh Bahadur had laid down a very heavy schedule for his son.

From an early age Gobind had to get up early, bathe and take part in the morning prayers and meditation. Then he received instruction from carefully chosen instructors. His subjects were the languages : Punjabi, Sanskrit, Persian and Arabic. The study of holy texts, not only of the Sikhs but of all major religions. He received instruction in arithmetic as well. He also learnt riding, archery, swordsmanship and shooting.

The morning after Guru Tegh Bahadur's funeral the young Guru woke at the appointed hour and went about his tasks as he had always done. He knew that this was the only way to help his people get over the grim tragedy of his father's death. He also knew that this was the best that he could do. His education was not yet complete and he must continue on the path that had been set for him by his father. As the days stretched into weeks and the weeks into months and the Sikhs saw the patience and courage with which the young Guru bore his great loss, they too learnt to accept this loss.

During this time the popularity and following of Sikhism increased manifold in North India. The story of Guru Tegh Bahadur's martyrdom, his great courage in sacrificing his life for the Kashmiri Brahmins spread far and wide. People wanted to know what had inspired this saint to do what he had done. They came to Anandpur to learn more about the Guru's teachings and about the Sikh religion. The Sikhs themselves had a new Guru and, as was the custom, each Sikh felt that he must come personally to pay homage to the new Guru. As a result there were thousands of pilgrims who came to Anandpur at this time. The Guru was very happy to meet his followers, to mingle with them and to listen to their problems and the news about their families. He suggested that they should all come once a year to meet him. His followers brought all kinds of gifts for the Guru. The Guru, like Guru Hargobind before him, indicated that the most welcome gifts would be weapons and horses and money with which he could raise a strong army.

Amongst the presents that he received at this time were two truly marvellous things. The Sikhs of Kabul sent Guru Gobind a beautiful canopy for his *gaddi* which would protect him from the sun and the rain. This wonderful canopy was made of heavy silk and was richly embroidered with a floral pattern. All the beautiful flowers and leaves were studded with precious and semi-precious stones of different colours. All those who saw the canopy were wonderstruck by its beauty and soon its fame had spread far and wide. While he was in Assam Guru Tegh Bahadur had befriended Raja Ram, one of the Assam princes, and helped him to gain influence in the king's court and to secure the future of his wife and his baby son, Ratan Rai. Raja Ram had died but his wife's position remained strong. She travelled all the way from Assam to Anandpur to express her gratitude. She was sad to learn that Guru Tegh Bahadur had died. But when she met Guru Gobind, she could see that the light of Tegh Bahadur had passed to the new Guru. She had brought many presents for Guru Tegh Bahadur; among those was a gifted elephant which had been trained by his mahout to do many things. This elephant too became very famous.

The growing popularity of the Guru and the growing strength of the Sikhs aroused the suspicion of some of the Rajas of the neighbouring hill regions, a suspicion which was further strengthened by the activities of the Guru. Guru Gobind had ordered the making of a huge drum which was named Ranjit Nagara and whenever the Guru wanted his followers together the drum would be beaten. On hearing the sound of the drum all the Sikhs of this area would collect at Anandpur. But a drum is normally beaten during battle and when the local Rajas heard of this they felt that the Guru was giving signal for battle and this aroused their fears.

The Raja who was most hostile and suspicious of the Guru was Raja Bhim Chand of Bilaspur from whom the land for Anandpur had been bought. He began to approach the other Rajas, seeking their help against the Guru.

The Guru's *masands* learnt of what Raja Bhim Chand was doing. They knew that the Guru was not yet ready for a battle and they advised the Guru to invite Bhim Chand to visit Anandpur. Once Bhim Chand came to Anandpur he would see that the Guru was only concerned with religion and with spiritual matters and had no intention of extending his territory and so the Raja would not be afraid of him any more.

The Guru's invitation was accepted by the Raja. He was looked after well when he came to Anandpur and made comfortable. For a while it seemed that Raja Bhim Chand had indeed been won over and he would become the Guru's friend, for when Bhim Chand was about to leave Anandpur he embraced the Guru and exchanged expensive presents with him.

No one could see that behind the smiles of friendship the Raja had a jealous heart. He knew that the Guru was not a threat to him because he was sure the Guru did not want any more land. But at the same time he had seen the thousands of people who came to visit the Guru. He had seen that the love and respect that the Guru commanded was far greater than what he got from his subjects. He carried this jealousy in his heart and it became stronger with each passing day and made him more and more determined to destroy the Guru and the Guru's popularity. He had seen that the Guru did not yet have a large or strong army. If he could provoke a fight with the Guru he would be able to destroy him. But to do this he needed an excuse.

He found an excuse soon enough. His son was due to be engaged and he invited the Guru to attend the festivities. He also asked for the loan of the wonderful canopy and the elephant to add colour to the festivities, a request that he knew would be refused, the refusal would give him the excuse that he needed to attack the Guru.

A messenger was sent with an invitation to the prince's engagement ceremony. In very polite and carefully thought-out words, a request was made for the canopy and the elephant. The Guru listened to the messenger; then he called a meeting of his *masands* and requested his mother to be present too. He explained the situation to the gathering and then sat back and listened to the advice and the suggestions that were given. "We are not yet ready for an open battle with the Raja," some of the senior *masands* pointed out. A battle at this stage could only end in our defeat. We must protect ourselves and protect our future and the only way out is to send these two things to the Raja. He will leave us in peace. We will then have time to organise ourselves."

"The matter will not end here," another group of *masands* said. "The canopy and the elephant are truly marvellous things. Any Raja would want to possess them. But Raja Bhim Chand's demands will not end with the canopy and the elephant. Once we have given him these he will ask for other things."

The Guru was not attached to worldly possessions. He would have been happy to give away the canopy and the elephant and would not have felt the loss. But he knew that these two things were symbols. The canopy was a symbol of the love and affection of his many followers in Kabul and the elephant was a symbol of the faith that Raja Ram's widow and countless other people like her had in the Guru. If he gave away these two things he would be striking against this love and this faith. Besides he knew that the second group of *masands* was right. The matter would not end there.

"It is not a question of the canopy and the elephant," Mata Gujri said.

"It is a question of accepting the Raja's authority. If we give him these two things we will accept his right to take tribute from us the way stronger kings take tribute from weaker kings. We have to decide whether we are willing to give him tribute."

There were loud murmurs of protest in the hall. It was obvious that when looked at in this way, none of the *masands* was willing to give up the canopy and the elephant, none of them was willing to recognise the Raja's right to take tribute from the Sikhs.

After considerable thought it was decided to accept the Raja's invitation. At the same time a polite refusal would be made to his request for the canopy and the elephant.

Bhim Chand's messenger returned to his court at Bilaspur with the Guru's messages and the Raja now had the excuse he sought. The Raja called a meeting of his generals and gave orders to prepare for a battle against the Sikhs.

All the hill Rajas were jealous and suspicious of each other. The more clever ones had their secret spies posted in the courts of the other Rajas who would give them information about everything that happened. The Raja of Sirmour had his spies in Raja Bhim Chand's court, who sent information back to Nahan and gave details of all the preparation that Bhim Chand was making for his war against the Sikhs.

The Raja of Sirmour, Medini Prakash, was a devotee of the Gurus. Ever since Guru Tegh Bahadur's martyrdom, he had felt himself drawn even closer to the Gurus. When his spies sent him the news of the impending war between Bhim Chand and the Guru, he was anxious and worried. It was true that Guru Gobind was a very brave and sensible boy. But it was also true that he was very young and inexperienced. He was not yet mature enough to lead his Sikhs into battle and the Sikhs themselves were not prepared for war. If Bhim Chand did declare war, the Raja of Sirmour knew that neither the Guru nor the Sikhs would turn their backs. They would make a stand and fight but in their present condition there was little chance of their being able to win.

This thought troubled him greatly. He had to help the Guru and the Sikhs but he did not know what he could do. At last he found the answer. He sent a message to the Guru and requested him to come and spend some time with him. Nahan, the capital of Sirmour, had a cool climate and the Raja suggested that the Guru would escape the intense heat of the plains. There were thick forests with plenty of game around Nahan and the Guru would be able to indulge in his favourite pastime of hunting.

The Guru knew what was behind the Raja's invitation. Once again he called a meeting of his senior *masands*. Once again he invited his mother to preside and once again different views were expressed. The Guru himself felt that it would be like running away from battle if he was to leave Anandpur now.

"But no battle has been declared," Mata Gujri pointed out. "At least not yet. So no one can accuse you of running away. You are young and inexperienced, you have no organised army. If you are going away now it is only to give yourself time to prepare, to prepare so well that when you do finally come face to face with the enemy there will be no doubt about your success." She paused for breath and realised that her son was not completely convinced. She continued:

"Remember what Guru Har Rai did. He was older than you. Yet he knew that he was not old enough, not organised enough, to go into battle. He went further into the hills where he got a chance to prepare himself. You too must take this chance. Accept this invitation — it will give you a chance to prepare yourself and your Sikhs for the battle that you know you will have to fight."

The Guru bowed to his mother's advice and wisdom. He accepted the Raja of Nahan's invitation and a few days later the Guru's party left Anandpur for Nahan. Now with the Guru's absence from Anandpur the tension between Bhim Chand and him was diffused for the moment and a battle had been averted.

Paonta

*B*efore leaving Anandpur the Guru called a meeting of all his senior disciples. He told them that even though he would be away from Anandpur the town must not be abandoned. Then in the summer of 1686, accompanied by his family and his bodyguard of five hundred Sikhs, the Guru left Anandpur.

The Guru's party moved first to Kiratpur where he stayed for a few days. He spent most of his time praying at the shrine of his grandfather Guru Hargobind. Now looking back,

Gurdwara Sri Paonta Sahib, Himachal Pradesh

after all these years, we can see the importance of this; of all the Gurus, Guru Gobind was closest in thought and feeling to Guru Hargobind.

The Raja placed soldiers as lookouts of points around Nahan and as soon as the Guru's party was sighted the Raja rode out from Nahan with an impressive escort to meet the Guru. They embraced warmly like brothers who were meeting after a long time. The Raja welcomed the Guru and placed an entire wing of his palace at the Guru's disposal.

The Raja was impressed with the Guru's bearing. He always walked tall and straight and was not afraid of anything. Even though he took an active interest in matters of the world, in the day-to-day problems of his followers and of his own family, there was an air of detachment in everything he did, and on his face there was a glow of saintliness.

Within a few days the Guru began to follow the same routine that he had followed in Anandpur. The Raja was impressed by the discipline of the Sikhs. They performed all their activities in a very orderly way, almost like an army which had been trained in every movement. He was impressed by their devotion to their Guru and their desire to carry out all his wishes. He saw that their faith was a faith which would stand up to the most difficult of tests. He listened to the recitation of Gurbani and tried to understand what he heard. When he did understand he realised the wonderful teachings which the Gurus had compiled for their followers. He listened to the *kirtan* and was overwhelmed by the beauty of the music and of the hymns. He went out hunting with the Guru and was impressed by the Guru's skill and courage. Within a few weeks he realised that he enjoyed having the Guru and the Sikhs with him and wished the Guru would remain with him for a longer time. At the same time he was mature and sensible enough to understand that the Guru would not be happy living with him in the palace for very long. He needed a place of his own — a place where the Sikhs would feel free to follow their own way of life, a place where he could receive all the disciples who had begun to visit him.

"You have brought so much happiness to me," he said to the Guru. "I would wish you to stay with me longer as my guest. At the same time I know that you have duties to perform as the Guru of the Sikhs which you cannot perform as well as you would like to while you live in the palace. I would like to make land available to you and to give you all possible help to build a place for yourself."

"You are very kind," the Guru said, "and your offer is a very generous one. Ever since I have come to Nahan your friendship and your love have filled my heart with happiness. I too would like to be with you for a longer period of time. But I would like first to discuss your kind proposal with my mother and my advisers."

The Guru's advisers and his mother unanimously decided to accept the Raja's generous offer. The Raja was pleased to learn that he would have his young friend with him for a longer period. What now remained was to choose the site for the Guru's centre. One day while the Guru and the Raja were out hunting they came to a beautiful spot which stood in a small curve of the river Yamuna. It was high ground with thick forest all around. At the base was the swift flowing Yamuna, its gushing waters bringing to the ears a beautiful music of their own. This was the place the Guru chose. Building plans were drawn up of a small fort and work started almost at once. When the Sikhs heard of this they came out in large numbers to help with the construction. The Raja's men also worked side by side with the Sikhs and in a very short time the fort was completed. It was called Paonta (foot-stool). Unlike a chair or a bed the footstool is used to sit upon only for a short time. So the Guru and his followers, whenever they used the expression, would know that they were only resting here — this was not their home. In a short time the Guru created a smaller Anandpur at Paonta and was absorbed once again in pursuing his education. He was determined that not one of his followers should remain illiterate. He engaged many tutors not only to teach all the children and young men and women of his *sangat*, but also all the grown-ups who did not know how to read and write.

He also realised that mere book learning was not enough. He knew that a healthy mind would only be found in a healthy body. So he insisted that all his followers should involve themselves in physical activity which would give strength to their bodies. So there were regular sports activities and athletic competitions. Just like in Guru Angad's time, there were prizes and honours for all the winners. The young men amongst his *sangat* learnt skills in martial arts and in riding and hunting and the use of arms like swords, bows and arrows, the spear and the discus.

By this time there were already strong well-organised Sikh communities from Kabul down to Ceylon (Sri Lanka) and from Karachi all the way to Assam. There were Sikh communities even outside India as far as Central Asia. All these followers regarded the Guru as the source, the fountainhead of all their spiritual strength.

Guru Gobind realised quite early that his greatest strength lay in the large number of his followers and he must organise them and give them a sense of unity so that when troubles came to the Sikhs they would be able to rise as one strong force against their enemies. He asked all the able-bodied amongst his followers to offer their services to the Sikh community by coming to Paonta and joining the Sikh army.

All those who joined his army had to undergo vigorous training which made them not only strong-bodied but also competent in riding, swordsmanship and shooting. They took part in mock battles and then in discussions about the mistakes that had been made during these battles. With each of these exercises the Guru's army came closer to being well prepared for a real battle.

Like all the Gurus before him, Guru Gobind was keenly interested in music. Music had always formed an important part of the Sikh religious ceremonies and no prayers could be complete without the singing of hymns.

Guru Gobind himself was very fond of playing the *rabaab*. He showed great skill in music and played the instruments both in solo performance and as an accompaniment to the singers. This encouraged the other members of the *sangat* to learn music. When Aurangzeb banned music from his court all the famous families of musicians and singers who had served the Moghuls for generations, sought the patronage of other kings and princes. Many of them heard of the Guru's interest in music and came to Paonta to seek employment with him. The Guru welcomed them with open arms and Paonta soon became the home of many famous musicians.

The Guru had made a deep study of classical literature and of mythology. This classical education and the beauty of his surroundings, the mountains, the forests and the rivers, inspired the poet in Guru Gobind and he began to write poetry in Hindi, Sanskrit, Persian and also in Punjabi. At that time Aurangzeb decided to ban poetry too from his court. Some of the court poets had heard how Guru Gobind had welcomed the musicians from Aurangzeb's court and given them employment. These poets also travelled to Paonta and came into the Guru's presence and told him of their woes. The Guru asked them to come and live in Paonta and work on their poetry. He would hold *kavi darbars* and *sammelans* on the banks of the Yamuna. Here the poets would recite their latest works and the best among them would be honoured with prizes. Finally fifty-two poets from the Moghul court came to live in Paonta and wrote their poetry there.

Once the poets knew that the Guru would look after them they competed with each other to write better and more beautiful poetry for the Guru. Inspired by all this literary activity the Guru himself wrote beautiful poetry. He took stories from Hindu mythology and rewrote them in the form of poems. His favourite themes were connected with the deeds of the Goddess Chandi. He wrote poems about the beauty of his surroundings, about the flowers and trees of the forest, about the mountains and about the beautiful rivers. His writings marked a clear break with the tradition of poetry set by the earlier Gurus. His poems were full of stories of warriors and of the war.

Again and again in these poems there were descriptions of battle, descriptions which stirred the heart and inspired the mind. Their purpose was clear. It was to teach the Sikhs that a glorious death in battle, in fighting for a cause that you believed in, was far better than a life that was lived in fear.

Paonta became the centre for literary and artistic activity in North India and the fame of the Guru and of the poets and musicians spread far and wide. The Guru gained many new disciples who came to Paonta to listen to the great poets and musicians.

Ram Rai, Guru Har Rai's elder son, had by this time established himself in Dehra Dun. He had given up all claims to being the Guru of the Sikhs and had become famous as a pious and saintly man and had gained many followers. Dehra Dun was less than a day's ride from Paonta and when Ram Rai heard that his uncle Guru Gobind was in Paonta, he felt an overwhelming desire to meet him. At first the memory of the difficulties he had caused for Guru Tegh Bahadur acted as a restraint. But then he sent a message to the Guru expressing his desire for a meeting and when he received a positive answer he rode out to meet Guru Gobind. The uncle and nephew met on the banks of the Yamuna. There was no trace of bitterness and hostility and when, after many hours, the two parted it was with mutual affection and respect.

Raja Fateh Shah of Garhwal was, at this time, having problems with some of the other hill Rajas, specially with Raja Medini of Nahan. His advisers advised Fateh Shah to go to

Paonta to seek the Guru's help and advice. Fateh Shah obtained a promise of safe conduct from the Raja of Nahan and arrived at Paonta with many declarations of devotion and friendship. The Guru gave Fateh Shah a patient hearing and then invited Medini Prakash to come to meet him at Paonta.

"Remember," he told the Raja of Nahan. "Fateh Shah and Bhim Chand will soon become relatives. If you have war with one you will have war with the other. You will have enemy soldiers on both your borders and they can easily move into your kingdom and force you out. It is far more sensible to talk to your enemy, to sort out your differences and to negotiate a peace."

The Raja of Nahan listened to the Guru and marvelled at the way the young Guru had matured and mellowed in a few years. He had been little more than a boy when he had first come to Nahan but now he spoke with all the wisdom and knowledge of a grown-up man. Of course, the Guru was right. He could not afford to have enemy soldiers on two of his borders.

"In poem after poem you tell of courage on the battle-field and praise the use of the sword in heroic acts. Would you now advise me to sheath my sword and seek a solution through a cowardly act of negotiation?"

"Using a sword is not always heroic and not wishing to fight is not always cowardly. Yes, I have in my poetry praised acts of valour. But I have also said that the sword should be drawn when all other means have failed."

"I will do what you advise, Guruji," the Raja said, "I will negotiate with my enemy."

Long negotiations followed between the two Rajas. They both gave vent to their complaints and grievances and one by one these were discussed and sorted out and in the end the Rajas embraced each other warmly and friendly relations were established between them.

In Sadhaura, a place close to Paonta, lived a Muslim saint, Sayyad Badruddin. Sayyad Badruddin was also known as

Budhu Shah and was greatly respected by people of all religions. Budhu Shah and Guru Gobind had grown to respect and love each other. At this time Aurangzeb disbanded a troop of five hundred Pathan soldiers on a charge of treachery. Amongst these soldiers were great warriors like Hyat Khan and Amir Khan. This troop of Pathan soldiers came to Sadhaura to seek the saint's help. They pleaded their innocence and asked the saint to help them to find employment. The saint was convinced that the charge against the soldiers was untrue and he gave them a letter of recommendation to the Guru. On the basis of this recommendation the Guru recruited the Pathan soldiers into his army.

One morning, just after the prayers, a messenger arrived from Dehra Dun. He had ridden through the major part of the night and had then crossed over to Paonta, a few miles upstream, in the early hours of the morning. The Guru knew that he had come from the *dera* of his nephew Ram Rai.

"What is the news from our nephew?" the Guru asked.

"Maharaj, my Guru is dead," the messenger said, lowering his eyes. Guru Gobind remembered their meeting on the banks of the Yamuna and was sad at the passing away of the saintly Ram Rai.

"So you were sent to deliver this sad news?"

"No Maharaj," the messenger said, again looking down at his feet.

"I have been sent by Mata Punjab Kaur to seek your help."

"Yes," the Guru said, "what is it that the good lady seeks from me?"

"Mata Punjab Kaur is afraid that some of the more powerful *massands* might try to set themselves up as the Guru. She asks you to help her to secure the succession for her son."

"I will help her," the Guru said, without a moment's hesitation.

The Guru rode out at the head of a small group of armed soldiers to Dehra Dun. There he defeated all opposition to Ram Rai's son, banished the troublesome *massands* and paid his respects to Punjab Kaur.

The years spent at Paonta were the most creative and important years in Guru Gobind's life. Here in those beautiful surroundings he completed his own education and worked to educate all his followers. A great deal of time was spent in religious discourses and military training and he was able to indulge in his favourite pastime like hunting and riding to his heart's content. The peaceful atmosphere of the place brought out the poet in him and, as we have seen, he composed a vast body of poetry.

But on his solitary walks along the river his mind turned to other more serious matters as well. He began to consider, with concern, the state of the country and he pondered over his own role as the Guru and what he could do to improve the conditions that existed around him. All through the period of his education he had read and re-read stories relating to the lives of the nine Gurus before him. He had learnt much from these stories. He had learnt how powerful the path of peace could be. Guru Nanak and his four successors had always followed a peaceful path and under them the new religion had grown from strength to strength. He had read of the martyrdom of Guru Arjun Dev and how Guru Hargobind had taught his followers that they should learn to defend their faith with the sword. Guru Hargobind himself had fought many successful battles against the might of the Moghuls. In his own young mind the image of his father's martyrdom was fresh and clear and like Guru Hargobind he too was training his followers for battle. Was he right in doing so? The path of the first five Gurus and the path that Guru Hargobind had followed seemed to be in conflict. But by thinking about it over and over again the young Gobind was able to see the unbroken thread and continuity of mission which ran through all that he had read and all that he had heard of the lives and teachings of the Gurus.

The Guru believed: Hate and revenge can never be as good as love and forgiveness. We must try always to follow the path of love. But once we are attacked and we know that the enemy means to destroy us and our beliefs, then we must resist him with all the strength that we can gather.

The battle is now a battle for survival, not only of our lives, but also of all the things that we believe in. It is a battle for righteousness, a *Dharmayudh*.

Guru Gobind, before he left Paonta to return to Anandpur, had worked out his future role as the Guru of the Sikhs, as a leader of his community. He would wage the battle of righteousness, he would uphold right and destroy sin and evil. This is a role he performed up to the very end of his life.

The Battles of Bhangani and Nadaun

The Guru's peaceful days in Paonta came to an abrupt end. Once the fort of Paonta had been built the Guru attracted Bhim Chand's attention again. Once again the Raja of Bilaspur's jealousy was aroused. He was considered the most powerful of the hill Rajas and, by tradition, the other Rajas had all come to him to help settle all their disputes and quarrels. Now the Guru had taken over this role.

The Raja sent carefully worded messages to each of the hill chiefs. Why should the Guru be building up his military strength? he asked. He went on to say that the answer was obvious, the Guru was going to use it to defeat the Rajas, one by one, and grab their kingdoms. Unless they all united to throw him out, the Guru would soon get rid of them. This struck a chord in the Rajas' hearts because it echoed their own fears and suspicions.

One of the main reasons why the Rajas wanted to throw the Guru out of the area was his influence with the poorer section of their people. For centuries they had treated the people of the lower castes as their slaves and had even had the power of life and death over them. As a result these poor people trembled with fear whenever they saw the Rajas and did whatever they were ordered to do. Now the Guru taught that there was no such thing as caste and that all men were equal. He taught those amongst his followers who had been born in the lower castes to stand up for their rights and to be afraid of none else but God.

The Rajas saw in this a lessening of their authority and a reduction in their strength and power and were quick to respond to Bhim Chand's overtures. They all pledged their support, except Fateh Shah and Medini, who were both great admirers of the Guru.

Bhim Chand blackmailed Fateh Shah to get his support against the Guru by threatening to break off his son's engagement to Fateh Shah's daughter. Fateh Shah had no option but to pledge his support even though it meant fighting against the Guru whom he admired above all other men.

Having secured Fateh Shah to his side Bhim Chand made one final effort to isolate the Guru. He sent a secret message to Medini Prakash. He said he knew that the Raja of Sirmour could not draw his sword against the Guru as the Guru was his guest. At the same time Medini Prakash should realise that all the hill Rajas including Fateh Shah were now on one side. If Medini Prakash fought against them on the Guru's side, he would become their enemy for life and his children would be the enemies of their children. Medini Prakash knew that this was not an empty threat because Rajputs never forgave an enemy. Sometimes revenge was taken a hundred years after a wrong was committed. Medini started staying away from the Guru. When the Guru sent messages to him he often did not send back any answers.

The Guru understood the reason for the cooling off both in Fateh Shah's affection and in Medini Prakash's friendship. He would have wished for them to have had more courage, but he did not blame them.

He knew that when the crisis came he could not expect help from anyone. So he began to make all the preparations that he could. He had among his followers one Ram Singh from Varanasi who was a skilled artisan in brass and an expert in the process of casting. With his help the Guru designed a canon which Ram Singh cast for him and before the battle the Guru was able to train a few of his soldiers in the use of this canon, till they could fire the canon with a fair degree of accuracy.

Bhim Chand heard of the Guru's preparations and knew that he had to strike at once. A council of all the Rajas was called and after much deliberation a message was sent to the Guru at Paonta asking him to leave the hills and promising him a safe passage if he did so. The Guru replied that he was a guest of the Raja of Sirmour. Only Raja Medini Prakash could ask him to leave Sirmour. When he did leave Paonta it would be to return to his home Anandpur. His father had bought the land on which Anandpur was built. As such no one had the legal or moral right to ask him to leave Anandpur. If the Rajas thought they could throw him out by force, they were welcome to come and do so.

Having sent off the message the Guru knew that there were only a few days left at his disposal. He had made a detailed study of the craft of battle and of different strategies and battle formations. He had practised all that he had studied and knew what movements would be suitable to his men and to the geographical area around Paonta. He knew that the occupation of a strategic position was of prime importance. Quickly and carefully the Guru made his choice of the battleground. He moved his men out of Paonta and positioned them in the area between the Yamuna and the Giri.

On the day of the battle when the sun rose the Guru's men saw the vast army of the Rajas that was drawn up against them and some of them felt fear build up in their hearts. The first group that gave in to their fear were the Udasis who had come from Anandpur as the Guru's escort. All of them, except their leader mahant Kirpal Das, ran away from the field even before the battle began.

The second group to desert the Guru were the Pathans. They had been offered rich rewards of land and money if they left the Guru's army and came over to the side of the Rajas. Now seeing the vast army arrayed against them the Pathans, forgetting all their promises of devotion and allegiance, gave in to the temptation of this offer and went over to the enemy.

The Guru had seen human nature in all its forms. He was familiar with all its strengths and all its weaknesses. He knew that those who overcame these weaknesses became men of God. But not all men could become men of God. Those who failed deserved our pity, not our hate or anger. He smiled when he heard the news of this desertion. He moved amongst his men, encouraging them, modifying his battle plans and rearranging his men's positions according to the changing needs.

The Guru's disciple Syed Budhu Shah who had heard about the impending battle collected all the able-bodied men of his *dera* and armed them with whatever weapons he could lay his hands on. With seven hundred armed men, including his own sons, he rode out to the Guru's assistance as fast as he could. On the way he learnt about the Pathans' desertion from a family of fleeing refugees. This only spurred the saint and his men to gallop faster.

They reached the battlefield well in time to help the Guru. The Guru was happy to see them but there was little time to lose in ceremony and welcome. Quickly the saint's soldiers moved to the positions the Guru assigned them. As the Guru's men heard of the new arrivals they felt a revival of their strength and morale. The news of the Pathans' desertion had travelled back to Paonta and as the first light broke in the sky every able-bodied man in Paonta, who could ride or walk, snatched up whatever weapons he could lay his hands on and came out to join his Guru. Shortly after the sun rose the Guru gave the orders for his men to charge against the much bigger army of the Rajas.

It was a short fiercely fought battle which the Guru's army won. Even in this, the first of the Guru's battles, there were many acts of individual valour. Mahant Kirpal Das carried into battle the burden of the desertion by all the other Udasis. He came into battle bare-bodied, carrying the only weapon he knew how to use, a wooden club, and with this he overcame Hyat Khan, one of the leaders of the Pathans.

Lal Chand, a cook in the Guru's *langar*, marched into battle with a sword and a shield. Like all the Guru's men he had received training in the use of these weapons. But he was not a soldier by profession and not really a match for the Pathans. Yet with his unflinching courage he overcame the redoubtable Amir Khan.

Budhu Shah felt that since he had recommended the Pathans to the Guru he was responsible for their treachery. He was determined that he and his followers make up for the absence of the Pathans. His sense of urgency was felt by his followers and they all fought with great courage, a courage that had not been seen before. One of Budhu Shah's sons was killed by an arrow fired by Raja Gopal.

Giving the lead to all these brave soldiers was of course the Guru himself. He engaged in personal battle with the brave Hari Chand. He has described this engagement in *Bachitra Natak*:

Angered by this, Hari Chand shot his arrows at me. One of them hit my horse. He shot another arrow. God protected me and this arrow only grazed my ear. Then Hari Chand fired a third arrow. This went through the buckle of my waistband. God Himself protected me and though this arrow touched my body it did not harm me. I was angered by this. I picked up my bow. I started raining arrows on the enemy. The enemy fled before this. I took aim and hit Hari Chand. As he collapsed, my brave soldiers rushed forward and destroyed them completely. Those who escaped my soldiers fled in terror. It was the mercy of God almighty that gave us victory. Having won the battle we sang songs of victory. I rewarded the deserving soldiers generously. There was rejoicing all around.

The Guru realised that it was now time for him to return to Anandpur. He had left Anandpur because it had been felt that he was not yet ready to face an open conflict with Raja Bhim Chand. This victory in the battle of Bhangani proved that this situation no longer existed. He had met the combined strength of all the Rajas and defeated it. He also did not want to stay in Sirmour as his continued presence there was becoming an embarrassment for his host. Medini Prakash had been very kind to him and had come to his help when he most needed it. The least he could do in return was to spare the Raja all awkwardness. So the Guru sent an affectionate message to Medini Prakash, thanking him for all he had done for him, shortly after the battle of Bhangani, and without returning to Paonta, the Guru and his followers made a quiet departure for Anandpur.

In the Guru's absence life seemed to have gone out of Anandpur. It is true that some people still lived there and the daily routine of the Guru's followers remained the same as when he had been there. But a large number of people had left. All the hustle and bustle, all the joy seemed to have gone. It was as if without the Guru, Anandpur had become a ghost of its former self. Now with the Guru's return Anandpur came alive once again. All those who had left Anandpur returned to live there again. News of the Guru's success at Bhangani spread far and wide and more and more people came to take up residence in Anandpur.

The Guru's victory won him the admiration of Raja Bhim Chand of Bilaspur as well. Whatever his personal feelings towards the Guru, specially after his defeat, the Raja had to admit that the Guru was a military genius. The Guru's army had been very much smaller than the army of the hill Rajas and yet with his skill at planning battles and his ability to inspire his followers, the Guru had won a resounding victory. The Raja admired him for this. He felt that it would be more sensible and practical to have the Guru as his friend rather than as his enemy.

A few months after the battle of Bhangani, Aurangzeb, who was still in the Deccan, sent an urgent message to Mian Khan, the Governor of Jammu. He asked Mian Khan to collect tribute from the hill Rajas.

As long as Aurangzeb was in Delhi, the hill Rajas had sent the tribute regularly to his court. Now that he had been away in the Deccan for so many years the fear of being attacked by the Moghul army became less real. So many of the kings, including the hill Rajas, stopped paying tribute and by so doing asserted their independence.

Aurangzeb realised that the refusal to pay tribute weakened his position greatly and action had to be taken immediately. He himself could not come away from the Deccan. Nor could he spare his army. So he wrote to the most powerful Governor in each region asking him to collect the tribute for the Emperor. The meaning of the message was clear. Those who did not pay the tribute should be destroyed.

Mian Khan sent messengers to the hill Rajas asking them to send their tribute to him in Jammu.

Bhim Chand wanted to function as an independent King and had no desire to pay the tribute, a stance that was shared by most of the hill Rajas. He also realised that on their own they did not have the skill to organise their army into an effective fighting force, a fact that the disastrous battle of Bhangani had proved only too clearly. The only person in the region who could help the Rajas was Guru Gobind. He alone could bring their armies together and make a strong fighting force with them. If he agreed to lead their army Bhim Chand knew that they could defeat Mian Khan. It was important that the Guru should be won over as quickly as possible. His *wazirs* agreed that it was more important to secure the Raja's position as an independent king than to avenge their defeat at Bhangani. It was decided to send an envoy to Guru Gobind asking for his help.

The Guru put all past differences aside and responded almost at once to the Rajas' request because he believed their cause was just. The hill Rajas had been ruling their little kingdoms for centuries and they had a right to rule without interference from the Moghul Emperor. He invited Raja Bhim Chand and his queen to visit Anandpur and at the end of the visit he pledged support to the Raja. With the promise of the Guru's support, the Rajas all united under one flag and they all refused to pay tribute to the Emperor.

Mian Khan sent his commander-in-chief, Alif Khan, supported by a strong army to collect the tribute. His instructions were simple and clear. If a Raja refused to pay tribute he was to be arrested and brought to Jammu in chains. If any of them tried to resist the arrest he must be killed. The first few Rajas he approached gave the answer that had been decided upon, they would do whatever Bhim Chand did. The Rajas got ready for battle and Bhim Chand sent a message to the Guru.

"We must give the Moghuls a fitting reply in war. They will then leave us alone and we will have long years of peace. If we give in, there will be no end to their demands." The Guru began to prepare for battle.

In the meantime the Rajas of Kanora and Bijharwal, filled with fear at the sight of the powerful Moghul army, gave in to Alif Khan's demands and paid tribute. This meant that in the coming battle they would be fighting on the side of the Moghuls against their own relatives.

Once again, after careful consideration the Guru chose the battlefield. The place was Nadaun, twenty miles south-east of Kangra, on the left bank of the Beas. This place would give the allies the greatest advantage in battle.

In the opening moments of the battle the Moghul army appeared to be very strong. Hussian Khan, the Moghul commander, fought with such great courage that it seemed that he would win, and Bhim Chand began to have doubts and wished to sue for peace.

Then the Guru himself rode into battle. The moment they saw their leader in their midst the soldiers were inspired to fight more fiercely. The first leader the Guru faced was Raja Dayal of Bhijarwal whom he killed in single combat. This heartened the allied soldiers and strengthened their will to fight. The Guru drew his bow and fired dozens of arrows, one after the other, at the enemy. These arrows killed many Moghul soldiers and this created panic in the enemy ranks. Sensing this the Guru and the other leaders of the allied soldiers doubled their efforts. Raja Bhim Chand saw that the tide of battle had turned in favour of the allies. He decided not to withdraw and even made a show of going into battle himself. The battle raged on and the Moghul soldiers began to fall back under the fierce attack of the allied soldiers. Darkness closed in and, as was the tradition of that time, the battle was called to a halt and the armies withdrew to their camps to rest and to tend to their wounded. When Alif Khan looked at the survivors who limped into his camp, he was frightened because he saw that many hundreds of his soldiers had been killed and many more had been wounded and he had very few able-bodied men left. As he sat eating his evening meal, he made his decision. He gave orders to

Hussain Khan to retreat. Collecting all the able-bodied soldiers around them, the two stole away from the battlefield under the cover of darkness and made their way back to Jammu.

The next morning when the allied army took up their position again, they found there was no enemy to oppose them. Great was the joy of Guru's army at this splendid victory.

The Guru describes the end of the battle in these words:

Then the almighty God hastened the end of the fight and the opposing host was driven away. Alif Khan fled in utter disarray without having the chance to care for his camp.

In spite of this great victory the Rajas could not overcome their fear of the Moghuls. As part of the victory celebration they had a council to decide what course of action they should adopt in the future. Many of the Rajas felt that their victory would not buy them peace for long because the moment Aurangzeb heard of this defeat he would send a much bigger and much stronger army against them, an army against which they could not hope to make a stand, and Raja Bhim Chand who had spoken up so loudly before that the Rajas should stand up against the Mughal force and try to give the Moghuls a slap in the face, now said that the Rajas should make their peace with the Moghuls by paying the tribute that Alif Khan asked for. So the tribute was collected from all the Rajas and one of Bhim Chand's ministers was appointed as an Ambassador to deliver this to Alif Khan in Jammu.

The Guru was disgusted by the Rajas' lack of courage and did not want to have anything to do with them. He withdrew from the court and from the celebration and returned home to Anandpur.

The Birth of the Khalsa

*A*urangzeb was angry both by the Rajas' initial refusal to pay tribute and by the defeat of the Moghul forces in battle. He was not satisfied by the settlement that had been reached and wanted the defeat avenged and the Rajas punished. This was the only way to reassert the authority and supremacy of the Moghuls. His son Muazzim, who later became Emperor Bahadur Shah, headed the campaign against the Rajas. The prince was assisted by General Mirza Beg, a very experienced and able soldier.

Though the prince fought a series of battles against the Rajas he left the Guru alone.

This was mainly because of the influence of Bhai Nand Lal. Bhai Nand Lal was not only a great poet but also a brilliant scholar in Persian and Arabic and had begun his professional life in the service of Prince Muazzim who at that time lived in Agra. The Prince was so impressed by Bhai Nand Lal that he made him his chief secretary and had complete faith and trust in the poet. So brilliant and learned was Bhai Nand Lal that he had once resolved a controversy regarding the interpretation of one of the verses of the Quran between two groups of scholars. In spite of his scholarship and the complete trust and faith that the Crown Prince had in him Bhai Nand Lal too, like many other scholars and poets, had fled from the Moghul Court in the face of Aurangzeb's discrimination against non-Muslims, and had taken up service with Guru Gobind at Paonta.

Now when the Prince began his campaign against the Rajas he talked to Bhai Nand Lal about the Guru and was convinced that the Guru only wished to be left alone to fulfil his responsibilities as the leader of the Sikhs and had no desire for territorial expansion. The prince also realised that when he became Emperor it would be useful to have the support of the ever increasing number of the followers of the Guru and this support he could easily get by keeping peace with the Guru.

The Guru welcomed this period of peace, but was also aware that the situation could change at any time. So he used these twelve years to strengthen his position. He bought the land around Anandpur and built a chain of four strong forts: Anandpur, Keshgarh, Lohgarh and Fatehgarh. These fortresses safeguarded Anandpur and also gave the Guru control over most of the area between the Sutlej and the Yamuna. The Guru prepared for war in many other ways too. He made his soldiers drill regularly and made them practice riding and martial skills everyday. Every evening the Sikhs gathered and listened to inspirational songs which praised the brave acts of soldiers and warriors who had fought against tyranny and oppression and had given their lives fighting for a right cause. Anandpur took on a martial atmosphere.

During this period of peace the Guru also continued the spiritual and literary activity that he had started at Paonta. His fifty-two poets wrote beautiful poetry. Some of this great poetry has come down to us. Among the better known works of this period are :

Gur Sobha by Saina Pat which gives details of the Guru's life and stewardship; *Bhagat Ratnavali* by Bhai Mani Singh who was later executed in Lahore in 1738: and of course the beautiful poems of Bhai Nand Lal. The poets also translated the Upanishads and other works of classical literature.

The writings of the Gurus were full of references to the Hindu religious texts and to Hindu mythology and this required an understanding of the Hindu religious texts. For this they required teachers who could teach Sanskrit and the finer points of the Hindu religion. The Guru sent some of his disciples to Pandit Raghu Nath for this purpose but the pandit refused to accept these Sikhs as his students because they belonged to the low castes.

Fort. Anandpur

Gurdwara Sri Keshgarh Sahib, Anandpur, Punjab

The Guru realised that he would have to create a group of Sanskrit scholars within the Sikhs and with this in mind he sent five of his disciples to Banaras. They were Karam Singh, Ganda Singh, Vir Singh, Saina Singh and Ram Singh. As was the custom among students they gave up all wordly pleasures and wordly attachments and spent all their time studying Sanskrit literature. On the completion of their studies they returned to Anandpur and the Guru gave them the title of "Nirmala" the pure ones. They founded a sect which exists even today. Their followers are called Nirmalas and they do not marry, wear white clothes and are strict vegetarians. They begin their studies with Sanskrit and the vedas and then use their knowledge to help people to understand the teachings of the Sikh Gurus.

Harjas, a Khatri from Lahore, who was a very devout follower of the Gurus, came every year to visit the Guru. When the Guru was eleven years old Harjas approached Mata Gujri and offered the hand of his daughter Jeeto to the Guru. Mata Gujri was impressed by Harjas' faith and his humility and accepted the offer. The Guru bowed to his mother's wishes and in 1677 Guru Gobind and Bibi Jeeto were married. Jeeto made an ideal wife for the Guru. She looked after Mata Gujri like her own mother and she supported the Guru in everything that he did. She made sure that the Guru's household ran smoothly and was by the Guru's side all through the period in Paonta and was a great help and support to him. The Guru loved her dearly and was happy to have found such a good wife. But as the years went by Bibi Jeeto's face sometimes took on a look of sadness and the Guru knew that this was because God had not blessed them with a child. He himself regarded all his Sikhs as his children and gave them all his love. But he could understand his wife's need for a child of her own.

When seven years had gone by, Mata Gujri was sure that Jeeto would never have a child and felt that the Guru should marry again. She thought of Sundari, daughter of Ram Saran from Labore, as a suitable bride. But when she spoke to the Guru about this he smiled and said in a quiet, gentle voice:

"Mother, I can understand your anxiety for a child. But I love Jeeto with all my heart and cannot do this to her. Besides, why do you look only for one child? See how lucky you are, how lucky I am — I have thousands of children who all look up to me as their father."

"What you say is true, my son. But I want a child who is flesh of my flesh and blood of my blood. A child who can carry on your name, your line."

"Why should you worry about this? I am no king and have no kingdom, so why should it be so important for my line to continue? As for my name — if my actions are not good enough for this, even a hundred sons would not be able to do this for me."

Mata Gujri knew what her son said was true but she longed for a grandchild held on her lap, a grandchild who she could shower all her love and blessings on. She knew that no purpose would be served by any further discussion at this point and she held her peace.

That evening when the Guru returned to his room it was a strange Jeeto who came to him. She was dressed in very simple clothes and came into his presence with her head bowed. She stood in the doorway as if waiting for his instructions. "What is this Jeeto," he said, "why do you behave so strangely? Come, come and sit beside me and tell me what the matter is?"

"I come to you as a humble supplicant and not as your wife," she said, without looking up, "so my place is not beside you but here on your doorstep."

The Guru was surprised but he decided to humour his wife. "Tell me, what is it you want. You know you only have to ask and if it is in my power it will be yours."

"It is in your power, my Guru. Give me your promise that you will accept Mata Gujri's proposal."

The Guru was stunned and could not find words to express his surprise.

"You, who give to all, and give without stinting do not turn me away empty handed." She held out the end of her *duppatta* the way beggars do when they ask for alms.

The Guru's heart was touched and tears came to his eyes. He got to his feet and went to Jeeto. "You are my wife," he said. "You are half of everything, I am. You have served me faithfully for seven long years, given me your undivided love and care. You have always been my strength and support, ask me for anything but this."

"There is nothing else I want." And still she stood with her head bowed, her hands held out in supplication. For a moment the Guru hesitated. Then he made up his mind.

"So be it," he said. Jeeto fell at his feet and broke into tears. The Guru drew her up and held her to his bosom.

So the Guru was married for the second time. Sundari came to Anandpur with all her innocence and her simple child-like heart. From the beginning she turned to Jeeto with everything that troubled her. There was nothing that she would keep from her and Jeeto with her advantage of age and experience gave her all the advice that an elder sister would give. In the same year Ramu, another devout follower of the Guru, belonging to Rohtas in the Jhelum district, came to see him with a very special request. Ramu had a daughter named Sahib Devan who was deeply religious and led a simple pious life. She was a follower of the Guru and spent her time in singing his hymns and bringing his teachings to people who had not read or heard of them. She had pledged herself as a bride to Guru Gobind and swore that she would marry no one else. Faced with this problem, Ramu came to see the Guru and begged of him to accept his daughter's hand in marriage. The Guru was polite but firm. He explained that he already had two wives, both of whom he loved dearly and had no wish to marry again. By doing this he would be doing a great injustice not only to his wives but also to the girl Sahib

Devan as he could not possibly give her the love and attention that a husband should give to a wife. Ramu said that Sahib Devan would be content even with this; all she wished for was to remain in the Guru's household and would lay no claim to any wifely rights.

The Guru did not accept this suggestion. But Ramu and Sahib Devan approached first Mata Gujri and then Bibi Jeeto and Sundari in turn. To each they repeated their strange request. The ladies were impressed and moved by the girl's great devotion to the Guru and they used their influence and persuaded the Guru to accept Sahib Devan into the household. He agreed on the condition that she would not make any claims on him as a wife.

So Sahib Devan became the Guru's 'wife'. But she was wife only in name. She remained a virgin all her life and the marriage is described by historians as the *kavara dola*. She was quite happy with this as she wanted only to serve the Guru and his *sangat*, to be near the Guru and to bring help to those in pain and need.

A year after her marriage, a son was born to Sundari in 1687 and was named Ajit. The Guru's household echoed with merriment and there was happiness that knew no end. Mata Gujri and Sundari loved Ajit as did all the members of the household but it was clear from the beginning that he was like Jeeto's son. As a baby when he cried and Sundari could not quieten him, she would carry him to Jeeto and place him in her lap."

"Here sister," she would say. "He is crying for you." And sure enough Jeeto would be able to still his crying. "Isn't he lucky?" Sundari would often tell her mother-in-law. "Other children have only one mother, he has two." When Ajit was four years old God finally gave Jeeto her first child, in 1691, a boy whom she named Jujhar. Two more sons were born to her : Zorawar in 1696 (or 1697), and Fateh in 1699. But till her death in 1701 Ajit remained her favourite and very special child.

All through his stay in Paonta and now during these years in Anandpur the Guru had studied the growth and development of the Sikh religion. He studied not only the teachings of the Gurus but also the entire history of the movement. He compared the Sikh movement as it was when Guru Nanak had started it with what it had become in his own time. He felt that a great deal of disunity had arisen among the followers of the Guru and there was a decline in the purity and strength of his followers and in their attitude towards their religion. He thought about this a great deal and finally realised that there were two main reasons for this. One was the functioning of the *masands* and the other was the disputes that often arose when a new Guru was appointed.

The *masands* had first been appointed to help the Guru in the task of administration. The Gurus' following had grown so large that administration could no longer be done from just one centre by the Guru alone and the *masands* worked honestly and looked after the welfare of all the Sikhs in their area and helped the poor and the needy. They collected all the offerings that people made to the Guru and brought them to the centre. But over the years many of the *masands* became corrupt and began to function independently. They kept a large part of the offerings for themselves and became rich and owned a lot of property. Some of them even had small private armies. With these they exploited the poor people : made them work on their lands and forced them to make greater offerings. In many cases they added to their power by making their office hereditary.

The death of a Guru had often led to a division among the Sikhs because claimants to the *gaddi* who did not succeed often set up their own *deras* and gathered large followings. Guru Gobind Singh had before him the examples of Datu, Prithi Chand, Dhirmal, Meharban and Ram Rai. While at Anandpur the Guru introduced many reforms in his organisation, the most important and far reaching of which was the solving of these two problems.

He sent out a *hukamnama* and invited all the *masands* to come to Anandpur. Once they were all there he announced that the order was being abolished once and for all. He had collected charges against various *masands*: these charges were read out and the *masands* were given a chance to explain their actions. Those who were found guilty of corruption and misuse of power were dealt with very severely. In this way the *sangat* was finally freed from the cruel power of the *masands* and the people were now directly linked with Anandpur and to their Guru.

The Guru's followers came to him for two reasons. One was to seek help and guidance in questions about religion and about spiritual matters. The other was to seek his advice regarding their day-to-day problems. It had been well established by now that the Granth contained all the religious and spiritual advice that any Sikh might need and it was only a matter of studying the sacred text carefully and the answer would be found. In their day-to-day lives the Punjabis had for many generations been taking their problems to the panchayat. The Guru felt that if the panchayat could be modified a little it would be able to help his followers the way the Guru had been able to help his followers. So between the Granth and the elected representatives of the community, the *panth*, the function of the Guru could continue to be performed even in the absence of a living Guru. The Granth would perform the spiritual function and as such would be the spiritual Guru, while the *panth* would perform the day-to-day functions and would be the secular Guru. So the Guru decided to end the line of personal Gurus and invest the Guruship in the Granth Sahib. In this way the Guruship would rest in something permanent, something which was sacred and above all dispute. He waited for a suitable moment to announce this decision to his followers.

Baisakhi, the first day of the month of Baisakh, has always been a very special day for the Sikhs. Guru Amar Das had declared this day as a special festival for all his followers and had said that all Sikhs should come to their centre to meet their Guru in person on this day. This practice had been followed ever since. As the following of the Gurus grew, the number of Sikhs coming to meet them on Baisakhi also grew. Guru Gobind realised that Baisakhi would be an ideal day on which he could give new life to the faith.

For the festival in 1699 he sent out a *hukumnana* to his followers very early in the year, asking them to make every effort to be present in Anandpur on Baisakhi day. As Baisakhi approached the visitors started pouring in : Everyone knew that there was something very special about this Baisakhi. So in addition to the normal excitement and joy there was also a feeling of expectancy.

On the morning of the main fair day, March 30, 1699, Guru Gobind rose early as usual. After his prayers and meditation, he returned to his room. When he came again before the huge *sangat* of more than eighty thousand, he came wearing the clothes he wore when he rode into battle, he came fully armed. He was greeted with great joy and reverence by all his followers. Then they all sat quietly waiting for him to begin his discourse. Instead he got to his feet and drew his sword and the steel flashed in the light of the morning sun.

"This is the moment of truth," he said in a voice that thundered down on his audience. "You are all my devoted followers. Which of my followers is ready to give up his life for me? I need a head that I can offer in sacrifice." The Sikhs were stunned. Never before had a Guru asked his followers to make such a sacrifice.

"Is there anyone who is ready to give up his life for me?" the Guru asked for the second time. Fear spread amongst the *sangat* and people began to murmur to one another.

"Am I to understand that not one of my followers is ready to prove his faith by sacrificing his life for his Guru?"

Daya Ram, a Khatri from Lahore, responded to the call. He got to his feet and made his way through the *sangat* till he was at the Guru's feet. He bowed his head and spoke in a clear loud voice.

"I am yours, *O Sache Padsha*, in life and in death. Take my head if it is of any use to you. For me there could be no greater honour than to die by your sword."

The Guru led him to a tent which had been erected nearby. The *sangat* sat in silence. They heard the swish of the Guru's sword as it flashed through the air and then the thud of a head falling to the ground. The Guru returned his sword covered with blood, his eyes flashing with a strange excitement.

"I need another head," he said in the same thundering voice. Fear turned to panic among the Guru's followers. But before the Guru could repeat his demand, Dharam Das, a Jat from Hastinapur, got to his feet.

"I am ready, my lord. I pledged my life to you when I became your Sikh. It is yours to do what you will with it."

Once more the Guru led his Sikh into the tent. Once more the *sangat* heard the swish of the sword and then the sound of the severed "head" as it fell to the ground. Some people became so frightened that they got up and fled. Some went to Mata Gujri and begged her to stop her son in this seeming madness.

Three times more the Guru repeated his call and three times brave and faithful Sikhs rose to answer the call. They were Mohkam Chand of Dwarka, Himmat of Jagannath and Sahib Chand of Bidar. With each sacrifice more and more of the congregation left. They had come to celebrate the festival of Baisakhi and now their Guru was "butchering" them in the most cruel and blood-thirsty manner. It was best to leave Anandpur and go back to their homes before any harm came to them.

A few minutes after the fifth sacrifice the Guru returned from the tent with the five Sikhs behind him, now dressed in beautiful new robes. For a moment the *sangat* could not understand what had happened. Then they remembered the

Guru's opening remark. This had indeed been the moment of truth; the Guru had been testing his disciples. Each time they had seen the fresh blood on the Guru's sword, it is said, it had been the blood of a sacrificial goat. Each time they had heard the sound of a falling head, it had been the head of a goat falling to the ground.

The Guru introduced his five faithful followers as 'Panj Pyare' or the Five Beloved Ones. He said that by offering themselves as sacrifice the five had come through the very last test that is possible for any man, and by so doing they had not only brought blessings to themselves but they had brought glory to the Sikh faith. He said that these five would form the heart of the Khalsa, the new order that he was going to start.

The Guru now took a bowl of steel in which he put pure clean water and stirred the water with his double-edged dagger. At this time Mata Sahib Devan came with a container of *batashas* (sugar crystals) as an offering.

"This is a happy coincidence" the Guru said.

"Your bringing of the sugar candy is indeed a timely gift. My dagger and your *batashas* are a combination of courage and kindness. My dagger will make sure that my Sikhs will be heroes when they go into battle and your *batashas* will make sure that they always spread sweetness wherever they go. Come, put the *batashas* into this water so that it can be changed to *amrit*. Sahib Devan put the *batashas* into the cauldron and the Guru stirred the water with his dagger till they were dissolved. While he was doing this the Guru recited hymns both from the Granth Sahib and of his own composition. Then he baptised the five Sikhs by pouring the nectar into their palms from which they drank. After which he asked them to drink in turn from a common bowl to emphasise that there was no distinction of caste between them.

By drinking the *amrit*, the Guru explained, the five had experienced a rebirth. They had left behind their previous family ties and now belonged to the family of the Guru. They had also left behind their previous professions which had given them their place in society. They were now all soldiers of the Guru, equal in rank, status and occupation. They had left behind their earlier beliefs and rituals and their worship, from now on, was to be addressed only to the one, timeless God, the Akal Purukh. Their father was Guru Gobind and their mother Sahib Devan and their birth-place was Anandpur. They had made a complete break with the past and made a new beginning.

These five Sikhs, one Jat, one Kshatriya and three out-castes, formed the heart of the Khalsa, the new order that the Guru founded.

The choice of the number five has a special significance. It is the same number as the number of the panchayat and the Guru himself has said:

"Where there are five, there am I, where the five meet they are the holiest of the holy."

The five were given the same powers as the Guru and by doing this the Guru had taken the first step in abolishing the tradition of a living Guru.

The Guru-Sikhs were to wear five symbols of purity. These became the symbols of the Khalsa. They were *kesh*: uncut hair and untrimmed beards: *kara*: a steel bracelet: *kanga*: a small comb: *kachha*: short, breeches — like underwear; *kirpan*: a sword. The Guru at the time of the birth of the Khalsa explained the importance of the five symbols. But there is no complete record of this speech and this has led to many different interpretations as to the meaning of these symbols. When we try to explain these symbols we must remember that the Guru's idea of a true Khalsa was of one who was both a saint and a soldier. Long hair in India has always been associated with saintliness. It can safely be assumed that all the Gurus from Nanak onwards wore long hair and all of them (with the obvious exception of Guru Har Krishan) had untrimmed beards. Many of the

Guru's followers must also have let their hair grow long, so when Guru Gobind asked his followers to keep long hair and beards they at once understood the significance of this. By keeping long hair and beards they were making a promise that they would lead good and virtuous lives. The *kanga* or the comb was to make sure that the long hair was kept neat and clean. This was to emphasise the difference between the Khalsa and the Jatta Sadhus. The Jatta Sadhus kept long hair but they never combed it — they allowed it to grow thick and matted as a symbol of their renunciation of the world. The Khalsa would keep long hair but keep it neatly combed to emphasise that though they were pledged to lead saintly lives, they had not renounced the world.

The *kara* and the *kirpan* both emphasised the martial nature of the Khalsa. The Khalsa was a soldier who would raise his sword to fight for right and defend the weak and the helpless. The *kara* was a thick steel bangle worn on the right wrist which gave strength to the wrist while flourishing a sword and protection against the enemy's weapon. The steel itself was a symbol of strength.

The *kachha* was a symbol of cleanliness and hygiene and also a symbol of restraint in sex.

The Guru then introduced a new greeting "*Whahegur-ji-ka-Khalsa, Wahegur-ji-ki-Fateh*": the Khalsa are chosen of God, victory be to our God.

The Guru now stood before the Khalsa with folded hands and asked them to give him *amrit* the way he had given them the *amrit*. The Khalsa and the *sangat* were stunned by this request. "You are our Guru, our guide. How can we give *amrit* to you?" "In my new order there is no high and low," the Guru said. "There is complete equality among men, even among the Guru and his disciples." On being given the *amrit* the Guru was also given the surname "SINGH" and he became Guru Gobind Singh.

After this the Guru turned and spoke to the *sangat*. "You must all follow one set of beliefs and get rid of all differences of religion. The four Hindu castes must forget all their differences and mix freely with each other. All men are equal and no man should think that he is superior or better than others. Let men of the four castes be baptised, eat from the same dishes and feel no contempt for each other."

He told the *sangat* that the path of the Khalsa was not an easy one: it was a path of faith and sacrifice and strict self-discipline. He invited those of the *sangat* who were ready to follow this difficult path to come forward and be baptised and thousands of the Sikhs came forward and were baptised.

The news-writer of the Moghul court was present in Anandpur and he sent a detailed report to the Emperor in which he says:

He has abolished caste and custom, old rituals, beliefs and superstitions. He has brought his followers together in one brotherhood. All men will be equal and no one will be superior or inferior to another. Men of all castes have been made to eat from the same bowl. Some orthodox men said they would never accept a religion which was opposed to the teaching of the Vedas and the Shastras. They would not renounce, at the bidding of a boy, their ancient faith which had come to them from their ancestors. But twenty thousand men and women have taken the baptism on the first day. They promised to obey him because they had the fullest faith in his divine mission.

The birth of the Khalsa brought into being Guru Gobind Singh's scheme for the uplift of his people. Through this one act he made a great change in the minds of his men. They had been weak and passive before but now their energies were aroused and directed towards positive goals. They were now aware of their own weakness and they gained strength to stand on their feet and fight against tyranny and oppression. They were able to get rid of the superstitions and divisions which had made them weak and kept their spirits in slavery for many centuries. They were given self-confidence and a belief that they could make their own destinies. The birth of the Khalsa led to many acts of courage and sacrifice which set an example to others and gave a new turn to Indian history.

Sparrows Meet Hawks

*T*he famous baptism ceremony in Anandpur had very far-reaching effects. The twenty thousand people who were baptised on that single day went back to their villages and towns and told of the new life that the Guru had brought to the Sikh religion and people who heard these reports were inspired to seek baptism as well. Anandpur became like a magnet attracting groups of people and there was an excitement which ran through the town as each new party arrived. A new brotherhood was created of those who had taken *amrit*. This sharing became a stronger bond than any other relationship.

The Guru had said at Anandpur that wherever five baptised Sikhs met, he would be present. So groups of five Sikhs went all over the north and baptised many thousands more. The Guru gained many new followers and the Sikh faith once more became alive and strong.

At one stage the Guru had written to the hill Rajas inviting them to join the new order. He had hoped that through this the people of North India would be united as one large family of brave and strong soldiers who would then be able to put up a joint defence against their common enemy, the Moghuls.

But the hill Rajas were jealous and suspicious, not only of the Moghuls but of the Guru and of each other. At this important point when the Moghuls had reduced them to petty chieftains they could not overcome their differences and come together for a common cause.

When the Rajas received the Guru's invitation, they sent back a message in which they said, "Each Turk can eat a whole goat. How can we, who eat only rice, cope with such strong men? Can sparrows kill hawks or sheep tigers?"

In this message the Rajas showed a lack of self-confidence and a lack of faith in the Guru's abilities to create a strong force from the material that came to him. All his followers were people who had lived in fear for hundreds of years and had never made a stand for their rights. Their bodies, their minds and their hearts had been made dead by generations who had lived in slavery. How could these men make good soldiers when their fathers and grandfathers had never even held a sword in their hands? How could these men ever kill the enemy when they had always been frightened by the shedding of blood? They were little more than sparrows and the Moghul soldiers were like hawks. The sparrows could never kill hawks.

The Guru took up this challenge when he received the Rajas' reply. He said that he would "train the sparrow to hunt the hawks and one man to fight an army." And this is exactly what the Guru did do. He knew that the Rajas were wrong in their assessment and that his men were in fact excellent soldier material. They came from a class of people who had lived lives of great hardship and knew the meaning of hunger and of pain. They knew what it was to struggle against great odds and had learnt long ago to accept the defeats and miseries of life without losing their balance of mind. These were important qualities for soldiers who would have to spend many months in battle. Their weakness was the lack of self-confidence, the fear of the ruling castes and the feeling that men had no control over their own destiny. The Guru began by showing them that all men were equal and that the divisions of caste were artificial, man-made divisions. As such they had no reason to be afraid of anyone. He taught them that their greatest strength was their faith in the Guru's teachings. If they had this faith there was no force either military or political that they needed to be afraid of. By giving them positions of responsibility and authority within the organisation he showed them that they did have a fair amount of control over their lives. He showed them that it was within their power to shake off the chains which had bound them for so many centuries and to live once again the lives of proud, free men. Once he had taught them this there was nothing that could hold them back. They had seen the joy of living in a casteless, unified society, they had tasted freedom and self-respect, they had become masters of their destiny. They would give up their lives rather than go back to the life they had led earlier. It was indeed a remarkable force that the Guru had created. There were thousands and thousands of turbaned, bearded soldiers, fully armed, each of them well-skilled in the use of arms, well-versed in the art of battle, each one of them ready to lay down his life at the Guru's command. Everywhere they went they showed a spirit of faith, confidence and optimism. They believed wholeheartedly in the Guru's injunction. "The Khalsa shall rule. Their enemies will be scattered, only they that seek refuge will be saved."

In the span of a lifetime Guru Gobind Singh had transformed the religious centre his father had built into a strong military base. The Guru himself was not only a spiritual guide but also a skilled military leader. The hill Rajas saw this change first with wonder and then with fear and all their old suspicions and jealousies were aroused again.

This hostility of the Rajas was to lead to four battles with the Guru, in all of which the Guru was victorious.

The first of these battles was a minor engagement.

Two of the Rajas, Alim Chand and Ballia Chand, attacked the Guru's camp while he was hunting. Their strategy was to attack the Guru while he had the least number of soldiers with him and when he was least expecting the attack. The manoeuvre was to be secret and swift and to be directed against the Guru's person.

The combined forces of the two Rajas far out-numbered the Guru's small escort. Yet the Sikhs fought with great courage and determination.

Balia Chand was shot dead by one of the Guru's arrows. So when the Guru's bodyguard charged down towards the advancing enemy it was Alim Chand who now led the combined forces of the two Rajas. There was fierce fighting which lasted many hours during which Alim Chand lost one arm and fled from the battle. Seeing this the soldiers realised that they had lost the battle and all fled from the battlefield.

This incident added to the growing fears of the Rajas. The Sikhs had been far outnumbered, yet they had succeeded in defeating the combined forces of the two Rajas. They were convinced that the Guru should be crushed once and for all and this conviction led to the second battle. The Rajas sent an appeal to the Subedar of Delhi.

Knowing that Guru Gobind was a successor of the holy Guru Nanak, we made no objection to his residence amongst us. When he obtained power we tried to restrain him. He went to Nahan and formed an alliance with the Raja. He then came into collision with Raja Fateh Shah of Srinagar which led to the battle of Bhangani where there was destruction of human life. After his return to Anandpur the Guru established a new sect as distinct from the Hindus and Mohammadens to which he has given the name of Khalsa. He has united the four castes into one and made many followers. He invited us to join him and promised if we converted then we should obtain an empire in this world and salvation in the next. He suggested to us that if we rose in rebellion against the Emperor, he would assist us with all his forces, because the Emperor had killed his father and he desired to avenge his death. As we did not think proper to oppose the Emperor, the Guru is displeased with us and now gives us every form of annoyance. We cannot restrain him and have accordingly come to crave the protection of this just government against him. If the government considers us its subject, we pray for its assistance to expel the Guru from Anandpur. Should you delay to punish or restrain him, his next expedition will be against the capital of your empire.

(Macauliffe — The Sikh Religion)

As was to be expected, when the Subedar of Delhi read this appeal he treated it as a matter of the greatest urgency and ordered two of the Panj Hazari Moghul Generals, Painda Khan and Din Beg, to move to the Punjab immediately. He also sent the Rajas' appeal to the Emperor along with a report of the action that he had taken.

When the Moghul soldiers reached Ropar they found the Rajas and their armies waiting to meet them. The combined armies were divided into two commands under Painda Khan and Din Beg. Reports of the approaching army had reached the Guru well in time. A large number of Sikhs had collected in Anandpur and the Guru had time to organise them and to plan his strategy for the battle. He decided not to wait for the enemy to come to him in Anandpur.

The Guru's Panj Piyare, who had shown such great courage in being the first to be baptised, were the commanders of the five divisions of the Guru's army. The battle was joined. The Moghul Commanders had been sure of an early victory because they felt that their men were better trained and were more skilled than the Sikhs. The Sikhs, though fewer in number, fought with great courage and determination and in the fierce battle that followed the Moghul soldiers began to falter. When it was certain that the battle had turned against the Moghuls, Painda Khan called for a temporary truce and rode out to parley with the Guru.

"Guru of the Sikhs," Painda Khan got immediately to the point, "I have many brave and famous soldiers in my army just as you have many brave and famous soldiers in yours. It would be a pity that they should lose their lives when there is a simpler way to resolve our conflict. Let you and I meet in single combat. As Allah is witness, let the better man win and let our armies abide by the outcome of this encounter."

The Guru smiled. "So be it, let the better man win and let our armies abide by the outcome of this challenge."

Painda Khan rode back to his camp to make preparations for the duel.

News of the challenge spread through the opposing armies. Both the generals prepared for the struggle ahead and when the preparations were complete they rode to the centre of the battleground with two escorts each.

"Since I held out the challenge it is your privilege to choose the weapons," Painda Khan said. He was an older and more experienced soldier than the young Guru and he had no doubt that he would be able to defeat and kill the Guru and thus ensure victory for the Moghul army.

"I choose the bow," the Guru said, without a moment's hesitation.

On both sides the army stood with bated breath, waiting for the outcome of the duel. A few of the younger Rajas were pleased. They had no doubt that they were going to see the end of their hated enemy at the hands of an older and more experienced soldier. But the older Rajas who had seen the Guru in personal combat at the battles of Bhangani and Nadaun were not so sure.

"Come Guru," Painda Khan said, putting on a brave front. "Strike the first blow so that neither you nor your people will have any regrets later."

"Oh Khan," the Guru said in a gentle voice, almost as if he was speaking to a child. "It is clear that you know nothing about my faith and my people. One of the most important principles that a Sikh lives by is that he never strikes the first blow. If we strike, it is always in self-defence when our enemy has already made the attack against us. So you must strike the first blow."

Painda Khan smiled with relief. The Guru saw the smile and understood the reason.

"You are a guest in my part of the country and a guest must be honoured in some way. So strike two blows before I strike my first blow."

The generals retreated to the prescribed distance. Painda Khan took careful aim and shot his first arrow. It whizzed past the Guru's head, narrowly missing his turban. He drew his bow a second time and took aim even more carefully. This time too he missed.

The Guru had been watching his enemy very carefully and had observed that Painda Khan was covered with steel armour from head to foot. The only part of his body that was left uncovered was his ear. So when Painda Khan's second arrow missed him, the Guru immediately picked up his bow and took careful aim. His arrow shot through the air and pierced Painda Khan's ear and in the blinking of an eyelid the great Moghul general fell from his horse dead. Breaking all the rules and customs of battle, the Moghul army refused to honour the outcome of the duel and shouting loud war-cries and calling for vengeance they charged at the Sikhs under the command of Din Begh.

The anger of the Pathan soldiers was great and they fought with even greater courage than before. But the Sikhs stood their ground firmly and met them blow for blow.

The hill Rajas saw that in spite of the fierce battle that was still being fought, the tide seemed to be flowing in favour of the Sikhs. They decided not to commit their armies to the fighting and suffer unnecessary losses, and calling them back they left the battlefield. This desertion weakened the morale of the Moghul soldiers. Din Begh fought very bravely and tried to hold the Moghul soldiers together. Then he was seriously wounded and could not continue to fight any longer.

He gave the call for retreat and the Moghul soldiers fled from the battlefield. The Sikh soldiers wanted to chase the fleeing army but the Guru held them back.

"They are fugitives and are weak and helpless. It is not right to chase them any further. It is enough that you have all fought with such great courage and been so firm in your stand. Let us pray and offer our gratitude to our maker for giving us this splendid victory."

There is a temple at Khizrabad which recalls this great victory of the Guru's Sikhs. This great victory of the Guru did not bring him any lasting peace. If anything, it increased the Rajas' fear and anger. They were now determined that the Guru should be pushed out from Anandpur as soon as possible. Once again a meeting was called and this time almost all the Rajas attended the meeting. They all felt that the defeat of the Imperial forces would lead to the Guru directing his attention against the Rajas.

The Rajas now decided to make a direct appeal to the Emperor and wanted to send Ajmer Chand on this mission to ensure that the Emperor saw how important it was to destroy the Guru's power as quickly as possible. This suggestion was opposed by Raja Bhup Chand of Handur. He felt that they should not depend upon the Mughals any more and should combine their strengths and make a determined all-out effort to defeat the Guru.

Bhup Chand spoke with such courage and conviction that his arguments won the day. This led to the third battle against the Guru. It was decided that they must mount another attack against Anandpur and this attack must be made with the greatest speed possible. The Rajas of Jammu, Nurpur, Mandi, Kulu, Keonthal, Chamba, Srinagar and Dadhwal moved their armies as quickly as possible to a place close to Anandpur where they were joined by the forces of the local Rajas. The Raja of Bilaspur, Ajmer Chand, was given overall charge of the combined forces and he sent a message to the Guru.

"You have been in illegal occupation of land that belonged to our father and now belongs to us," Ajmer Chand wrote in his message. "We have tolerated your presence as your father was a saint and you are a successor to Nanak. But now we cannot allow this state of affairs to continue. You are given two choices : You must either abandon Anandpur and move out of our territory, or if you choose to live on in Anandpur you must recognise our ownership of this land and pay us rent for its use. If you fail to follow either of these alternatives we will have no choice but to use force to evict you."

The Guru received the messenger with all due courtesy and sent back a polite but firm message. He said that the land in question was freehold and had been bought by his father against payment in cash. As such it had become his father's property and now, by the laws of inheritance, his property. As such there could not be a question of payment of rent : a man did not pay rent for living in his own house. If they tried to force any decision on him he would meet them with force and answer blow for blow. He desired only to live in peace and if the Rajas put aside their pride and came to him in peace they could take from him whatever they wanted. The Guru's house was open to all.

The Rajas had come with the intention of destroying the Guru and they were not prepared to acknowledge that what the Guru said was reasonable. Many of the Guru's Sikhs had, after the last battle, gone to visit their families. But as news of the impending battle spread they hurried back. The Sikh army was also helped by the arrival in Anandpur of 500 soldiers from Majha. Sher Singh and Nahar Singh were put in charge of the fort of Lohgarh while Ude Singh was entrusted with the defence of Fatehgarh. Ajit Singh, the Guru's eldest son, now fourteen-year-old, was given the command of a company.

The Guru advised his Sikhs to keep to the forts and not to venture out into the open. The armies of the hill Rajas formed a cordon around Anandpur and laid siege which lasted for many days. The Sikhs in small groups would ride out at night and attack and loot the enemy's camps and carry away their supplies. Ajit conducted many of these raids. His acts of courage and fearlessness soon became common topics of conversation amongst the inhabitants of Anandpur. From time to time the Rajas too attacked what they felt were weak points in the fortification. But they were always pushed back and they were not able to break through.

When months had passed with little success, some of the senior Rajas advised that they should make their peace with the Guru. "There is no dishonour in making your peace with the house of Nanak," the Raja of Mandi advised. "All things said and done, the Guru is a man of God, a holy man, and there is no shame in coming to terms with him. I am sure he will give us terms that do not bring us dishonour." His advice was supported by a few of the other senior Rajas who had begun to feel that they could not win against the Guru. But by and large the Rajas listened to the Raja of Mandi in sullen silence and it was clear that in spite of the failure of their efforts they were not willing to negotiate a peace. "Far better an honourable peace now than a disgraceful defeat later."

"It is only old men who talk of defeat," once again it was the outspoken Raja Bhup Chand. "With all due apologies to my respected uncle, I am sure that we can still break through if we make one final determined effort."

"I am sure of this too," Raja Ajmer Chand said, supporting Bhup Chand's stand. Plans were discussed and Ajmer explained that a concentrated and determined attack, on a point which he felt was the weakest part of the fortification, would see them through.

The Rajas did make a very determined attack and for a while it seemed that they would break through. It was the young Ajit Singh who pushed them back and with his band of brave soldiers he caused havoc among the enemy forces.

An enemy arrow wounded his horse but without the slightest hesitation he dismounted and continued to fight on foot.

At last the hopelessness of their attempt began to stare the Rajas in their face. But before they abandoned their attack they made one desperate effort to batter down the great gate of the Lohgarh fort. They got hold of a huge elephant and covered him in thick steel. Then the elephant was fed a very heavy dose of intoxicants to ensure that he would feel no fear or pain. The elephant was set on a ramp leading to the great gate and the Rajas' armies formed up behind him. Meeting little opposition the elephant battered at the gate and for a while it seemed that this scheme might meet with success. Guru Gobind Singh sent one of his bravest Sikhs, Bachittar Singh, son of Bhai Mani Singh, to deal with the elephant. Bachittar thrust at the elephant with his spear and with the very first thrust pierced the steel plate and injured it in the head. It was a deep injury and the poor animal felt the pain in spite of the large dose of intoxicants he had been given. The soldiers did not have a chance to turn around and many of them were trampled to death.

The Guru's army came out into the open and fell upon their enemy. Both sides suffered heavy losses. But the army of the Rajas had lost many of its important leaders and generals. Among them were Raja Kesri Chand of Jamwal, Jagatullah the great leader of the Gujjar and Ranghar tribes, Raja Chamund Chand of Kangra and Raja Bhup Chand of Handur, who had played a very important part in the battle, were both seriously injured. Without these leaders to lead them, the allied army was crippled and at last the Rajas, accepting the bitter truth of their defeat, lifted the siege and fled from Anandpur to safety.

All the Rajas, except the Raja of Bilaspur, were content to lie low in their own states and to lick their wounds. The Raja of Bilaspur, who had been the commander of the allied forces, took this setback as a personal insult and was determined to avenge this defeat. He tried to approach some of the other Rajas individually and in secret. From a few of them he received taunts about his poor leadership, from the others very lukewarm support. He realised that if he was to fight the Guru he could not expect any help from his former allies, the hill Rajas.

But he was not put off by this. He had made up his mind and was quite determined that he must make a fresh attack on the Guru as soon as possible. If the Rajas were not willing to help him he would turn to another source for help. He approached the Faujdars of Sirhind and Lahore and was pleasanlty surprised to receive positive replies from both of them.

The combined forces of the two Faujdars and the Raja of Bilaspur marched on Anandpur. This was to be the fourth battle against the Guru.

The Guru had learnt a very valuable lesson from the last siege. Anandpur was very well fortified but it could stand up to a siege only if they had been able to stock up a sufficient supply of food. In the last siege they had been saved by the supplies that Ajit Singh and his band of brave soldiers had looted from the enemy camp. But this was not a very dependable source of supply. If the enemy had continued the siege for very much longer they could have been in very serious trouble. Now when the Guru heard of the fresh forces marching towards Anandpur he realised that there had not been enough time to prepare for a fresh siege and they did not have enough supplies to last them for more than a month or two. So the Guru, with his usual skill, decided not to meet the enemy at Anandpur. Instead he took up position at Nirmoh, a small village near Kiratpur. A quick fierce battle took place and both the armies fought with great courage. At the beginning it seemed the allies would win but the Guru's forces held their own and finally broke through the cordon and the allies were thrown back. They made one last effort to hold the Guru by trying to throw a fresh cordon around his force. But this effort was also defeated. The Faujdars of

Sirhind and Lahore called off the battle and retreated with their armies.

The Guru now moved to Basali and sought refuge with the Raja who was his friend and who had often invited him to come and visit him in Basali. Now the Guru appeared at his gates, tired after the series of battles and the Raja was happy to give him refuge.

The young Raja of Bilaspur was still not ready to accept defeat. Even though all his earlier efforts had failed he was not prepared to give up. He called his men and followed the Guru to Basali and made a desperate last effort by leading an attack against the Guru. The Guru led his tired soldiers out against Raja Ajmer Chand. Once they marched on to the battlefield all their exhaustion and their wounds were forgotten. They fell upon the Raja's men and inflicted heavy losses. The hill people fled before such fierce fighting and the heavy losses that they had suffered. The Sikhs also lost heavily. Sahib Singh, a brave soldier who had covered himself with glory in every battle that he had taken part in, fell in this action after fighting valiantly to the very end.

The Guru returned to Anandpur and was blessed with a short peace which gave him some breathing time to prepare for the second phase of his military struggle.

Vichora — Separation

*R*aja Ajmer Chand now realised that he could not prevail against the Guru and felt it was better to be on friendly terms with the Guru rather than to be at war with him. He wrote to the Guru asking for peace between them and suggesting that the Guru should accept his ambassador at Anandpur. Guru Gobind Singh did not trust Ajmer Chand and was sure that the so-called ambassador would be a spy. Yet he accepted Ajmer Chand's offer because he knew that as the victor in the recent battle it would be ungracious of him to refuse an offer of peace from the loser.

The other Rajas too followed Ajmer Chand's example and made overtures of friendship to which the Guru readily responded.

Peace seemed to have come back to the area and the Rajas and the Guru appeared to be on friendly terms. But in his heart the Guru knew that this was a prelude to more trouble. He began to prepare for this even before the dust had settled on the battlefield after his last battle.

The first thing he did was to strengthen Anandpur. Till now Anandpur had used the steep hill terrain on which it stood as a natural fortification. Now the Guru built a strong wall around the town and Anandpur became a fort in the real sense of the word. The forts of Keshgarh and Lohgarh were repaired and made stronger and stocked with food supplies and ammunition to last many months. Smithies were set up and weapons of all kinds made by the hundreds.

He knew that the excitement that all these preparations generated could breed an eagerness for war and the desire to strike the first blow. So in all his sermons to his followers he preached again and again the teachings of the Gurus from Guru Nanak down to Guru Teg Bahadur. He explained to them that Sikhs were men of peace. Their task was to serve the *sangat* and to work for the uplift of the weak and the suffering. Soldiering was not their occupation and so they must never look for war. All the battles that they had fought so far were not of their making but had been forced upon them. They had fought these battles not to win lands or to bring fame to the Sikh community but in self-defence. They had fought to defend their right to live their lives according to their beliefs and be able to continue to serve humanity. If someone tried to take this right away from them they should be ready to fight again to the last drop of blood. Once they had gained victory they must turn again to what was their real aim in life : to live a life of peace, doing useful deeds for their fellow men.

There used to be an annual fair at Rawalsar, near Mandi, which was very popular and to which all the hill people from the areas around went. Most of the hill Rajas, their queens, their families and courtiers also attended this fair. The Guru was invited to come to this fair by the Rajas and he felt that this would be the ideal chance to meet the Rajas and convince them that he did not wish to encroach on their land or to threaten their security. So he accepted this invitation and the Guru and his family and a band of faithful Sikhs reached Rawalsar where they set up camp like the other Rajas had done.

Soon the Rajas and their queens came by turn to visit the Guru's camp and to invite him to come and visit them. Many of the Rajas and Ranis were impressed by the Guru and were sure that he was a deeply religious man and that he was honest and sincere when he said that they should all live in peace and friendship. Princess Padma, who belonged to the family of the Guru's old friend Medini Prakash of Nahan, was an ardent devotee of the Guru.

Raja Ajmer Chand came on a surprise visit to Nahan and Padma overheard him plotting and scheming against the Guru.

"There is no point waiting passively for the Moghul army to come to our aid," Raja Ajmer Chand told the Raja of Nahan. "While we wait the Guru is growing from strength to strength and weaning our own people to his side. We must attack him immediately and crush his growing power. For this I have been able to enlist the aid of two of Aurangzeb's bravest generals, Sayyad Beg and Alif Khan, who are on their way from Delhi to Lahore. For a thousand rupees a day they are ready to fight the Guru's forces."

Late that night, when everyone in the camp was asleep, disguised as a poor old woman, Padma stole out of her camp, dodged the sentries and made her way to the Guru's camp. Here she was stopped by the guards. "I have to see the Guru," she said crying in the manner of an old woman.

"I am in trouble and only the Guru can help me. I have to see him at once."

"The Guru is asleep," the sentries explained patiently.

"Why don't you too rest, mother, and I will make sure that you meet him first thing in the morning."

"I have come a very long way," she said showing them her dust covered feet. "I have walked day and night and I must see my Guru now."

The noise had woken the Guru and he sent instructions that the woman should be sent into his quarters at once. When she was alone with the Guru she told him who she was and everything that she had heard. The Guru thanked her and made sure that she got safely back to her camp.

The Guru returned to Anandpur as quickly as possible to prepare for the battle which was being thrust upon him.

While the Rajas waited for the Moghul army to reach Anandpur they fought two battles with the Guru. In the first, they depended on the two Moghul Generals Sayyad Beg and Alif Khan to lead them to victory. Sayyad Beg was so impressed by all that he saw and heard of the Guru that he became a follower of the Guru and fought on the Guru's side and the combined forces of Alif Khan and the hill Rajas were defeated. In the second engagement the hill Rajas combined their armies and attacked the Guru at a time when the Guru had only eight hundred men with him. This time too the Rajas' army was defeated.

At last news came that the Moghul army was approaching Anandpur. This army was led by Gen. Sayyad Khan, one of the most famous generals of the Moghul army. He was a brave and experienced soldier who had never shown any fear while fighting. He had risen steadily in the Moghul army because of his personal courage and because of his skill in battle. He had brought success to the Moghul forces in many battles and was greatly respected and admired by the Moghul Emperor. He was devoted to the Emperor and was ready to lay down his life for him.

Sayyad Khan looked forward to pitting his wits against a worthy enemy. He had heard about the Guru, heard about the Sikhs. Now he cast his mind back and pieces of information that he had gathered over the years came back to his mind and he built up a picture of his opponent. All the reports he had heard had said that the Guru was very handsome, strongly built, with clear bright eyes. They talked of his famous blue horse which ran with the speed of the wind and of the white hawk he always carried on his wrist. Then there were reports of his love for hunting and the tigers he had killed in single combat with his sword. It was the picture of a brave fearless man, skilled in the use of weapons with almost limitless stamina.

He had also heard reports of the Guru's kindness and compassion and of the help that he always gave to the weak and the oppressed. He had heard of his teaching and once he had even heard a beautiful hymn that the Sikhs sang and been moved by its beauty.

He had never heard of another man who was both a religious leader and a warrior. He was very keen to meet this man face to face, look into his eyes and try to understand how anyone could be both these things — a saint and a soldier.

There was another reason why Sayyad Khan was looking forward to this expedition to the north. He had been away in the Deccan for so long that he had lost touch with all his family and friends. He missed them all but he missed most of all his sister Nasiran. She was older than him and as a child he had got from her not only the love and friendship of a sister but also the care and protection of a mother. They had been very close. Then his sister had married the holy man Pir Badruddin, who was called Budhu Shah and gone to live with him at Sadaura. They had met from time to time but as the years went past these meetings became less frequent. Now with the Emperor's wars in the Deccan it was many years since he had met her. He had heard reports that she was now a widow, that she had lost her sons in war and his heart had longed to be with her but he was helpless. The battlefield is one place that does not give you leave of absence.

Now as he moved with his army towards Anandpur he found his mind going again and again to his sister and his chance of meeting her again. Childhood memories came flooding his heart and mind and this strong brave man who had not cried in years found the tears come to his eyes.

He planned his march in such a way that his army rode quite close to his sister's home. He gave his army a much needed rest in the camp they set up. Then handing over responsibility to his deputy Ramzan Khan, accompanied by a handful of soldiers, he went to visit his sister.

He had hoped to give his sister a surprise but such a large army could not move in secret and news had already come to her of the large Moghul army that was moving to Anandpur under the command of her brother Sayyad Khan. She was sure in her heart that he would come to see her before he marched into battle. This meeting was of the greatest importance to her. She had not met him for so many years and wanted to know everything that had happened to him during this time. She had missed her "little brother", missed all the love that they had shared and now she waited eagerly to be with him again. But this meeting was important to her for another reason. Like her late husband, the Pir, Nasiran too had become a great admirer of the Guru and her life was filled with her love for the Guru and in following the Guru's teachings. She was proud that her husband and her sons had given their lives for the Guru and if the need ever arose she knew that she too would gladly give up her own life for him, and here was her brother leading a mighty Moghul army against her Guru. She knew that her brother was a loyal and devoted soldier of the Moghul Emperor and believed that his duty was to fight against the Guru and to defeat him. For this he would give his life. Yet, Nasiran also knew that, futile as it seemed, she must try everything to persuade her brother from going out on this venture.

Sayyad Khan found his sister waiting for him and for a long moment they stood looking at each other, just looking at each other, the feelings between them so strong that they needed no words.

Much later after Sayyad had been fed and they had exchanged all their news, he said at last:

"Appa, I have come for your blessings, I go on the most difficult expedition of my life and I seek your prayers and your blessings for my success." Narsiran was silent and he saw a cloud of sadness pass over her face.

"What is it, my sister, what is it that troubles you?"

"I cannot give you either my prayers or my blessings." Her voice broke and she stopped to gain control of herself.

"My prayers are with the Guru, with every part of my body and soul, I pray for his success, it cannot be otherwise. If you love me, my brother — you will give up this venture. Tell your Emperor that you cannot lead his army, he has generals enough, he can find someone else to do your work."

Sayyad Khan looked away from his sister's face and cast his eyes into what remained of the fire. He knew that this would indeed be the most difficult expedition of his life, he would be going into battle without his sister's blessings on his side. But he had no choice. He looked back again into his sister's face.

"If I do this, I can only be one of two things, a coward who is afraid of the Guru's strength or a traitor who will not obey his Emperor's commands. What would you have me be? Tell me, appa, tell me." There was such pain in his voice that Nasiran felt the pain too. The famous, mighty general of the Moghuls was once again a little lost child looking to his elder sister for help. But for once she could give him no help. "I do not know," she said gently. "I cannot tell you anything. All that I know is that every arrow you aim at the Guru or at his men will be an arrow aimed at my heart. Every time you raise your sword it will be raised to strike off my head." She got up quickly and went into her room, locking the door behind her. Then she unrolled her prayer-mat and prayed to the powers-that-be to step in and resolve the difficult situation that they had created.

Sayyad Khan knew his sister well enough to know that she would not see him again before he rode out into battle. He rolled himself up in his blanket besides the glowing embers and tried to sleep. But sleep came only fitfully and he was aware in the early hours of the morning that his sister knelt besides him. He kept his eyes closed. When she was sure that he slept, he heard her muttering a prayer and then she tied something around his arm. He knew what is was, it was a *taviz* for his personal safety. He forced himself to lie still, not to let her know that he was awake. He felt the brief touch of her hand on his forehead and then she was gone. This is all that she could do for him, she could not pray for his success, could not wish that he succeed because her prayers and wishes were already given to his enemy. But as his dear beloved sister, she could not help but wish and pray for his personal safety. With his left hand he touched the *taviz* and smiled to himself. Then in the cold of the early morning he at last slept for an hour or two.

The battle was joined. On one side was the combined army of the Moghuls and the hill Rajas. On the other was the small Sikh army led by Sayyad Beg and Maimun Khan. "Remember," the Guru told his men before the fighting started. "Finally it is not your weapons or the number of your soldiers that will lead you to victory — it is what is in your hearts."

The fighting raged furiously. Through the smoke and dust of battle Sayyad Khan at last saw the Guru. He was indeed a handsome figure. He rode on his famous blue horse from group to group of his soldiers giving them courage and strength. All around him there was a rain of arrows and musket shots and he rode through it all as if he did not notice it. Sayyad Khan's heart filled with adoration for this remarkable man. He was everything that he had heard of him and even more. Then he checked his thoughts. He was his enemy and it was not right that he should think such thoughts of his enemy. It would weaken him. He thought of his duty, he thought of what the Emperor had said to him at their last meeting. His soldiers will come back. He raised his bow, and with carefully practised aim he aimed an arrow at the Guru. But as he aimed Nasiran's words came back to him.

"Everytime you aim an arrow at the Guru or his men you will aim it at my heart," and when the arrow at last left the bow it went wide off the mark. This upset him very much. He could not remember when he had last missed his target. His fame as a marksman had spread far and wide for in battle after battle he had never failed to hit the target. He was angry with his sister for making him so weak. He would show her that he was still a man, still a great shot. He pulled out his musket and loading it took careful aim at the Guru. He would get him now and the whole thing would be over and done with and he could go again to his wife and children. But when he had steadied his musket and taken careful aim, he saw in the sights not the Guru but his sister Nasiran and she smiled sadly at him almost as if she was mocking him. He fired and again his aim was wide off the mark and he knew at last that this was one battle he would not win.

The Guru rode out to him and when he was within ear-shot he called out to him. "You are a great and famous general and I have all respect for you. You have shot at me twice but for some strange reason your weapons have not found their mark. You are famous for your marksmanship. What made your aim miss? Was the distance too great? I am before you now. Pull out your sword and perhaps your sword will be able to do what your bow and your musket have not been able to do."

Sayyad Khan looked closely at the Guru. He saw the Guru smiling gently at him and knew at once why his sister followed this great man. The Guru waited and alongwith him all the soldiers who had heard the Guru's challenge waited. But instead of drawing his sword Sayyad dismounted from his horse, walked up to the Guru and put his face against the Guru's stir-up. The Guru too dismounted and drawing Sayyad into an embrace gave him his blessings. Sayyad got back on to his horse. Without a word, without a backward glance, he rode away from the battlefield. Seeing this his soldiers lost heart and also left the battlefield.

Sayyad Khan gave up his leadership of the Moghul army and retired into the hills to meditate. It is said that when the Guru went to the Deccan, Sayyad Khan was amongst the band of followers who went with him.

In a little while the allied army had regrouped. This time it was led by Wazir Khan, the Governor of Sirhind. Wazir Khan had already been defeated by the Guru in battle and was seeking revenge. Since he had lived for a long time in Sirhind, which is close to Anandpur, he knew of the strengths and weaknesses of the forts which the Guru had built. He also knew all the Rajas and knew which Rajas could be trusted and which Rajas could not be trusted. In the battle which was about to begin he knew exactly what tasks each of the Rajas could be trusted with. He was assisted by the Governor of Lahore who had also brought a very large force with him.

In the winter of 1705 the huge allied army marched towards Anandpur. The Guru's army came out to meet the advancing allied army and a heroic battle was fought in which both sides suffered heavy losses. The Guru realised that the enemy's number was so great that the Sikhs, in spite of all their courage, could not defeat them in open battle.

So he gave orders that the Sikhs should withdraw into Anandpur. Keshgarh was placed in the charge of his son Ajit Singh and Lohgarh was given to Nahar Singh and Sher Singh to defend. Seeing that the Sikh forces had withdrawn into Anandpur the allied forces laid siege to the town. Wazir Khan had learnt from his earlier defeat. He decided to put a cordon of soldiers around Anandpur and keep anyone from either entering or leaving the town. He made no effort to break through the walls. Slowly he tightened the siege. Following Wazir Khan's instruction the hill Rajas also realised that they should not think of an immediate victory. They should wait patiently. They must make sure that no one came in or went out of Anandpur and victory would be theirs.

The days stretched into weeks and the weeks into months. The food stock ran so low that wheat began to be sold for one rupee per seer and even this was not always available. At the beginning, bands of brave Sikh soldiers rode out at night and captured food and supplies from the enemy camp which helped to ease the food shortage a little. Then the allied forces became more vigilant. Most of the Sikh soldiers who rode out were killed and the quantity of food they brought back was so small that it did not lessen the suffering of the people. The Guru decided to abandon these attempts.

The people of Anandpur suffered greatly, specially the children and the old people. The Guru was pained by this suffering but he knew it was a price that had to be paid if the Sikhs were to keep their freedom. People ate whatever they could get hold of — grass, the leaves of trees and even the bark of the trees after they had been made into a powder. And yet the siege went on.

The allied soldiers began to get impatient. They had nothing to keep them occupied. They had come ready for battle and now they had been turned into little more than guards. It seemed to them that they would not be able to force the Guru out even after years of waiting.

There was a small mountain stream gurgling and singing as it made its way down the hills. This stream flowed through Anandpur bringing to the Sikhs not only its very special music but also the life-giving force of its sweet fresh water.

In fact, it was this mountain stream which was one of the reasons that had made Guru Tegh Bahadur decide to build his centre here. The people of Anandpur had got so used to its presence that they had begun to take it for granted. Now when the siege of Anandpur had lasted for many months, those inhabitants of the town who had been able to sleep that particular night, woke to a strange silence, the absence of a familiar sound. For sometime in their confusion, they could not say what it was. But their instinct told them that there was something terribly wrong. At last they realised what it was, they could no longer hear the music of their stream. The people poured out to the banks of the stream and what they saw filled their hearts with dread. There was no longer any water in the stream and they knew without asking that this was a fresh blow struck by the enemy. It was in fact the latest move that Wazir Khan had made in tightening his control over the town.

He was aware of the suffering and hardships that the population must be going through when no food was coming in. Yet the months dragged on and there was no sign of any weakening on the Guru's part. He decided that something more would have to be done. When he talked to the hill Rajas he found out about the stream and how important it was for the people of Anandpur. So he had diverted the stream away from Anandpur to deprive the inhabitants of its life-giving waters. Some water had been stored in tanks but once the supply stopped this stored water did not last long.

The condition of the people came unbearable. First the animals began to die of hunger and thirst and the Guru lost his favourite horses and then the famous elephant Prasadi. Then people started dying and yet the Guru refused to give up the battle. Some of the Sikhs began openly to talk of giving up the fort and moving out and even went to Mata Gujari and asked her to plead with her son. Everywhere people lay sick or dying.

It was at this point in the siege that a messenger arrived at the gates of Anandpur. He carried the sign of peace and the Guru gave order that he should be allowed to enter the fort. He was a special messenger from the Emperor Aurangzeb and brought a message signed by the Emperor himself. The Emperor praised the Guru and the Sikhs for their great courage and bravery and went on to say that he knew of the difficulties being faced by the Sikhs of Anandpur. He knew that there must be great suffering inside the fort without food and water and invited the Guru to leave Anandpur. He gave a personal promise that the Guru, his family and his Sikhs would be given a safe passage from the town. The Guru did not believe that the Emperor was sincere in his promise though some of the Sikhs began to feel that the Emperor's offer should be accepted. The Guru was not yet ready to give up his beloved Anandpur and the siege continued.

Forty Sikhs formed a group and asked the Guru for permission to leave the Fort.

"You will have to give me in writing that you are giving your Guru up : that from now on you will have nothing more to do with me. Then you can go," the Guru said. This was a difficult thing for the Sikhs to do: they could not bear the hardships of living in Anandpur, but at the same time they loved their Guru deeply and could not give him up. Then they realised that if they wrote this disclaimer the Guru would let them go and with their departure he might think again about his decision not to leave the fort. So they signed a disclaimer and the Guru permitted them to leave. It made the Guru sad to see them go because it was the first sign of the weakening of the people — but he was not one to hold them by force. When the Moghuls saw the band of forty Sikhs riding out of the fort with the sign of surrender, they knew that the siege was successful. All doubts vanished and they renewed the siege with greater vigour.

For sometime more the brave band of people tried to hold on in the fort. The Sikh soldiers had seen their children and their women, their old and their sick suffering the pangs of hunger and had turned their face away and ignored their suffering. But now when they saw people dying of thirst it was too much for them to bear. In the stillness of the night the soldiers would take turns to steal out in small bands to the now distant stream and bring small amounts of water back to the fort. The price they paid was heavy because at least half of each band never returned. But they willingly paid this price every night because even the little water they brought back gave the gift of life to a handful of people for at least another twenty-four hours. It gave relief to those who were weak and ill and also showed the Moghul forces that the people of Anandpur had not yet given up.

But the misery of the people increased with every passing hour. People became mad with the suffering and the number of the dead and dying became far greater. The Guru could not bear the scenes that he saw everytime he went out into the streets. He at last gave in to the pleading of his mother and his advisers and decided to leave Anandpur. Before he left he destroyed and burnt what was left of the town so that the enemy would not be able to use it as a stronghold. Then on the night of 5 and 6 December 1705, the Guru left his beloved city. The first party was made up of his mother, his wives, his two young sons and all the women and children, the sick and the wounded. Before he mounted his horse to leave Anandpur, for the last time the Guru made one final visit to the little shrine that he had built in memory of his father. He stood there in silence, his eyes closed, his lips moving in prayer. All the wonderful memories of his great father passed through his mind one by one, all the great lessons that the Ninth Guru had taught him while he lived and the greatest of lessons he had taught through his death. He placed the shrine in the care of Gurbaksh, a member of the Udasi sect, and then rode out with the *Panj Pyare*, his two elder sons and what remained of his forces.

As he rode away the Guru reined in his horse and turned to look, one last time, at the town. He could see the tall towers looming as shadows against the sky. This town had been his home for thirty years and most of what he had achieved had been here in this town. The short happy period of his boyhood when he had been so close to his father had been spent here and it was here that the head of his martyred father had been brought to him and, in a moment, he had grown from a boy to a man. Here in Anandpur he had grown to adulthood and proved that the light of Nanak's lamp had indeed passed on to him. In this beautiful little town he had transformed the peaceful Sikhs into a militant force that could make the mighty Moghul army tremble. Much of his poetry had been written here and it was here that he had spent long hours in meditation. The hills around had echoed with the shouts of his men as they practised their skills at riding and in the use of weapons. And it was in the hills that he had developed his own skills as a military genius.

His eyes ranged over the outline of the hills and of some of the fortifications. There was little that he could see at the time but he knew each fold in the hills, each curve in the wall so well that he could see every little detail in his mind's eye. He wondered if he would come back again, if that golden period would ever be given back to him and to his Sikhs. Then he turned and rode away, never to look back again.

The two groups of Sikhs joined up on the banks of the river Sarsa. While the Guru was thinking of the best way to cross the river the Moghul forces broke their promise and attacked the retreating Sikhs from the rear. Ude Chand, one of the five faithfuls, collected a brave band of soldiers and turned to hold the Moghul forces back for a little while to give a chance to the rest of the party to cross the river. There had been heavy winter rains up in the hills and the stream was swollen. The river waters roared in anger as they flowed between the banks that contained them. On this winter night the waters were cold. But the Guru and his group had no choice. The only other choice was to face the attacking army and face certain death. So while Ude Chand held the enemy back the Guru made an uncertain crossing. The mules carrying his precious books and manuscripts were all swept away by the strong current. The Guru's party too was broken up as they came out on the opposite bank at different points. The Guru's wives Mata Sundari and Mata Sahib Devan found themselves separated from the Guru. There was great danger all around and they were persuaded by a faithful Sikh to go to his house in Delhi where they could live in safety till they were able to rejoin the Guru.

Mata Gujari and her two younger grandsons Zorawar Singh and Fateh Singh were washed out of the waters further downstream and found themselves separated from the rest of the party. But Mata Gujari felt they had nothing to fear. They had with them some money hidden in Mata Gujari's saddle bag and even more important they had with them Gangu, a Brahmin cook who had worked in the Guru's household. Gangu offered to take them to the safety of his village, an offer which they accepted.

The Guru when he crossed the river found that he had only forty soldiers with him. These included his two elder sons Ajit Singh and Jujhar Singh.

Though the survivors did not know of it at the time many of the party had been swept away in the icy cold water. It was also much later that they learnt of Ude Singh's death.

He had died fighting, given up his life so that others would have a chance to save their lives.

The Guru decided to make a fresh stand. He and his brave band of forty soldiers galloped as fast as they could to the little fortress of Chamkaur near Ropar. They took up positions inside the stockade and in the little time that they had did everything they could to strengthen the defences. The attack was not long in coming. A detachment of the Moghul army had come in hot pursuit and this was joined by fresh troops which had been sent out from Delhi and also by the local Ranghars and Gujjars who were looking for a chance to avenge their earlier defeat.

Now began the story of what must surely be one of the greatest acts of courage and sacrifice in the annals of all history. Those inside the fort could see the enemy all around them, like the waves of an angry sea. Yet they were not afraid. Their Guru had decided to take a stand and they would gladly give their lives to carry out his wishes.

The Guru and a few other brave warriors rained arrows on the enemy. Since they were shooting from a higher point they were able to keep the enemy soldiers at bay. In the meantime the other soldiers rode out, one small band at a time, and engaged the enemy in close-quarter battles. Death was certain. But it was the only way that they could inflict the greatest loss on the enemy forces. The enemy realised that the defenders were very few in number and there was no hope of any reinforcements coming to their help and was content not to attack the little fort. When the second brave band of soldiers had been killed, Ajit Singh and Jujhar Singh, the Guru's elder sons, asked for permission to ride out and face the enemy. Ajit was seventeen years old at the time and Jujhar fourteen. The Guru gave his permission and blessed them both. With them was Alam Singh who had made a name for himself as a brave warrior. From the upper storey of the fortress the Guru watched his sons engage the enemy soldiers and fight with the skill of experienced soldiers, determined that their deeds should make their father proud of them. They killed many enemy soldiers before they themselves were slain. The Guru, who had remained so calm and strong when he heard of his father's death, remained calm and strong when he saw his sons being killed. He said a little prayer, then turned again to the defence of the fortress.

The Moghul soldiers now realised that they were paying a very heavy price in terms of loss of life and decided to storm the little fortress. One group of Moghul soldiers, led by Nahar Khan, tried to climb up the wall of the fort but he was shot down by an arrow and the others fell back.

The battle was waged through the day without any sign of letting up till the Guru's force was reduced to five. Among those who died were Mukham Singh and Himmat Singh, two of the *Panj Pyare*.

The five surviving Sikhs decided that the Guru's life must be saved at all costs. The *panth* was passing through a difficult phase and only the Guru could give it the leadership that was needed for its survival. They passed a resolution, a *Gurmata,* to say that the Guru must leave Chamkaur and seek refuge in a place of safety. The Guru had at the birth of the Khalsa declared that the word of five faithful Sikhs was the word of the Guru. So, much against his will, the Guru had to bow to the resolution.

Two Sikhs, Sant Singh and Sangat Singh, rode out to fight the enemy. Sant Singh had dressed in the Guru's clothes and even wore the Guru's *kalgi* in his turban and the enemy soldiers were taken in by this deception and all attention was concentrated on Sant Singh. Taking advantage of this situation, the Guru, accompanied by Man Singh and the two surviving members of the *Panj Pyare*, Daya Singh and Dharam Singh, slipped out of Chamkaur.

Darkness had gathered. The Guru and his followers tried to cover as much distance as they could and get as far away from Chamkaur as possible. Finally, tired and footsore they came to the forest of Machiwara between Ropar and Ludhiana. Here they rested for a while. It is said that it was here that the Guru composed one of the few poems that he wrote in Punjabi, the beautiful hymn, *Mitar pyare noo hall muridan da kahna.*

One of the Guru's Sikhs saw a detachment of Moghul soldiers camped outside the forest and realised that it was not safe for the Guru to remain in the forest any longer. They found refuge in the house of a Sikh named Gulaba. By now the Moghul soldiers had realised their mistake and knew that Sant Singh, whom they had killed, was not the Guru. They also knew that the Guru had escaped, and began to search for him. Reports of this search were brought to Gulaba, but he felt that the Guru was quite safe in the upper storey of his house and no one would find him there. The Guru, however, did not want to stay in Gulaba's house any more as he did not want to endanger Gulaba.

At this time the Guru was visited by the Pathans, Ghani Khan and Nabi Khan. They were both horse traders, who had often brought horses for Guru Gobind Singh in Anandpur and had learnt to respect him and love him. Now they had heard that the Mughal forces were chasing the Guru and he was hiding somewhere near the forest of Machiwara and they came to look for him and to offer him their services. The Guru was very happy to see his old friends again.

The two Pathans found Mughal soldiers everywhere. They realised that in spite of the great love that the local people had for the Guru and their intense desire to protect him, it was only a matter of time before his whereabouts were discovered by the Moghuls. It was imperative to move the Guru to a safer place. But to do this they would have to break through the cordon of enemy soldiers and the only way this was possible was to disguise the Guru. But when they sought to buy the means with which they could disguise the Guru they found that the Moghul soldiers checked each purchase that was made and questioned everything that seemed of the slightest suspicion. If, while making their purchase, they aroused the soldiers' suspicion, their plan would fail even before they had begun to put it into operation. They would have to try and get what they needed from some of the Guru's well-wishers. When they were returning to Gulaba's house they glanced through the open door of his neighbour's house and saw a middle-aged woman sitting at a loom weaving a piece of very fine cotton cloth. The two Pathans looked at each other and smiled: they had found what they were looking for. They stopped at the door and greeted the woman. She stopped in her work to answer their greeting.

"That is very fine cloth that you are weaving," Nabi Khan said.

"Yes," she answered proudly, smiling at them as she spoke.

"It is very fine cloth indeed."

"We would like to buy it," Ghani Khan offered. The woman smiled again.

"It is not for sale," she said firmly and turned back to her work.

"We will pay you three times, four times the cost of the cloth because it is such fine cloth," Ghani Khan said. The woman only shook her head from side to side and went on with her work.

"You do not understand," Nabi Khan was getting irritated and his voice was a little sharp. Again the woman stopped in her work and looked at them.

"We will pay you in silver." Then he shot a quick look around the house. "I can see from the condition of your house that you need the silver."

"Yes, I am a poor woman," she said in a soft voice, "and I need the silver. But I will not sell this cloth for that need. This cloth is for my Guru. When I began to weave it I told myself that I would weave it for my Guru. Don't you understand, this is why it has come out as such a fine cloth.

I have never woven such fine cloth before." The Pathans knew that they were defeated, they would never be able to make the woman part with the cloth. They looked at the cloth one last time, then turned and walked away. They walked a dozen steps when Nabi Khan stopped and turned back.

"And who is your Guru, mother?" he asked. The woman held the cloth to her chest. "My Guru is Guru Gobind Singh," she said and there was such love, such joy on her face that the Pathans' hearts beat with excitement. They had found their answer. They looked at each other again. With the look that passed between them they had taken the decision to share their secret with the woman.

"If it is Guru Gobind Singh that you want to give the cloth to you will not have to go far," Nabi Khan said gently. They saw the excitement leap like wild fire in the woman's eyes. She jumped to her feet letting the precious cloth fall to the ground. She took a few steps to the door. "Oh, where is he? Take me to him, take me to him please." Nabi Khan took the two steps to the door in one leap. He held the woman's arm gently and seated her down again. "First we have something to tell you. It is very important and you must listen very carefully." He made a signal towards the open door with his eyes and head and Gani Khan, understanding the signal, closed the door.

It was dark inside the room and the two Pathans sat down at the woman's feet. Very patiently and simply they told her of the Guru's position and the danger he was in. They told her of their plan to disguise him and get him away to a place of safety. They told her of their difficulty in trying to make this plan work. Her devotion to her Guru, her awareness of the danger he was in, gave her mind a sharpness that she had never before possessed. She gave the Pathans some food to eat. It was simple, rough food and very little even of that. But they ate it with gratitude and listened to her as she wove her plans and almost immediately after the meal put them into action.

The only dye that was available was a deep blue dye — the blue that is the honoured colour of most Muslim saints. So the dye was mixed in an earthen pot, the cloth was dyed, dried and then cut and stitched into a robe.

So it was that the Guru was dressed in the robes of a saint, put into a palanquin and carried by the palanquin bearers — his three faithful Sikhs and Gani Khan, out of Gulaba's village. The doors of the palanquin had been veiled by thick curtains to guard them against curious eyes. Whenever they were stopped and asked as to who was in the palanquin, the palanquin bearers would reply "Uch *da Pir*" — or the holy man from Uch. Uch was very famous centre of Muslim saints or Pirs, thirty-eight miles from Bahawalpur. The moment the Muslims heard the name they fell on their knees and asked for the Pir's blessings.

The small group stopped for a few days in the village of Hehar. Kirpal Das, the head of the Udasis who had fought so bravely for the Guru in the battle of Bhangani, lived here. He welcomed the Guru and his companions. The Guru said goodbye to his two Pathan friends and in recognition of their courage and all the difficulties they had faced to help him, he gave them a certificate in which he praised them. This certificate or *hukamnama* is still in the custody of the descendants of the Pathans. Sikhs even today go to see this and express their thanks to the family of those who helped their Guru when he needed help the most.

After a few days the Guru noticed that Kirpal Das was behaving in a strange way. It did not take him long to understand what was on the Mahant's mind. He realised that this was not the Kirpal Das he had once known. Now Kirpal Das was the head of a rich *dera* and was used to a luxurious, settled life. He was worried about what would happen to him when the Moghul authorities discovered that he had given shelter to their enemy. To spare the Mahant any trouble the Guru decided to move on.

He came at last to Jatpura where he was received by Rai Kalha, the Muslim chief. Rai Kalha welcomed him to his home and treated him with great respect and affection. The Guru was tired after all the travelling but his spirit was still strong and full of hope. This strength remained even after he heard the news of the terrible death that his two younger sons had suffered.

Mata Gujari and her two younger grandsons, Zorawar, aged nine, and Fateh Singh, aged seven, had been brought by Gangu to his village, Sahar. At the beginning he looked after them well. Then he noticed that there were three things that Mata Gujari never let out of her sight, her two grandsons and her saddle bag. He was sure that the saddle bag had something very valuable in it. One night while Mata Gujari lay asleep, her dear grandsons hugged closely to her heart, Gangu came quietly into the room and stole the saddle bag. He was very happy to see that the bag contained a large number of gold coins. In the morning Mata Gujari saw that her bag was missing. It contained all the money that she had and now she would have to depend on the charity of others to look after her grandsons.

"Gangu," she said when he brought their food to them.

"You remember that saddle bag that you carried up for me when we came here? It was here last night, but it is missing this morning."

"Are you saying that I stole it?" Gangu asked, pretending to be angry.

"I am not saying that," Mata Gujari said, patiently, adding, "I am only saying that it was here last night and it is not here now."

"This is the reward you are giving me," Gangu began to shout: "After all that I have done, I have risked my life to protect you and the two boys. I have brought you to my own house but instead of expressing gratitude and thanking me for all this, you call me a thief."

He left the room and went down the street shouting at the top of his voice.

"Look at these people from the Guru's household," he said.

"I did everything in my power to help his mother and his two young sons and see what I get in return : I am accused of stealing their gold." In this way the villagers learnt that Gangu's guests were the Guru's mother and his two young sons and this news was carried to the village headman. The headman knew that he would get a generous reward if he brought this news to the officials. Mata Gujari and her two grandsons were apprehended and brought before Wazir Khan, the Governor of Sirhind and were locked up in a tower in the fort of Sirhind. It is said that Nawaz Sher Mohammad Khan, the Nawab of Malerkotla, appealed to Wazir Khan to spare the young lives.

"It is against the teachings of the Prophet to take the lives of helpless women and innocent children. You can hold them as prisoners or send them to the Emperor's court. But do not take their lives."

It seems that for a while Wazir Khan was inclined to listen to the Nawab's advice. But then another nobleman intervened:

"Do not forget they are Guru Gobind Singh's sons. When they grow up they will be like their father and will cause much trouble to us. Far better to kill them now, while they are still harmless."

Wazir Khan ordered that the two boys should be brought before him. When the messenger came to fetch them Mata Gujari feared the worst. She held them close to her heart and would not let them go. Zorawar, the elder of the two, felt his grandmother's frail thin body trembling with fear as she held him close. He kissed her and said:

"Do not be afraid Mataji. The worst that they can do to us is to put us to death." For a moment it was as if her young Gobind was speaking to her. She was proud that the little boys had already learnt to be so much like their father. She wiped the tears from her eyes, blessed her grandsons and let them go.

The two young boys entered the Governor's presence without a sign of fear in their bearing or on their faces.

"Have you no manners?" Suchanand, one of Wazir Khan's ministers, asked them. "You have come into the great Subedar's presence and you do not bow before him."

"We have been taught from an early age to bow only before God and before the Guru." Zorawar answered in a quiet but firm voice. "We cannot go against what we have been taught."

Wazir Khan tried to work out a compromise. If he could convert the boys to Islam he would not have to put them to death and God would not be angry with him. If they accepted Islam as their religion the Moghul Emperor too would be very pleased with him.

"I can see that you are brave young boys. You will grow up to be fine men and will be famous throughout the Moghul Empire. I know that you will occupy high position first here with me in Sirhind and then later at the Emperor's court. All you have to do is to accept Islam and become Muslims."

The two boys looked at each other and exchanged a smile. Then Zorawar turned back to Wazir Khan.

"You forget to whom you speak." His voice was louder now.

"We are the grandsons of Guru Teg Bahadur who gave up his life rather than give up his faith. The blood of Guru Arjun Dev, Guru Hargobind and Guru Gobind Singh runs in our veins. Like our grandfather, we will give up our lives but not our faith."

Wazir Khan ordered that the boys should be taken back to the fort. He tried every trick he knew to persuade the boys to change their religion. He tried to offer them all kinds of rewards if they would accept his proposal. "Nothing that you can offer will tempt us. Nothing that you can offer can be equal to the joy of knowing that we carry out our Guru's will.

Take our lives if you wish to, but we will never change our faith."

Wazir Khan now knew that the boys would not change their minds. The *qazi* advised Wazir Khan that the boys should be bricked up alive. And the boys were made to stand side by side and the wall was built up on both sides of them. When the wall reached their chests Wazir Khan asked the masons to stop. "It is not too late," he said as gently as he could. "There is still time. Even now if you agree to become Muslims your lives will be spared." The boys looked at one another again and smiled. Then they looked back at Wazir Khan and shook their heads. Wazir Khan signalled to the masons who completed their work. This terrible crime was committed on December 27, 1704. Part of this wall still stands in the Gurudwara at Fatehgarh Sahib. Three days later, Mata Gujari, overcome with the grief of her tragic loss, left this world.

News of this tragedy was brought to Guru Gobind Singh while he was at Jatpura. The Guru's cup of grief was now full to the brim but he took this tragic happening in his stride like he had done everything else and remained calm and strong. He was always a source of strength to his followers and inspired them to remain calm and brave and not to waver in their faith. He showed through his great courage that there was still light in the darkness that seemed to have gathered around them.

The Final Years

*F*rom Jatpura the Guru moved on to Dina, a village near Nabha where he stayed for some time. As the news of the Guru's presence in Dina spread through the Punjab, his followers flocked to the village. The news of the murder of the Guru's young sons had spread like wildfire and angered all the Sikhs, and they were determined to avenge this terrible crime. They came, armed with whatever weapons they could lay their hands on, and offered their services to the Guru. The core of the new army was provided by three brothers, Shamira, Lakhmira and Takht Mal.

When Wazir Khan heard reports of this new gathering of the Sikhs, he sent a message to Shamira to surrender the Guru to him failing which Shamira himself would be killed. Shamira wrote back to say that he was ready to give up his life in his Guru's defence. Wazir Khan now began to prepare for battle.

The Guru heard of Wazir Khan's preparations. He had been welcomed by the people of Dina with open arms and had been given great love and affection by them. He did not wish to turn their home into a battlefield and moved on to Kotkapura. Here, too, large numbers of Sikhs came to offer their services to the Guru. During this time he was able to bring together all the Sikhs who had been scattered after the desertion of Anandpur. In addition, many non-Sikhs were influenced by the Guru and his teachings by his great courage and calm in the face of such intense suffering, and had become his followers. After a while the Guru moved on from Kotkapura. It was during this time that he made peace with the descendants of Prithi Chand, the eldest brother of Guru Arjun Dev. Baba Kaul, the direct descendant of Prithi Chand who lived in Dhilwan, received Guru Gobind Singh with affection and gave him new robes. It was here that the Guru finally discarded the blue robes that he had worn to help him to escape from Gulaba's house. These tattered robes were taken up by a group of Nihangs and it is from them that the blue dress of the Nihangs came into being. Baba Kaul's grandson took *amrit* and so this branch of Sikhs was brought back into the mainstream.

When the Guru reached Khidrana, the forty Sikhs who had abandoned him in Anandpur, came back to fight on his side again. They had been consumed by feelings of guilt and shame ever since they had deserted the Guru and did not have the courage to offer their services to the Guru again. It was the woman warrior, Mai Bhago, who convinced them that the Guru would forgive them and led them back to the Guru.

The enemy was approaching. The Guru placed a small band of Sikhs in the grove of trees around the water tank and asked them to spread sheets and coverlets over the trees so that from a distance it seemed that the Guru's army was camping here. The Guru and his main army took up position on a hill nearly a mile away.

Wazir Khan and his army drew near and stopped a little way away from the water tank. Seeing what looked like tents Wazir Khan was sure that the Guru himself had camped amongst the trees. He exhorted his men to give of their best in this final battle of their war against the 'infidel'.

A fierce battle followed. The Guru and his soldiers rained arrows and spears on Wazir Khan's army. The Moghul soldiers were confused because they had not expected an attack from this quarter. The small band of Sikhs in the forest fought with great courage because they were determined to show the Guru that they were not cowards and to wipe away the memory of what they had done at Anandpur.

The Moghul force suffered great losses because they did not know how to cope with the Guru's attack from the hill. At the end, overwhelmed by thirst and exhaustion, they retreated from the battlefield.

There was great rejoicing amongst the Guru's soldiers, but when they came down to the tank they were greeted with a dead silence. As they rode among the trees they found that every single member of that band of brave soldiers had been killed. As the Guru rode among the bodies he heard a soft moan. He dismounted and searched amongst the bodies and found Maha Singh, the leader of the band of forty, seriously wounded, and almost at the point of death.

The Guru wiped his face and blessed him. "Ask what you want," the Guru said, cradling the wounded man's head in his lap. "For your family, if not for yourself. Ask for anything and I will ensure that it is granted." Maha Singh smiled through his pain:

"All I seek is your forgiveness, my lord. It is all that my colleagues desired. Give us back the letter with which we deserted you." It was a letter that the Guru had always carried on his person. He took it out now and tore it into small pieces, pieces which the wind picked up and scattered all around. Maha Singh watched the tiny pieces of paper flutter away. He looked once at his Guru, then still with the smile on his lips, he closed his eyes, and went to join his companions.

The Guru found Mai Bhago, the leader of these Sikhs, severely wounded but still alive. She was carried back to the camp and her wounds were tended to: She was the sole survivor of the Khidrana Sikhs.

The Guru said a special prayer for the forty martyrs and blessed them as the *Chali Mukte* (the Forty Immortals). They are remembered by all Sikhs in the *ardas* that is said at the conclusion of all Sikh religious ceremonies. Khidrana came to be known as Muktsar, or the pool of salvation in memory of the *muktas* and every year a big fair is held in Muktsar in memory of this battle and of the redemption of the forty Sikhs. Thousands of pilgrims come from far and near and the great acts of heroism of the *muktas* are retold again and again and in each retelling the *muktas* come alive again and are truly immortal.

The Guru spent a year travelling in the country around Muktsar. This region is the Malwa region and the inhabitants are mostly Jats, simple, hardworking and straight forward people, people who like freedom of both thought and action. They found that the Guru's teachings were very simple and practical and gave freedom to people who had been bound by caste and by ceremonies and rituals. As a result many people from this region joined this new faith.

The Guru camped in Lakhi jungle, a forest between the towns of Bhatinda and Kot Kapura, for a while and then moved on to Talwandi Sabo where he was greeted with great warmth by Bhai Dalla, the landlord. Dalla extended all hospitality to the Guru and made the Guru and his followers welcome to his home and the Guru decided to stay for some time in Talwandi. Talwandi soon came to be known as Damdama, the breathing place, and the Guru was visited by a large number of followers who brought him gifts and horses and weapons. New followers continued to join the Khalsa in ever-increasing numbers. Dalla himself took *amrit*.

Damdama also became the centre of great literary and cultural activity. Many of the poets and musicians who had been with the Guru at Paonta and Anandpur came here and joined the Guru and it seemed that the spirit of Anandpur had now come to abide in Damdama.

It was at Damdama that Mata Sundari and Mata Sahib Devan rejoined the Guru. They had been all this time in Delhi and when their host was sure that the troubled times were over he escorted them from Delhi to Damdama. The two ladies were overcome with grief when they heard of the loss of their four sons. But the Guru consoled them. "Look around you," he said, indicating the thousands of Sikhs who lived in Damdama. "You have thousands of sons still alive. Do not mourn for what you have lost. Instead, rejoice at what still remains to you."

From Damdama the Guru wrote a long letter to Aurangzeb who was still in the Deccan. He told the Emperor the story of his leaving Anandpur and how he was attacked by the Moghul forces from the rear. He accused the Emperor of betrayal as the Emperor had promised him a safe passage if he left Anandpur. He also described in the letter the cruelty of Wazir Khan towards his younger sons, which was an act against the teachings of Islam. This letter was carried to Aurangzeb by Daya Singh and Dharam Singh.

Guru Gobind Singh's stay in Damdama was marked by the fortunate arrival of Bhai Mani Singh, a great scholar and a childhood friend of the Guru. The Granth compiled by Guru Arjun Dev had been copied over and over again and these copies were not always rechecked against the original Granth. As a result many mistakes and discrepancies had come into these copies and there was great need for making a new, authorized copy of the Granth, which would be free of all these mistakes. The Guru asked Bhai Mani Singh to undertake the task of writing this work.

Months were spent in copying out the Granth and correcting all the mistakes and differences. The Guru also added one hundred and fifteen hymns composed by his father Guru Teg Bahadur to the original text compiled by Guru Arjun Dev. He did not include any of his own compositions.

The Guru wrote many poems while he was in Damdama. These poems along with much of his earlier work were compiled by Bhai Mani Singh into another Granth called Dasam Granth, or Dasven Padsah ka Granth. Most of the works included in the Dasam Granth were written in Anandpur. The Dasam Granth is made of eighteen works, among them Bichitra Natak, Chandi di Var, Shabad Hazare, Zafarnama and Jaap Sahib. They are written in four languages: Braj, Hindi, Persian and Punjabi. They contain stories from Hindu mythology, poems which are religious in nature and are used in Sikh religious ceremonies. Some works are philosophical. There are also some works like the Bichitra Natak and the Zafarnama which are autobiographical and tell us about the Guru's life and personality and about his times.

Bhai Mani Singh took nine years to complete this work which he undertook after the Guru's death. There are many versions of the *Dasam Granth* in existence but the one written in Bhai Mani Singh's own handwriting is the one that is generally recognised as authentic.

The work on the new version of the Granth and the Guru's own poetic work inspired all the other scholars and writers in his group. There was great literary activity and Damdama soon came to be known as Guru ka Kashi, after Kashi (Benaras) which has always been a great centre of scholarship. For a long time after the Guru's death Damdama continued to live up to this title and there was a very strong and distinct tradition of scholarship specially related to Sikh studies. Teachers and scholars from Damdama were regarded with special respect and copies of the Granth which had been written in Damdama were much sought after.

Looking back now the literary achievements in Damdama seem almost miraculous because of the couple of years that the Guru lived in the area around Muktsar, his stay in Damdama was not more than a few months. In a few short months, men who were known mainly for their skills in battle, for their courage in the face of the enemy, had set up a centre of learning and literary activity. Damdama is thus a measure of the strength of the inspiration that the Guru gave his followers.

The day of the Baisakhi festival came while the Guru was at Damdama. From Guru Amar Das's time Baisakhi had become the most important festival for the Sikhs and Guru Gobind Singh had added a special dimension by making it the birthday of the Khalsa. The past year had seen a resurgence in the Sikh faith, the number of devotees had increased manifold and the devotion of the Khalsa to their Guru and to their faith had grown from strength to strength. After having fought a series of fierce battles the Sikhs at last had peace. All this found expression in the fervour and joy with which the Sikhs celebrated their festival. Thousands of people thronged to Damdama and the fields around the town became one big fair-ground. The celebration of the festival became a celebration of life itself — the Sikh way of life. Perhaps never before and never since has the Baisakhi festival been celebrated the way it was celebrated that year. Ever since the celebration of Baisakhi at Damdama has become a very important occasion for the Sikhs.

Aurangzeb was at this time still in the Deccan, in Ahmednagar. He was now ninety years old and had become frail and was so ill that he was largely confined to his bed. With his age and his long illness his mind had begun to wander. He would confuse the past with the present, talk about things that had already happened as if they were happening at that time and repeat himself over and over again.

His son Azam was with him in the Deccan and took care of his father. Azam was an ambitious man and hoped to be the next Emperor after his father's death. He knew that his brothers Muazzam and Kam Baksh nurtured a similar ambition. By keeping the news of the Emperor's illness and of his impending death a secret, Azam would keep the initiative in his own hands. When the Emperor did finally die his brothers would be totally unprepared; he would declare himself Emperor and strengthen his position even before the news of the Emperor's death could reach his brothers. Because of this Aurangzeb was kept under very strict guard and only his very close relatives and attendants were allowed to meet him. All other communications with the Emperor had to be made through Azam. Daya Singh and Dharam Singh said that their Guru's instructions were to deliver the letter to the Emperor himself and refused to hand it over to Azam. As a result Azam gave orders that they were not to be allowed to meet the Emperor. The two Sikhs waited patiently and came to the court and requested to see the Emperor and each day this request was refused. The days rolled into months and at last when it seemed that they would never be admitted into Aurangzeb's presence, they sent a message to the Guru explaining their predicament. He wrote back to advise them that they should stay on in the court till such time as they were able to meet the Emperor. The Guru also wrote to some very influential Sikhs in Ahmednagar asking them to use their good offices in the court to get permission for Daya Singh and Dharam Singh to meet the Emperor. One of these Sikhs knew an official from the Emperor's court whom he requested to put in a word with the Emperor so that the Guru's messengers would be able to deliver the letter personally. The official waited for the right moment to speak to the Emperor.

The moment the official had been waiting for at last presented itself.

"Wazir Khan, Wazir Khan," the Emperor called in one of his troubled moments. He was constantly doing this — calling out for people who were far away or who were long dead and gone. His attendants had learnt how to deal with this situation. The official stepped forward.

"Your Majesty, Wazir Khan has gone out on some important business. He will be back in a little while. But if there is an urgent message to be sent, tell your servant, he will be honoured to deliver it for you."

"Tell him he must not do it." His voice took on a great urgency, his eyes burned with an intense light. "On no account must he do it. I do not want the blood of two innocent young boys on my hands. Allah will never forgive me for being a party to this sin. He will not admit me into his presence when my time comes." His voice became louder and stronger as he spoke, the intensity of his speech communicated itself to those around him and there was dead silence in the room, a silence into which his words fell one at a time like pebbles in a still pond of water, and touched the hearts of all the listeners. "No matter what Gobind Singh does, the boys are innocent. They must not be harmed in any way." With a supreme effort the Emperor raised himself up. His old authority and strength seemed to have come back.

"Go, go tell him my wish. Tell him that if he violates it, it will be upon the pain of death." The command was clear and strong, the command of an Emperor to his subject. His voice at last gave way and he broke into a fit of coughing. On and on the coughing came, wracking his feeble frame. His attendants lowered him to the bed. One of them held up his head, another held a glass of water to his lips. The sick man tried to take a drink of water. A few drops went down his throat, most of it dribbled down into his long flowing beard. At last the coughing ceased. The Emperor closed his eyes and it seemed that he had drifted off to sleep. The courtiers looked at each other. It was obvious to them that the Emperor was troubled by a strong feeling of guilt at what had been done to the Guru's sons.

Suddenly the Emperor's eyes flew open. His bony hand searched out and caught the official's wrist. The grip was strong as steel.

"Tell me," he said in a firm quiet voice. "Why doesn't anyone come to see me?" The official had no answer and looked away.

"You do not need to be afraid," Aurangzeb said in a gentle voice. "We have known each other for many years and there are a few secrets between us. Tell me why none comes to see me anymore."

"You are sick, my lord. You need all the rest that you can get. This is why Prince Azam has forbidden any visitors from coming in to you. It is out of consideration for you." The Emperor chuckled and once again he broke into a fit of coughing. When the coughing ceased he looked up into the official's eyes.

"Consideration for me or consideration for himself?" he said with a smile.

"Has he already set himself up as an Emperor? Or is this merely a way of keeping my sickness from his brothers?" The official realised that at this moment the Emperor's mind was as lucid and clear as it had ever been. He realised that this was his chance and he grabbed it immediately.

"If it is the lack of visitors that troubles your Majesty, this can be corrected immediately. You have two visitors outside who have been waiting for three months for an audience with you."

"Three months? They are really persistent visitors or perhaps their need is pressing. Who are they?"

"They are messengers from Guru Gobind Singh, the Guru of the Sikhs. They bring a letter from him."

"A letter from Guru Gobind Singh." The Emperor's face darkened and his eyes took on a far-away look. He was silent for a long while and the official thought he had lost him again. "Bring them to me." Aurangzeb said. "Wait, first straighten my cap and my bed clothes. When they go back to their Guru they must not report that they met a battered old man. They must report that they met the Emperor of Hindustan, slightly infirm no doubt, but still the Emperor."

He looked up at the official and there was a twinkle in his eyes which had not been there for many, many years.

The two Sikhs, who had been waiting for so long, were finally admitted to the Emperor's presence. Greetings were exchanged and the Emperor asked if they had had any trouble at his court. The two Sikhs said that there had been no trouble, they were quite comfortable. "You have a letter for me from your Guru," the Emperor asked, stretching out his hand. "Give it to me." The official took the letter from Daya Singh and brought it to the Emperor. Aurangzeb opened it and scanned a few lines. Then he looked up again.

"These eyes grow old and tired and cannot read such fine writing. Manzar Khan, come and read this for me." Manzar Khan was the Emperor's favourite scribe. He also had a beautiful deep voice and the Emperor loved to listen to him when he read aloud. Now Manzar Khan came forward to read the Guru's letter.

"Hail to Aurangzeb, Emperor of Hindustan," the letter began. Aurangzeb smiled and nodded his head with satisfaction.

"King of Kings, expert swordsman and rider, Aurangzeb you are handsome and intelligent. You have proved that not only are you skilled in battle but also a clever administrator. You are generous to people who follow your religion and firm in crushing your enemies. You have given away much land and wealth. Your generosity is great and in battle you are as firm as a mountain. You are the king of kings and ornament of the thrones of the World." Manzar Khan paused and looked at the Emperor. The Emperor lay there, eyes looking straight ahead, a smile playing at his lips. He was old and experienced enough not to be fooled by flattery. But this praise came from an enemy, an enemy who had fought many battles with the Emperor's forces, an enemy who himself was recognised as a great soldier, a generous leader, one whom his people called the true Emperor. This praise could only be true praise and it acted like a balm to the Emperor's tired soul. For a long while he lay there letting his mind go over the Guru's words. Manzar Khan had a chance to glance through the rest of the letter. He hoped that he would not have to read it. He hoped that the Emperor would drift off to sleep and the rest of the letter would remain unread. But this was not to be.

"Why do you stop? Go on."

The scribe hesitated for a moment, then he cleared his throat and read on.

"You are the monarch of the world, but religion remains far away from you. He who respects his religion never breaks his promise. I have no faith in your promises. Anyone who respects your oath will be a ruined man. You made God your witness and gave me a promise. Yet you broke this promise. This means that you do not know God and believe not in Muhammad. If the Prophet was present in this world I would make it my special mission to tell him of your treachery."

The scribe had tried to keep his voice soft and neutral. But the vigour of the epistle, the passion of the feeling would not be denied and soon he found himself reading the Guru's words with some of the Guru's feelings.

"Because you are not a man of God, your Governors and officers are not men of God. They deny Mohammad, everyday they go against the teachings of Islam. They violate the basic rules which have made Islam one of the greatest religions of the world. What Wazir Khan did to my children is common knowledge, every one knows of this. Was this in keeping with the teaching of Islam? And yet he remains unpunished. He rules as the Governor of Sirhind and is marked for special favour by you. Perhaps he did what he did at your command..."

"No, no," the Emperor had pushed himself up again. His voice was almost a shout and his whole frame was shaking with emotion.

"I swear I had no knowledge of this terrible deed. I swear I was not party to it." His voice came in gasps and it seemed that the coughing would come upon him again. His attendants hurried to his bedside but he pushed them away.

"Believe me Gobind Singh," his voice was quieter now, quieter and more controlled. "I know not who I am, where I shall go and what will happen to this sinner full of sins. My years have gone by profitless. God has been in my heart but my darkened eyes have recognised not His light. I have greatly sinned and know not what torment awaits me in the Hereafter. But believe me Gobind Singh, sinner as I am that is one sin that I am not guilty of — I did not kill your sons, I did not kill your sons." His body shook with sobs but no tears flowed in his eyes to give him relief. Many of his listeners wept, even the Sikhs were touched by the old man's remorse.

He lay back again and closed his eyes. The silence stretched on for a long while. The official indicated to the Sikhs that they should leave as quickly as they could, and

Daya Singh and Dharam Singh shuffled backwards towards the door. But the Emperor had not finished yet.

"Wait," he said when they were almost near the door.

"Gobind Singh's letter must not go unanswered. Manzar Khan have you your pen and ink ready?"

"Yes my Lord," once more the scribe came forward. He took his seat close to the Emperor's bedside.

"Address the letter to Mun'im Khan, my Wazir at Delhi." The Emperor spoke slowly, a few words at a time, so that the scribe would be able to write it all down.

"Tell him that we are very impressed by Gobind Singh's honesty and courage. By his deep and abiding faith in God and his justice. Tell him that henceforth, all friendliness is to be shown to Gobind Singh and to his Sikhs. He must invite Gobind Singh to Delhi. Here he must convey to him our Royal *farman,* inviting him to come to us here in the Deccan.

"Instruct Mun'im Khan to give him as much money as may be needed for his expenses and also to give him a royal escort so that all will know he comes as our cherished guest. Muhammad Beg, you will personally carry this letter and see that it is delivered to our Wazir. Now go," he said waving impatiently to all those around him. "Go, we are tired and wish to rest."

They all bowed to the ailing Emperor and stepped away from his chamber, the two Sikhs amongst them. They were happy that their mission had been accomplished. Mohammad Beg, the Emperor's trusted macebearer, left for Delhi with the Emperor's letter and shortly afterwards Daya Singh and Dharam Singh also set out to bring the good news of the Emperor's change of heart to their Guru.

At Damdama the Guru waited for news from his two disciples. He knew that he had told them to be patient, to wait till they could see Aurangzeb. But as the months went by without any news from them, the Guru became anxious. During these months the only news from Ahmednagar that reached Damdama were reports of the Emperor's growing illness. Each report confirmed the fact that Aurangzeb was drawing quickly towards his end. Some inner restlessness seemed to possess the Guru. Aurangzeb and he had been enemies for long and Aurangzeb had done everything in his power to harm the Guru and his family. Yet the Guru knew that he had to say what was in his heart, he had to let Aurangzeb know before the end. If he could be sure that his letter had been read he would be content. But there had been no further news from Daya Singh and every day seemed to bring Aurangzeb's end closer. He felt that he himself must go to the Deccan. Once having taken his decision the Guru wasted no time in carrying it out.

Dalla Singh and the other Sikhs made every effort to dissuade the Guru but at last they knew that they could not hold their Guru in Damdama any longer. They bowed their heads in grief and accepted the Guru's decision to leave.

The Guru knew that the journey would be difficult. He was also not sure of what awaited him once he reached Ahmednagar. So he decided to spare Mata Sundari and Mata Sahib Devan the difficulties of the journey and the uncertainty of the future. He decided that the ladies would go back to Delhi where they would remain till it was safe for them to join him.

Mata Sundari went about making preparations for the departure with self-confidence and authority. She carried her grief at her impending separation from the Guru with quiet dignity. Watching her as she worked the Guru marvelled at how far she had come from the shy confused girl who had first come to Anandpur, the girl who had been so helpless that she had had to turn to Mata Jeeto for help to look after her son. There was now a great maturity and mellowness in the way she conducted herself ever in the way she made her farewell to her lord when he came down to the courtyard where his horse waited for him.

Mata Sahib Devan stood on the fringe of the crowd to catch one last glimpse of her lord as he rode away. As the

Guru turned to mount his horse he caught sight of her and hesitated. Once again she had merged herself into the crowd. She knew that she might not see him again for a long time and yet she had made no deliberate effort to come into his presence. She had remained as self-effacing as she had always been, content to go about her work, content merely to be under the same roof as her Guru. The Guru raised his foot to the stirrup and found that he could not go away like this, he had to acknowledge her presence, acknowledge all that she had done. He pulled his foot down and turned to her.

"You wait on the fringe of the crowd to see me go," he said speaking to her. "Yet you make no effort to come and meet me, to say goodbye. You know that is your right."

"No my lord," Sahib Devan said with lowered head. "That is not my right. It never was. I gave that right up in order to marry you and I have never desired it, never needed it. It was enough for me to know that you were there."

The Guru's heart filled once again with emotion at the greatness of this lady's sacrifice.

"And now when I am not there?"

"It will be enough for me that I am allowed to wait for your return."

"This is all?" The Guru asked in a gentle voice. "That is all that you seek? Don't you ever feel cheated, feel that your husband has been able to give you so little compared to what other husbands give their wives?" Sahib Devan's head came up with a start and she looked at last into the Guru's eyes and smiled. "It is enough that you should question this. In the flush of your generosity you forget how much you have given me. Till the end of time whenever a Khalsa receives *amrit* and you are named as his father, I will be remembered as his mother. You have made me immortal, you have made our relationship immortal, and you have made my motherhood immortal. Can any wife be given more, can any wife ask for more?"

There was nothing more to say. The Guru placed his hand on Sahib Devan's head and blessed her. Then he turned and mounted his horse and rode out of Damdama.

The Guru was accompanied by a small band of selected Sikhs. He had forbidden all others from accompanying him. The Guru rode through Rajasthan and camped at a place called Bhangaur. It was here that he was met by Daya Singh who was returning from Ahmednagar. Daya Singh gave the Guru details of his meeting with Aurangzeb and of the Emperor's orders to the Wazir of Delhi. Shortly afterwards news came of the Emperor's death.

Almost at once a war of succession broke out. Azam lost no time in declaring himself as the Emperor and began to make preparation for the battle that he knew he would have to fight with his brothers and marched towards Delhi.

Muazzam, the eldest son, was away in Afghanistan, fighting a campaign. When news of his father's death reached him he too marched back immediately towards the imperial city. Both brothers knew that whoever gained control there would strengthen his claims to the throne. Bhai Nand Lal, who had at one time been Muazzam's secretary and close friend, wrote to him, advising him to seek the Guru's help in his fight against his brother. The Guru was close to Delhi when he received Muazzam's appeal.

Muazzam was the eldest son of the Emperor and the throne was rightfully his. When he had come to the Punjab to subdue the hill Rajas he had carefully maintained his peace with the Guru and this had given the Guru twelve valuable years in which to prepare his army. Muazzam was influenced by the teachings of the Sufi saints and was not only liberal-minded but also tolerant of other religions. The Guru decided to help Muazzam.

A detachment of Sikh soldiers under the command of Dharam Singh was sent to help Muazzam. The two brothers met in battle at Jajau near Agra, on June 8, 1707 and a fierce battle raged for three days in which Azam was defeated and killed. Muazzam became the Emperor and took the title of Bahadur Shah and sent a special messenger to the Guru to convey the news of his victory and also to thank him for his help.

The Guru set out to visit the holy cities of Mathura and Brindaban. While he was camping in a garden outside Agra the Emperor heard of his arrival and sent a special invitation to the Guru to visit him.

It was a very warm and cordial meeting. The Emperor showed a lot of affection and respect for the Guru and thanked him for accepting his invitation and for his timely help in the battle of Jajau. Cordial relations were established and the Emperor requested for another meeting. When they parted the Emperor gave the Guru many costly presents, including a *kalgi*, a jewelled dagger and a robe of honour.

The Guru felt that this was the beginning of a new chapter in the relationship between the Moghuls and the Sikhs and was hopeful that under the liberal Bahadur Shah the Sikhs would, once again, be allowed to live in peace. With this hope the Guru stayed on in the area and met the Emperor a number of times. He hoped that some positive agreement would be reached between him and the Emperor before he returned to the Punjab.

But news came that Bahadur Shah's youngest brother Kam Baksh had risen in rebellion against the Emperor and the Emperor left for the Deccan to suppress this rebellion. He invited the Guru to accompany him at least part of the way and the Guru, hoping for some positive commitment from the Emperor, accepted this invitation.

Their subsequent meetings did not fulfil the promise that the earlier meetings had held out. The Emperor talked vaguely of liberalism and tolerance but was not prepared to make any concrete promises and the Guru soon realised that further meetings would not serve any purpose. It also became apparent that the Emperor had asked the Guru to accompany him because he hoped for the Guru's support not only against his brother but also against the Marathas. The Guru realising that no purpose would be served in accompanying the Emperor's party any further, said goodbye to the Emperor and broke away.

The Guru reached Nanded and was charmed by the beauty of the place. One of the most beautiful sounds to the Guru's ears was the sound of flowing water. At Patna, from the moment of his birth, he had heard the sound of the Ganga as it flowed past the city. At Anandpur during his childhood he had heard the murmur of the Satluj and at Paonta where had had spent some of the happiest years of his life, he had found pleasure in the sound of the Yamuna as it raced down to the plains. Here in Nanded it was the soft, sleepy tone of the Godavari that came to his ears. He decided to rest here for a little while.

It was at Nanded that the Guru met a *sadhu* who had renounced the world, a Bairagi by the name of Madho Das. He was born in Kashmir and had been very fond of hunting. One day he killed a deer and found two young ones in her womb. This affected him so much that he renounced the world and moved down to Nanded where he set up a hermitage on the banks of the Godavari. His fame as a religious and holy man had spread far and wide and it was said that his spiritual power was so strong that he could perform miracles.

Madho Das came often to listen to the Guru and was greatly influenced by his teachings. One day he fell at the Guru's feet and said, "I am your Banda." The Guru gave him *amrit* and he entered the Khalsa Panth and was given the name of Banda Singh. But he was to become famous as Banda Bahadur, one of the most heroic figures in Sikh history.

Once the news of the Guru's presence began to spread. Sikhs in ever-increasing numbers flocked to Nanded to get his blessings. Many Hindus and Muslims also came to listen to the teachings of the Guru. Meanwhile in Sirhind, Wazir

Khan had heard reports of the help that the Guru had given to the new Emperor and of the Emperor's growing affection for the Guru. He felt that at some stage the Guru might ask the Emperor to punish Wazir Khan for the cowardly murder of his two young sons and the Emperor in a burst of affection might agree to do so. The only way to forestall this was to take the initiative in his own hands and to murder the Guru.

He called upon the services of two loyal young Pathans, Gul Khan and Jamshed Khan. These two Pathans travelled from Sirhind and caught up with the Guru's party at Nanded. They were frequent visitors to the Guru's daily prayer-meetings and even accepted *prasad* from the Guru's hands. In this manner they allayed all suspicions and they were soon allowed free access to the Guru's chambers.

After a few days the two entered the Guru's room while the Guru was resting. Gul Khan stabbed the Guru twice with his dagger. The Guru reacted with the speed of lightning and with one stroke of his sword he beheaded the Pathan. The Sikhs outside the room heard the noice, came rushing in and killed Jamshed Khan.

The Guru's wound was deep and there was a lot of bleeding. The Guru remained calm and told his followers not to panic.

Almost as soon as the attack was made, one of the Guru's visitors galloped off to Bahadur Shah who was camping nearby. Bahadur Shah immediately despatched his most experienced surgeon, Dr. Cole. The surgeon examined the wounds, stitched them up and gave the Guru some medicines. When he came again to examine the Guru after a few days the wounds had healed completely and bandages were removed. The Guru now began to go about his normal task. The *sangat* thanked God for his quick and complete recovery.

One of the Guru's devotees had presented him with a strong, heavy bow. The Guru who had always had a special love for weapons of all kinds could not resist the temptation

to try out his new bow. When he stretched the bow the
wounds burst open again. He bled profusely. He was given
the best medical aid but he knew that his end was near and
yet he remained calm as he had remained calm in the face
of all difficulties.

He asked his Sikhs to collect around him and when they
had all assembled he spoke to them:

"The one thing men dread most is death. I have always
lived close to death and looked it in the face. So should
everyone of you who claims to follow me. I will ride to my
death as a bridegroom rides to the house of his bride. So
do not grieve for me."

He recited the Japji Sahib, the morning prayer and said
the *ardas*. Then he went four times around the Granth Sahib,
and as was the custom when a new Guru was appointed,
he made an offering of five copper coins and a coconut. He
told the Sikhs that they should now look upon the Granth
as the spiritual representation of the Guru. The Granth would
be their Guru and the teachings contained in it represented
the spirit of the Gurus. He reminded them again of what he
had told them at the birth of the Khalsa in Anandpur.

"Where there are five true Sikhs assembled, there will I
be. Henceforth the Guru shall be the Khalsa. The spirit of
the Gurus has passed into the Khalsa."

The Guru breathed his last in the early hours of October
7, 1708. The Sikhs put their grief behind them and
conducted the funeral with great dignity. The sacred body
was placed on the funeral pyre, hymns were recited, prayers
were said and the pyre was lit.

For the first time the Sikhs were without a living Guru
to lead them, to give them a sense of direction. This gave
them a feeling of emptiness and of helplessness. Then they
remembered what Guru Gobind Singh had told them before
he died and turned with renewed faith to the Guru Granth
Sahib. They read the teachings of their Gurus with great
care and practised these teachings with firmness and

dedication. This helped to fill up the emptiness within them and they realised that their Guru had been right; they were as strong as they had been when he was alive.

Conclusion

Guru Gobind Singh was one of the most attractive personalities that history had thrown up in Northern India. He had captured the imagination of the people of this region as no other person had and this attracted people to Anandpur and Paonta in thousands, both the faithful and the casual visitors. They saw the Guru and took back with them a very striking picture of the Guru in their minds. They saw him with his handsome face, his intense eyes and his beautiful clothes. They saw him with his lean, sinewy body walking straight and erect and proud, his *kalgi* seeming to sweep the heavens as he walked. They saw him riding out to battle on his beautiful blue horse, his sword flashing in the sun, ready to swoop down and strike his enemy. They saw him set out hunting, his white hawk perched on his left wrist, his horse galloping with the speed of the wind till it seemed that the Guru and his horse had merged into one and there was one life that beat in both their hearts. This was the image that the people took back with them and painted for others who had not had the good fortune to see the Guru, and this is the image that has come down over the years, fixed and unaltered. Little wonder that even today the Guru is often referred to as *Kalgidhar* — the one with the *kalgi, Chityan bajawale* — the one with white hawk and *Nile ghore da asvr* — the rider on the blue horse.

The people of the north are a virile people who have faced the brunt of a hundred invasions, the anger of a hundred conquerers. They value physical strength, courage and valour in battle above all else and this the Guru showed in more than ample measure. He killed tigers in hand-to-hand fights with a few strokes of his sword, he fought against great odds and, through his personal example, led little bands of farmers against the mighty Moghul army in battle after battle. He showed great skill with the sword and with the bow and arrow, and he showed true genius as a military leader. Stories of this valour and leadership were carried far and wide and became legends in the Guru's own lifetime and over the years they have become a household heritage. They fired people's minds then, they fire people's minds now. But the image of the Guru that people carried in their minds was not all an image of blood and thunder. There was another side of the image too, a softer image, an image of kindness and of compassion even to his enemies. They had seen the tips of his arrows when he rode into battle, mounted with solid gold to give support to the dependants of the enemy soldiers who would fall to these arrows; they had seen him stopping his soldiers when they wanted to chase the fugitive soldiers of the defeated enemy, and they had seen him give to all who came to his doorstep all that was in his power to give.

For the educated and the literate there was the image of the Guru as a patron of music and learning and poetry and was a great poet himself. There was the image created by his poems themselves — the soft lyrical poems of the early days in Paonta, the poems of inspiration and of faith, the poems of defiance, the poems of heroism. Through all these poems ran one note of strong unchanging hope.

For the weak, the weary and the oppressed he had the image of a saviour. He reached out to them and gave them strength, courage and confidence till they were able to hold their own against the very forces that had exploited them.

The people saw in him the coming together of all that was heroic and chivalrous, a representation of everything that is good and beautiful. He was what all men desire to be but few, very few, succeed in becoming.

When we think of Guru Nanak we think first of all of a pacifist — a man who loved peace. When we think of Guru Gobind Singh we think first of all of a warrior, a man who fought many battles. Little wonder then that many people think that the roles of the two Gurus contradict each other and to the layman Guru Gobind Singh appears to have taken the Sikhs away from the path of Guru Nanak's teachings. But this appearance is deceptive. When we compare their teachings we see that Guru Gobind Singh believed in everything that Guru Nanak taught. If there seems to be a change it is only in the extension to these teachings which became necessary because of the change in times and without which the *panth* may not have survived the difficult period.

In the basic and important beliefs Guru Gobind Singh believed what Guru Nanak had believed and taught. Like Guru Nanak, Guru Gobind Singh believed that there was only one God, a God who was without form, who was present everywhere and for all time. Like Nanak he believed that men must live in the world of men and must not shirk their worldly duties, but must work towards salvation by attending to these duties. He too believed that men should strive to be like the lotus, pure and clean, even when it grows in muddy water. As a result, like Nanak, Guru Gobind Singh disapproved of people renouncing the world and going up into mountains or jungles to live the life of ascetics. Guru Gobind Singh shared Guru Nanak's belief that the cure for all the miseries of life was to lead a life of prayer and that prayers were the answer to all life's problems. Guru Gobind Singh did not even alter the form of the prayers : these were the same prayers that Guru Arjan Dev had included in the Granth. Like Guru Nanak, Guru Gobind Singh felt that the caste system was evil and worked to abolish all feelings of caste amongst his followers. Three of the original *Panj Pyare* belonged to the so-called low castes and went on to prove by their courage and their devotion that they were equal to people belonging to the higher castes. Guru Gobind Singh's favourite saying was : *"Manas ki jat sabe eko pahchanbo"* — he knew all mankind as one caste.

Guru Gobind Singh believed like Guru Nanak that death was the merging of the individual's soul with God and as such death was an event to be welcomed and not to be feared.

Nanak preached that all men should be good: Gobind preached that all men should be good and should also destroy evil. As a result, whereas Nanak said that God loved his saints and all those who lived good lives, Gobind said that God loved his saints but he also punished the doers of evil. It was the duty of every Sikh to fight against evil and tyranny. Guru Nanak said that we must always do what is right; Guru Gobind Singh went one step further. He said that not only must we always do what is right, we must also protect those who were doing right even if it meant giving up our lives while doing so.

The three important developments that Guru Gobind Singh brought to the Sikh faith were the creation of the Khalsa, the delegation of authority to the five faithful and the installation of the Guru Granth Sahib as the permanent Guru of the Sikhs. Each of these developments was made necessary by the need of the times. Certain weaknesses had crept into the faith and the followers were beginning to be awed by the strength of the Mughuls. By creating the Khalsa Guru Gobind Singh made the Sikh faith pure and strong and gave his followers strength and courage and self-confidence so that they could stand up against all odds. It is true that by asking his followers to wear the five "Ks" he changed their appearance. But though their looks had changed, their beliefs had not. They still believed in what Guru Nanak had taught. They had only become more assertive in their defence of these beliefs.

Guru Gobind Singh gave total authority to the five faithful, their decision was to be binding even on him. It was one such decision that he bowed to when he left the fortress at Chamakur. By doing this the Guru strengthened the ancient institution of the Panchayat and introduced an element of democracy into the administration of the day-to-day affairs of his followers. By declaring that henceforth the Guru Granth Sahib would be the Guru of the Sikhs, Guru Gobind removed the need of a living Guru and gave the Sikhs a permanent and unchangeable point on which they could focus their devotion and from which they could gain spiritual strength. He was able to get rid for ever of the wrangles and rivalries that had resulted with each change of leadership.

Two hundred years passed between the time Guru Nanak first preached his new faith (1499) and the time when Guru Gobind Singh created the Khalsa (1699). In these two hundred years Sikhism gained strength from year to year and thousands had joined the new faith. In the first hundred years of its existence Sikhism was basically a movement of social and spiritual reform. All distinctions based on economic class or social caste were abolished amongst its followers. The Sikh Gurudwaras were open to everyone and in the Guru's *langar* the high caste Brahmin and the lowborn Shudra sat side by side to eat their meals and all Sikhs were members of one family. The Sikh faith worked to free the society of hypocrisy. It also worked for the uplift of women, abolished *sati* and encouraged widow-marriage. Religion was made simple, and empty ceremonies and rituals were dispensed with and, as a result, the faith appealed to both Hindus and Muslims. The bridge it had provided between the two religions was symbolised by its most sacred shrine, the Harimandir, and by its holy book, the Guru Granth Sahib. The foundation stone of the Harimandir was laid by a Muslim, Mian Mir, and the building itself was raised through the labour of Hindus, Sikhs and Muslims working side by side. The Guru Granth Sahib contains not only the writings of the Gurus but also the compositions of both Hindu and Muslim saints.

In the second hundreds years of its existence Sikhism found itself being strengthened by the addition of a new dimension. It continued to be a vehicle of social reform but the martyrdom of Guru Arjan Dev gave it a new direction. Guru Hargobind gave a call to arms and made the Sikh movement a movement of resistance, resistance to tryanny and oppression unleashed by the powerful Moghul rulers. Like all resistance movements this movement too taught its members to match superior military and numerical strength with greater determination and dedication. It taught its members the spirit of selflessness and self-sacrifice. So strong and popular did this movement become that it was able to stem the rise of Islam in India and prevent India from becoming a Muslim State inhabited only by Muslims.

There are many stories about Guru Gobind Singh and about his followers that have come down to us. Though most of these stories are based on history, some of them do not have historical evidence to support them. But they are all beautiful stories and they bring close to us some features to the Guru's personality and of his teachings. There, perhaps, could be no better way to conclude than by retelling some of these stories.

Amongst the thousands of Sikhs who thronged Anandpur was one called Bhai Kanhaiya. He was a very meek and humble man and there was nothing to single him out from the other Sikhs. Like thousands of the Guru's followers he went about his work quietly, seeking no reward, no recognition, doing whatever duty was assigned to him with complete and total dedication. Like so many of the other Sikhs, he would offer his services wherever they were needed and would perform chores that needed to be done without waiting to be asked to do them. His favourite task was to supply water to the *langar* and to the Guru Mahal. This became his special duty and people became familiar with the sight of Bhai Kanhiaya making frequent trips to the stream to carry water back in his *mashk* (leather water-bag). This was a sight that was seen so often that it would have been difficult for people to imagine Bhai Kanhaiya without his *mashk*.

He continued to perform this task even when the Guru's soldiers rode out to battle and carried water out to the detachments of the Guru's soldiers as they fought. The soldiers, tired and thirsty, welcomed Bhai Kanhaiya's visits because he brought them the welcome relief of a drink of cool water. Up and down Bhai Kanhaiya would go from the fort to the battle-field with his *mashk*. He could easily have been killed by a stray arrow or a stray musket shot, but he was unafraid of the danger he exposed himself to, unmindful of the risk that he was taking.

He found special happiness when he gave water to the wounded as they lay on the battlefield, waiting to be carried back to the camp. He would lift their heads on his lap and give them a much needed drink of cool water. He would wipe the sweat and the dust of battle from their faces, caress their foreheads and murmur a few words of comfort and hope. He moved from one wounded soldier to the other like an angel of kindness who gave these wounded men the strength to bear their pain.

It was the second day of the battle for Anandpur. The battle raged fiercely and Bhai Kanhaiya, as was his habit, moved among the soldiers on the battlefield bringing them a little relief with the water that he brought. He moved among the wounded murmuring prayers and offering solace when he knelt beside them.

That evening when the fighting ended a group of Sikhs waited upon the Guru and it was obvious that they wanted to speak to him on a matter of great importance.

"Yes", the Guru asked. "What troubles you, my friends?"

"It is Bhai Kanhaiya," the leader of the group said.

The mention of Bhai Kanhaiya's name brought a smile to the Guru's face. He knew of the special task that this Sikh performed and of the love and comfort that he brought to the wounded.

"He brings water to the soldiers in the battlefield. He risks his life and moves from one wounded soldier to the next.

Yet today he was doing a terrible thing. All through the day he was busy on the battlefield, but he was bringing water not only to our soldiers but also to the enemy soldiers."

"Is this true? Who saw him?" The Guru's face did not show any emotion.

"We all saw him Maharaj," the Sikhs spoke in a chorus.

"He treated the enemy's soldiers with the same gentleness that he gives to our soldiers. He wiped their faces and gave them water to drink," the leader of the group went on. "He even spoke words of encouragement of them. I was close enough on these occasions to hear what he said," one of the younger members of the group went on.

"And what did he say?" the Guru asked.

"He said, *'Rab sab da rakha'* — May God protect everyone."

"If our own Sikhs start helping the enemy in this way it will weaken the morale of our people." The leader of the group spoke on and there were anger and indignation in his voice and the other Sikhs nodded their heads in agreement.

"Send for Bhai Kanhaiya," the Guru ordered and two Sikhs ran to carry out this order.

"Bhai Kanhaiya," the Guru said when Kanhaiya had been ushered into his presence. "A very serious charge has been made against you, you have been accused of helping the enemy soldiers during battle." Bhai Kanhaiya's head came up with a start and even in the light of the torches the look of intense shock and disbelief could be seen by everyone. The colour had drained from his face and he had lost his ability to speak. He shook his head from side to side in denial.

"Did you not bring water to those of the enemy who were wounded?" the Guru asked. "Did you not lay their heads on you lap and comfort them?"

Bhai Kanhaiya hung his head in shame and the Guru knew that the charge was true.

"Speak," he said, "what do you have to say in your defence?" Bhai Kanhaiya took two steps forward and knelt at the Guru's feet. "It is true my Guru, I did give water to those of the enemy who were wounded. I did slake their terrible thirst and comfort them. But when I moved among the wounded on the battlefield, I could not tell which of them were ours and which were theirs." He looked up at last into the Guru's face. He continued:

"When I looked into the faces of those wounded soldiers, I did not see the Moghul or the Sikh. I did not see the enemy or the friend. I saw only you. Whichever way I turned, whoever I attended to, I saw only you."

The Guru got up from his seat and drew Bhai Kanhaiya up and held him close. Then he turned to the group of Sikhs.

"He is my true follower, this Bhai Kanhaiya, and he has understood my mission aright. Where there is misery make it your duty to bring relief. Where there is pain bring comfort without thought of yours or mine." Then he spoke to Bhai Kanhaiya.

"Go Bhai Kanhaiya, go and get what rest you can. Sleep so that you will be strong tomorrow to carry on with your mission. May God give you strength and may you always bring comfort and relief to all those who suffer. May your children too be blessed with this compassion and this gift."

It is said that Bhai Kanhaiya went on to spend the rest of his days in prayer and in bringing relief and the message of hope to all those in pain. His children carried on the good work and made a study of herbal medicines and specialised in the treatment of wounds.

One of the very remarkable figures to come out of the *bhakti* movement was the saint, Dadu. Dadu was known for his saintliness and for various social and religious reforms that he brought about. He was also a very fine poet. His poems and his teachings had spread far and wide even during his lifetime and he had become a very famous and popular personality. He lived in a place called Naraina, not very far from Pushkar. Even after his death people who read his teachings and his poems regarded him with great respect and

Naraina became a place of pilgrimage and was often referred to as Dadudwara. Guru Gobind Singh had read Dadu's poems and his teachings and he too had great regard for this poet saint. On his way to Nanded, Guru Gobind Singh camped at Dadudwara. The Guru's tents were put up very close to the place where Dadu was buried. A *dargah* had come up here and there were many pilgrims who visited this shrine every day. While the Guru and his followers were riding past the *dargah* the Guru remembered all the wonderful things that Dadu had said in his beautiful poems. The Guru's heart was filled with respect for the long-dead saint and as an expression of this respect he raised an arrow to his forehead and saluted the shrine.

When they returned to their camp Dharam Singh, one of the original *Panj Pyaras*, called a meeting of the Khalsa *panth* of the five faithfuls. The Guru was asked to appear before the *panth*. The Guru himself had given them an authority which was higher than his and in deference to this authority appeared before them. They bowed to him and then they all took their seats. "Today while we were riding out Guruji, you saluted the tomb of Dadu."

"Yes," said the Guru. "He was a very great and pious man. My heart filled with respect for him and I had to express this respect, I could not help myself, I saluted the tomb. But you yourself have said: *Gor marhi mat bhul na mane* — worship not even by mistake cemeteries or places of cremation." Bhai Man Singh reminded the Guru, quoting from one of the Guru's own hymns. "Yes I have said this. It is one of my teachings and an important teaching," the Guru said.

"Then you have violated the Guru's teachings and you must be punished." Bhai Dharam Singh pressed on.

"It is true, my Khalsa," the Guru said in all humility. "I have violated the Guru's teachings and I will willingly undergo any punishment that the *panth* may decide to impose upon me."

A fine of one hundred and twenty-five rupees was imposed upon the Guru, a fine the Guru immediately paid, admitting thereby that he had been wrong to salute Dadu's tomb, no matter how holy or pious the saint had been.

The Guru having given authority to the Khalsa was willing to submit himself to this authority even when the Khalsa had decided to punish him. The democratic set-up that the Guru had wished to introduce in the day-to-day affairs of his people was already in place and functioning efficiently even during his lifetime. In spite of his towering personality and great military strength the Guru remained a very humble man at heart and was willing to admit his mistake in public without a moment's hesitation.

The Guru, as we have seen, was very fond of music. He was very kind and generous to his musicians and was able to attract the best musicians both to Paonta and to Anandpur. Amongst his musicians, the most favoured and easily the best were his *raagis*, who sang hymns at both the morning and the evening prayer meetings. These *raagis* sang the holy hymns with so much beauty and so much feeling that they moved the hearts of all who listened to them. These *raagis* were famous all over North India and people came from far off places to listen to them.

One day a group of the Guru's faithful happened to pass by the *raagis'* quarters. The time was about eleven in the morning, the *raagis* were free from their duties and usually spent this time in *riyaz* or practice. To lighten their mood a little they were singing the story of the two legendary lovers of Punjab: Sohni and Mahiwal. The music was beautiful and their voices, as always, were full of feeling. The Sikhs were forced to stop and listen. As they listened to the words they were shocked to hear that the *raagis* were singing a love song. For a while they could not believe their ears, the *raagis* who sang such beautiful hymns, who sang of God and truth, of life and death, were singing of the profane love of a man and a woman. This was sacrilege, they thought.

That evening, after the evening prayer meeting, the band of devoted Sikhs stayed on to speak to the Guru. They told him of the sin that the *raagis* had committed. "Yes," the Guru said, shaking his head. "I agree with you, this is a terrible sin that they have committed and they deserve terrible punishment to it."

The group of Sikhs looked at each other and exchanged knowing glances. They had been sure that the Guru would share their feelings.

"In fact, this is such a terrible thing, I feel it should be brought to the notice of the entire *sangat*. The *sangat* should decide what punishment should be given to these great sinners. After the morning prayers tomorrow I will ask the *sangat* to stay back and then we will take up this matter."

The Sikhs bowed and withdrew, quite happy in the knowledge that the Guru would deal with this matter with the seriousness that it deserved.

Sometime during the early hours of the morning, it began to rain and the rain continued for a long time. It was a cold winter, and the rain made the morning even colder. The Sikhs, each in his own house, woke up for the morning prayers, but seeing the rain and the cold each of them was convinced that very few of the *sangat* would attend the prayer meeting that morning. Seeing the thin attendance the Guru would not take up the matter of the *raagis*. Each one of them went back to bed, wrapped himself snugly in his quilt and slept for a few hours more. That evening when they did go to attend the prayer meeting the Guru greeted them with a smile.

"Why my faithful Sikhs, what happened this morning? We were to discuss a very important and serious matter but all of you failed to turn up."

The leader of the group looked at his friends. It was clear that they wanted him to be their spokesman. "My lord, it was raining heavily and it was very cold. We thought that

very few of the *sangat* would come and so we went back to
bed too."

"So you got frightened by a little rain and a small blast
of cold wind?" the Guru asked gently. "You who swear to
give your lives for me were put off by a slight change in the
weather?" The leader of the group shuffled his feet uneasily
and all the Sikhs stood with their heads bowed. "What kind
of faith or love is it that cannot stand up against a little bad
weather? Think of this and think of that young woman's faith,
her love. A young woman who was little more than a girl.
Think of the raging storm, the lashing rain and the biting
wind. Think of the thunder and lightning and think too of
the river Chenab swollen and angry, the waves tearing at the
banks, the water one vast body of raging fury. Remember
that she did not know how to swim and the only support
she had was an earthenware pitcher which she knew had not
been baked and which would dissolve in the water. Yet all
that the girl could think of was her *mahi*, her *mahiwal*,
waiting for her on the other bank. Because he waited she
had to fight against all odds to try and get to him. Because
he waited she threw herself into the raging waters, fully
knowing that she would meet her end there." The Guru's
voice had become gradually louder and now when he stopped
speaking there was a hushed silence. "Think of this my
friends," he continued gently. "Think of it carefully then
answer my question. Were her faith and love stronger or were
yours? If my *raagis* sing of her it is because her story deserves
to be sung. Go, go all of you and if you can, you too sing of
her. Perhaps with this singing you will learn from her the
meaning of true love and of true devotion."

The Guru was not an orthodox man and was not tied
down by a rigid scale of values. He was an extremely sensitive
man and had the ability to see beauty and strength even in
the most unconventional situations. Above everything he had
the ability to draw upon everyday incidents to illustrate his
teachings. Little wonder that he could see in Sohni's devotion

to her lover a parallel of the true devotion that a disciple
should have for his Guru, for his God. He could see in Sohni's
sacrifice a symbol of the ultimate form of worship.

Bibliography

Aarshi, P.S., *The Golden Temple*, Laneer, New Delhi, 1989.

Bal, Surjit Singh, *Life of Guru Nanak*, Panjabi University, Patiala, 1969.

Duggal, K.S., *Sikh Gurus: Their Lives and Teachings*, UBSPD, New Delhi, 1993.

Guru Gobind Singh Foundation, Chandigarh, *The Tenth Master: Tributes on Tricentenary*, 1967.

Kohli, Surinder Singh, *Travels of Guru Nanak,* Panjabi University, Patiala, 1969.

Singh, Dr Gopal, *History of the Sikh People,* World Sikh University Press, New Delhi, 1979.

Singh, Fauja, *Guru Amar Das: Life and Teachings*, Sterling Publication, New Delhi, 1979.

Singh, Harbans, *Guru Gobind Singh,* Sterling Publication, New Delhi, 1979.

—— *Guru Nanak,* Panjabi University Press, Patiala, 1971.

Singh, Kartar, *Life of Guru Gobind Singh,* Ward Lock & Co., New York, 1967.

—— *Guru Gobind Singh and the Moghuls,* Ward Lock & Co., New York, 1967.

Singh, Khushwant, *A History of the Sikhs (Vol. 1),* Oxford University Press, New Delhi, 1977.

Singh, Puran, *A Book of the Ten Masters,* Panjabi University, Patiala, 1989.

Singh, Raja Daljit, *Guru Nanak,* Lahore Book Shop, Ludhiana, 1979.

Singh, Shanta Sarabjeet, *Nanak, the Guru,* Orient Longman, New Delhi, 1970.

Singh Tirlochan, *Life of Guru Har Krishan*, Delhi Sikh
    Gurdwara Management Committee, Delhi, 1981

Talib, G.S., *An Introduction to Sri Guru Granth Sahib*,
    Panjabi University Patiala, 1991.

——— *Guru Tegh Bahadur: Background and Supreme
    Sacrifice*, Panjabi University, Patiala, 1976.

——— *The Impact of Guru Gobind Singh on Indian
    Society*, Lahore Book Shop, Ludhiana, 1984.

Index